RILKE

Rilke

THE ALCHEMY OF ALIENATION

edited by
Frank Baron, Ernst S. Dick, and Warren R. Maurer

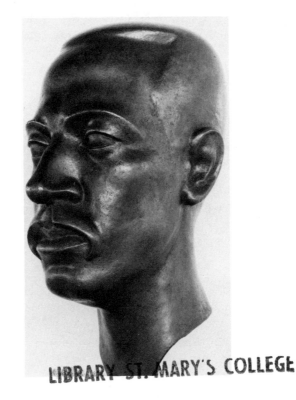

THE REGENTS PRESS OF KANSAS

Lawrence

Library of Congress Cataloging in Publication Data

Main entry under title:

Rilke, the alchemy of alienation.

Includes bibliographical references and index.
1. Rilke, Ranier Maria, 1875-1926—Criticism
and interpretation—Addresses, essays, lectures.
I. Baron, Frank. II. Maurer, Warren R.
III. Dick, Ernst Siegfried.
PT2635.I65Z8433   831'.9'12   79-19759
ISBN 0-7006-0198-8

Contents

Preface   vii

Foreword   ix
  Ulrich Fülleborn

1   Rilke's Letters   3
  Bernhard Blume

2   Rilke: Nirvana or Creation   15
  Walter Kaufmann

3   The Poet and the Lion of Toledo   29
  Hans Egon Holthusen

4   Rilke and Eliot   47
  Stephen Spender

5   Rilke and Ponge: "L'Objet c'est la Poétique"   63
  Walter A. Strauss

6   Alienation and Transformation: Rilke's Poem "Der Schwan"   95
  Herbert Lehnert

7   Rilke and Russia   113
  Lev Kopelev

8   Rilke's Poetic Cycle "Die Zaren"   137
  Daria Rothe

9   Rilke's "Das Bett"   151
  Andrzej Warminski

10 The Devolution of the Self in *The Notebooks of Malte Laurids Brigge*   171
      Walter H. Sokel

11 Rilke and the Problem of Poetic Inwardness   191
      Richard Jayne

12 Rilke's and Walter Benjamin's Conceptions of Rescue and Liberation   223
      Andras Sandor

13 R. M. Rilke's Dreams and His Conception of Dream   243
      Erich Simenauer

    List of Contributors   263

    Index   265

Preface

Rilke's exile from his native land was self-imposed, permanent, and necessary to his existence as a poet. Rilke was not at home with traditional literary forms and themes. From his intense alienation he undertook the transmutation of the physical world into visions of permanence.

>   . . . Zeiten brauchte er,
> Jahrtausende für sich und diese Birne
> in der es brodelte; im Hirn Gestirne
> und im Bewußtsein mindestens das Meer.
>   ["Der Alchimist," *Der neuen Gedichte anderer Teil*]

>   . . . he needed ages,
> thousands of years for himself and his pear-shaped,
> bubbling flask; in his brain he needed galaxies
> and an awareness as great as the sea.

This book illuminates the alchemy of Rilke's alienation.

Originally inspired by the outstanding Rilke collection in the Spencer Research Library at the University of Kansas, this volume has grown out of a number of related projects, including exhibits, bibliographies, translations, collections of poetry, and a symposium in the fall of 1975.

We have attempted to approach Rilke through a wide range of topics. Biographical, philosophical, religious, political, and psychological questions—all relevant to Rilke's image—have been dealt with by our contributors. At the same time, we responded to the need for close interpretation of literary texts, comparative analysis, and the study of literary influences. Above all, we have tried to offer a balanced representation to a broad spectrum of views, touching the salient problems of Rilke's work.

Although Rilke was, as he asserted, "thoroughly and permanently opposed to being visually portrayed," in 1915 he sat four times for the Swiss artist Fritz Huf (1888–1970). In 1925 Rilke stated: "Fritz Huf's bust, from the museum of Winterthur, which, if it absolutely must be so, I come closest to authorizing." The editors are indebted to Klaus W. Jonas for supplying information about this unique bronze bust of Rilke and to the Deutsche Schillergesellschaft for permission to use it in this book.

For encouragement and generous support of our efforts to complete this as well as related Rilke projects, we are grateful to Helmut E. Huelsbergen, chairman of the Department of Germanic Languages and Literatures; Alexandra Mason, Sarah Hocker, and L. E. James Helyar of the Spencer Research Library; Henry Marx and the Goethe House in New York; H. R. Kiderlen and the German Consulate in Chicago; Willard B. Snyder and the German Consulate in Kansas City; and Patricia Brodsky, Gerald E. Mikkelson, Alice Percival, Tamerlan Salaty, Janet Sharistanian, and John Brushwood.

F.B.

Foreword

Rainer Maria Rilke is one of very few German language authors of the twentieth century to have found a secure place in world literature. The present volume, which combines the work of specialist scholars and renowned essayists and critics from America and Europe, confirms this status; a status, incidentally, which was not brought about by German criticism and German readers, but by the reception of the author's works by an international public. While, at first glance, this may not appear to be unusual, it is, nevertheless, rather astonishing that literary creations like *The Book of Hours*, *The Notebooks of Malte Laurids Brigge*, *Duino Elegies*, and *Sonnets to Orpheus*, which in their etherealized esotericism strike one as typically German, have achieved such recognition. The works published as *New Poems* are, to be sure, somewhat more easily accessible, but they would never alone have led to the generous reception from which we can proceed today.

Naturally, it is possible to find in Rilke himself attributes which help to elevate his work to world-wide significance. From his early period to his death he expended a large part of his energies on overcoming the narrowness of his Prague origins and the limitations of the German cultural sphere. Few other poets have opened themselves so decisively to foreign influences. Russia and the Paris of Rodin, Cézanne, and the Symbolist tradition were more important for his development than any native landscape or literary movement. Even for the later work his experiences of Provence, Spain, and Egypt may well have been more important than his return to a specific German poetic tradition, namely, the elegiac and hymnic modes of Klopstock and Hölderlin. As a result of such a broadened outlook, Rilke's work, with its unique problems, experiences, and creative insights, finds resonance throughout the world: in America and Japan as well as in Europe.

How is it, then, that Rilke's accomplishment is, nevertheless, frequently questioned, especially from within Germany itself? The present volume also reflects this problem. Characteristically, many views of Rilke are subject to intense fluctuation—either from enthusiasm to indifference and rejection, or from serious reservations and objections to a steadily growing respect. Hans Egon Holthusen exemplifies the first possibility, both in his person and in his essay; for the second, one may point to Eudo C. Mason's lifework.

The world-wide recognition and the repeated questioning of the Rilkean achievement apparently derive from a single source. A poetic *oeuvre* that, like Rilke's, is consciously built upon contradictions, is obviously greater in its impact but makes a less harmonious impression than one in which, intellectually or artistically, unity is achieved or even simulated. (Unity, to be sure, exists in our century only at the price of one-sidedness.) The reception of such work proceeds accordingly: unified, "closed" poetry attracts a homogeneous readership and, in extreme cases, creates an elitarian circle of like-minded followers—as with Stefan George. In today's complex and contradictory social and intellectual environment a large part of the public is, thereby, automatically excluded from the start. Those who are excluded can, to be sure, respect the accomplishment of the author in question but may not sense the need for a more sincere confrontation and interaction with him.

A lifework such as Rilke's—work with repeated new starts, which nevertheless fails to resolve its inner tensions, which offers solutions but then supersedes them, proceeding in this way to a wide-ranging "openness" of form and content—is quite a different story. Such a work appeals to readers with very different expectations. Partial identifications arise; some with intellectual significance, others with specific aesthetic experiments. Always, however, the "yes" also seems to require a "no"—a "no," namely, to those dimensions of the work with which identification fails. The evaluations that fluctuate in this manner must, to be sure, always be seen before the background of a more universal change in taste and interest, which Holthusen stresses.

A justification for the present essay collection is provided by the general reception and scholarly preoccupation with Rilke sketched above. It is clear that the nature of his work demands the cooperation of many critics and scholars, working from as many divergent premises as possible. Only in this way, perhaps, can the tension-filled complexity of the work, with its contradictions, gradually be comprehended. Individuals will always treat only individual aspects or will concern themselves with the problem of interpretation per se. It is, therefore, to the credit of the editors of this volume that they have brought together authors who proceed from widely differing perspectives.

Such a procedure, naturally, requires a great deal from the reader of these thirteen contributions. He must try to integrate seemingly divergent strands of scholarship. The result should be a total overview that obviously ought not to be a simple synthesis, nor, on the other hand, should it include unassimilated contrasts. And aid in the form of a foreword to the collection, therefore, would not seem superfluous. I have gladly accepted the challenge to try and provide such an introduction since (on the basis of my own earlier efforts relating to the history of Rilke's reception) I can perhaps help readers avoid some of those false turns that I myself once took.

Regardless of the extent to which the various standpoints and results colliding here must at first confuse us (especially since each is individually significant), one must not allow oneself to be deceived by surface appearances. Beneath the surface, in their nuclei, many of the questions and results converge; and for an understanding of Rilke, none are irrelevant. To be sure, there are *topoi* relating to the appraisal of Rilke that, being matters of taste, must remain on the level of mere opinion. On the other hand, certain constants have crystallized over the years and can be accepted today as indisputable. Such progress is most clearly seen in the break with an exclusively narrow focus on Rilke—a break which often makes it possible for the first time to substantiate critically definite positions in the interpretation of his work.

In the present volume such productive expansions into larger literary contexts occur again and again, and are frequently referred to programmatically in the titles of the essays concerned. Rilke is compared with T. S. Eliot by Spender, with Ponge by Strauss, and with Benjamin by Sandor. Historical links and processes are uncovered; the face of an epoch, which makes unqualified, impressionistic criticism impossible, is evoked. The old theme of Rilke and Russia also gains new weight in that Kopelev, a Russian, confirms the authenticity of the encounter.

The contributors to this volume do not avoid an intellectual confrontation with the past or with Rilke's place in it. That applies as much to Sokel, who uses the example of *Malte* for a contribution to the theme of the modern disintegration of personality, as to Jayne, who, following in Erich Heller's footsteps, locates Rilke in the tradition of romanticism and Hegel and subjects his inwardness ("Innerlichkeit") to criticism as a historical phenomenon. It also applies *eo ipso* to Lehnert's augmentation of Rilke scholarship by sociological approaches, as well as to Simenauer's continuing analyses using the tools of depth-psychology. In each case a definite phenomenon of Rilkean poetry is clarified and evaluated within a larger historical context. In what follows I should like to point out, under three categories, several such clarifications and, in so doing, stress the points of contact that exist between such independently conceived efforts. This procedure should show how well all of the contributions, including those which have not yet been mentioned, serve to complement each other.

1. *Aestheticism and extra-aesthetic content:* This theme seems to me to be one of the most important and controversial in all of the literature dealing with Rilke. Holthusen takes it up with appropriate emphasis, and for Jayne it is central. Kopelev too sees it as a problem. He, Strauss, and Simenauer oppose a one-sided, aestheticized Rilke image with an emphasis on the high "reality content" of his work. Spender elevates the problem to the very theme of his comparison with Eliot in order to show that *Four Quartets* and *Duino Elegies* realize the goals of the aesthetic movement of the last century but that beyond this they aim for a "religious vision" in which aesthetic substance serves the religious meaning of life. Warminski demonstrates the complete, indissoluble coincidence of these aesthetic and extra-aesthetic goals on the basis of a single poem from the *New Poems*. "The Bed" is the simultaneous evocation—possible only in a poem—of sexual union, birth, death, and—by no means last—the birth of a poem. Because of its structural uniformity it is impossible to say what the poem "really" is. For this reason too, no attempt is made to speak of its religious significance.

2. *Alienation and salvation:* The concept of alienation ("Entfremdung"), which has become imprecise through excessive use, needs special clarification when applied to Rilke. Sokel and Warminski in particular concern themselves with its genuinely Rilkean variants. They recognize the positive attributes here associated with the concept as "absence" ("Abwesenheit") and "withdrawal" ("Entzug"). Both refer to Rilke's dictum that whatever is most distant and estranged from man—love, birth, death, creativity—most concerns him and most belongs to him.

It is, simultaneously, that which questions and negates the normal modern ego most radically. The positive thrust of this concept is that it renders the existential conditions and basic experiences of mankind inaccessible to objectivizing and egocentric thought.

Jayne illuminates a further aspect of the theme when he reminds us of the process of the alienation of the work of art from concrete reality (begun during Romanticism), which has its basis in the discovery that reality is no longer capable of expressing the truth of the spirit. It would be pertinent to add here that the "things" which Rilke conjures up as contrast to the empirical reality of the twentieth century are not self-present and self-sufficient nor is the poetic language in which he does it. Both, rather, are rooted in a constitutive difference from themselves—something which again must not be seen negatively (Warminski).

Lehnert's thesis, which is based on a socially critical stance and which postulates a causal connection between "alienation" ("Entfremdung") and "transformation" ("Verwandlung"), looks quite different: "Rilke transformed the theme of alienation from society into artistic form." This is interpreted as "redemption and justification of human existence in the poem" and criticized by means of politicohistorical arguments.

Now, it happens that "salvation of the things" ("Rettung der Dinge") and "salvation (or self-salvation) of the artist (or man)" in literary work by means of the written word are themes that have always been energetically discussed in regard to Rilke, especially within those tension-filled areas between aestheticism and religiosity or art and existence. In our volume their continued topicality is confirmed, yet most of the authors treat them without bias, *sine ira et studio*, as it were. The sociologically based criticism is perhaps still closest to earlier existentialist criticism in that it sees in aesthetic attempts at achieving salvation an escape from the concrete social situation.

The value and the historical context of Rilke's attempt to intercede, as a poet, in the historical situation as "rescuer" stand out with surprising clarity in Sandor's comparison with Benjamin. Here we learn that Rilke and Benjamin did not wish to rescue the world of things ("Dingwelt") without accepting the world of time ("Zeitwelt") in its sociohistorical manifestations. But both men, Sandor adds, lacked the aggressive "power that can constitute a world"—the late Rilke, to be sure, less so than Benjamin. That Russia—as "land of the future"—already provided the early Rilke with the belief in the possibility of a "salvation" is shown by Daria Rothe's interpretation of the "Czar" cycle.

For the background of intellectual history for a "salvation" of the earth and man through art in the twentieth century, one must, naturally, seek first and foremost in Nietzsche (cf. Jayne).

Kaufmann adds a very precise context of motifs to this general theme, tracing the interplay of the concepts of "peace" and intensity" through the short poems to their ever-greater congruence in the latest works. He sees intensity as an elemental law of life, especially of creative life, to which a longing for peace, for redemption, is a complement. The dialectic of needs and experiences indicated here becomes totally clear when Blume, in reference to the letters, indicates a tangible biographical parallel. For the sake of concentration and artistic productivity, Rilke sought protection and loneliness, for example, in the empty castles of nobility; but extreme loneliness had to lead inevitably to isolation.

The reader of these essays, insofar as their content is concerned, finds himself *vis-à-vis* a multifaceted image, which is nevertheless illuminated from a central source. In Rilke's work we are apparently dealing with the exploration or design of a spiritual world that makes human life possible in the face of a historical situation in which the ability to live can by no means be taken for granted. To accomplish this a type of writing is invoked in which ideas are not expressed simply as such, or merely rhetorically; but instead, they appear to be endowed with inimitable linguistic, poetic structures. The significance of such poetry certainly lies in the fact that questions are kept open and thinking about them continues. Intellectual content always relates to intellectual traditions, even if it strives in the opposite direction; within these traditions, it follows, one is most likely to notice historical limitations. Structures, on the other hand, can rise above conventional thinking and represent real innovation. This too is demonstrated by the volume at hand.

3. *The linguistic-poetic structure.* Of importance here are, first of all, the negative determinations that have been made: the poetry of the mature Rilke is no longer the poetry of personal experiences (Sokel), nor is it based upon traditional symbolism or allegory (Sandor)—which, certainly, manifests a break with tradition. In what new ways a poetic Rilkean language tries to assert itself is not as easily shown. On the one hand, there are allusions to "mythopoesis" and "magic" imagery (Rothe, Kopelev) inspired in Rilke by Russia, and, on the other hand, to his "mannerism" (Holthusen). Structures of space and time are described which simultaneously signify "uncovering" and "hiding," "presence" and "absence" (Warminski). Corresponding to the latter is

Sandor's conclusion that Rilke's poetry seeks to realize two opposite aims at the same time. Rilke "identified on the one hand"—something which, in itself, could be equated with the practice of symbolism—"and kept apart on the other," enforcing a greater and different type of distance of poetic designation from its object than is possible with allegory. In this, according to Sandor, there is a correspondence to Benjamin's attempt to free himself from allegory and symbol by means of "metaphoric blending, montage"; that is, to bring together quite different things while maintaining their distance from each other. Both techniques are evident in much of twentieth-century literature.

What was creatively possible for Rilke and modern literature in the face of social and intellectual contradictions is, therefore, universal "relationship" ("Bezüglichkeit") as structure. This structure bridges the contrast of alienation and salvation without overcoming it; just as pain, complaint, and mourning are not "overcome" but endured, although Rilke's poetry attempts to realize an all-encompassing conceptual space of "celebration" ("Rühmung") as an affirmation of existence. We are familiar with this from *Duino Elegies* and *Sonnets to Orpheus*. And even in *Malte*, structurally, the most extreme negativity (as in an electrical potential) keeps open the possibility of the most extreme positivity (cf. Sokel). It is not "either/or" writing, then; but rather one of complementarity. It is precisely this which has, again and again, irritated Rilke's readers and, at the same time, stimulated them most strongly. Justifiably, Holthusen demands that the relationship between the aesthetic and ethical be re-thought. Insofar as Rilke's writing is not concerned with relieving anyone of the ethical decisions he must make in life, but presents instead a profusion of possible modes of thought and existence, it is quite able to function as an ethical challenge, as a challenge to achieve authentic existence, to "change your life" (cf. "Archaic Torso of Apollo"). If the reader wished to follow him, he would not find himself deserted, for the direction of historically possible and humanly desirable change is marked clearly enough in Rilke's work.

ULRICH FÜLLEBORN

RILKE

1

Rilke's Letters

BERNHARD BLUME

Some time ago, *Neue Zürcher Zeitung* published some heretofore unknown letters that Rudolf Kassner had written to Lili Schalk, the wife of the director of the Vienna Opera. In one of these letters, dated September 19, 1908, Kassner mentions that he had just received a letter from Rilke and then goes on: "You know how I admire his poetry, but his letters are unpleasantly pretentious, well, really, quite silly. Sorry. If you ever should be on very good terms with him, tell him. Or maybe not. Things like that are really just deplorable and can hardly be changed anymore."[1]

It may sound startling to hear Rilke's letters called silly, but it is no sacrilege. We ponder this judgment because the man who rendered it was not just anybody, but a thinker and essayist of great distinction. The irony of it is that Rilke considered Kassner his only true friend, among men; he even went so far as to say that among all living writers (including himself), Kassner was perhaps the most important.[2]

Affectation is a quality that has been ascribed to Rilke's letters and to Rilke himself by more than one critic; and if one wanted to, one could easily support the claim. For instance, there is the letter Rilke wrote in October, 1900 (to be sure, a much earlier date), to the sculptress Clara Westhoff, whom he was to marry half a year later. It is a sort of fantasy: Clara and Rainer would be together in their cottage in Worpswede, and Rainer would prepare supper for the two of them. It would all be grouped around "a fine vegetable or cereal dish." Of course, there would be honey, and "cold, ivory-pure butter would form a gentle contrast to the gaiety of a Russian table-cloth." And then bread and "'Westphalian ham, streaked with bands of white fat like an evening sky with long-drawn-out clouds. Tea would stand ready . . . and . . . great lemons, cut in disks, would sink like suns into the golden dusk of the tea, dimly shining through it with the radiant flesh of their fruit. . . ."[3]

What strikes us as ludicrous is, of course, not the tempting meal, but the false "poetry." It is, however, no different from the false poetry of Rilke's early poems. The whole letter reads like an unsuccessful attempt to transpose a Dutch still-life into a prose poem. One has only to read the marvelous letter on Cézanne that Rilke wrote to the same Clara seven years later, to discover how superbly Rilke learned to master tasks of this kind. Nevertheless, throughout his life, occasional streaks of this preciosity permeated, like the white fat of the Westphalian ham, both his poetry and his letters.

This, I think, is something one has to realize and to accept. What is really startling is not that there is an occasional weakness in the fiber of Rilke's work and person, but that, out of the *total* weakness of Rilke's beginnings, such great poetry grew. Studying the enormous quantity of Rilke's early writing, one cannot help being amazed by this mass of triviality. A purely formal talent at best, one would think: derivative, sentimental, thin, without a trace of originality, without strength, ideas, or substance.

As far as it is possible to attribute the great "breakthrough" in Rilke's development to the impact of any one human being, it was probably Lou Andreas-Salomé who, more than anybody else, helped him overcome the inanities of his early phase. For this reason alone, his correspondence with her, in spite of its incompleteness, appears to be most important in his development.

Rilke was barely twenty-two when he met her. Lou, fourteen years older than Rilke, was superior to him in every regard. Highly intelligent, beautiful, emancipated, experienced in the ways of the world, with social and literary connections everywhere, she took him out of the provincialism of his youth, changed his standards, and gave him confidence, if for no other reason than the mere fact that she loved him. A few years later, she dropped him. Although Rilke succeeded in reestablishing the broken relationship and in maintaining it, though with interruptions, for the rest of his life, it had changed. Rilke, to be sure, looked up to Lou as before; he confided in her, wrote to her, and came to her with his crises, his troubles, his great self-doubts, his fears; Lou remained the one person to whom he spoke with complete openness. Lou, on the

4

other hand, never realized that Rilke outgrew and surpassed her. He outgrew her in depth, in range, in insight, in kindness. Yet, Lou, although she did not love Rilke anymore, still believed that she understood him. And so she explained him, to himself and to others, in terms of her psychological and psychoanalytical theories. This resulted in a strange mixture of brilliant insights and startling obtuseness. Even so, there is no one to whom Rilke owed so much as to her. Except, of course, to himself.

It seems a miracle that Rilke was able to shape, out of the conventional poetic language of his epoch, the highly differentiated and individualized idiom of his mature achievements. It was the result of determination, ruthless discipline, critical intelligence, courage, resilience, and staying power, and it was a task that demanded the last ounce of his energy. But this was only the first great miracle of Rilke's life. The second was the fact that he managed, in this same century, to *live* as a poet. I am speaking here of simple, material survival. To subsist, and sometimes even to live well, on the proceeds from plays or novels is indeed possible; to subsist on the sale of poetry does not seem possible. It is regrettable that, not just in Rilke's case but in general, the material conditions that form the basis of all literature so far have been explored only insufficiently. When Schiller's sister-in-law, Caroline von Wolzogen, wrote Schiller's biography, she declared in her introduction that she had omitted in her book everything that had to do with economic matters, as she did not wish to tarnish the ideal image that the German nation had of its great poet. Reticence about such matters has hardly diminished since then. Clearly, we need a major study entitled *The Financial Side of Literature* or *Poetry and Money*, in which Rilke could be the subject of a major chapter. But whoever wanted to write such a chapter would derive little help from the Rilke correspondences that so far have been published.

In 1926 another great poet of the twentieth century, Gottfried Benn, published a financial accounting of his literary income. It comprised the time from his twenty-fifth year when he had published his first poem, to his fortieth year when he wrote this accounting. The total with which he came up was 975 marks, or 4 marks and 50 pfennigs per month.[4] Naturally, not even a poet can live on 15 pfennigs per day. Benn did not either; he made his living as a medical doctor, a specialist on venereal diseases.

Benn understood that in our society a piece of literature is, like anything else, a piece of merchandise which has to be marketed. From the point of view of the artist, it is, of course, a very unsatisfactory system; but when we look at the alternatives, we do not find them exactly ideal either. There is patronage, a system during feudal times whereby the artist depended on his lord or prince or a rich burgher for support. Or there is the twentieth-century version of patronage practiced by authoritarian systems whereby the state or the party takes over the function of the patron. The ruling bureaucracy exercises control over literary production, deciding what is desirable or undesirable, and which authors are to be promoted and which suppressed.

In view of this situation, Benn's solution looks neat. It frees art from the rigors of the marketplace, for which it is ill-equipped, and makes it independent. At the same time, it is a desperate solution, desperate because it exceeds the strength of most who try it. Benn is one case, Rilke is quite another. It is true, Rilke at times thought about making a decision similar to Benn's. But when we hear him talk about his desire to become an obscure country doctor, we cannot visualize him in such a role. He simply did not have the stamina for two professions.

When Rilke made the decision to stake his existence upon nothing but his poetical resources, he made it against all odds, yet with open eyes. Viewed within this context, his life can be seen as the solution of a seemingly insoluble question, and his letters as the record of his unending struggle to solve it. Rilke, as we know, took his letters very seriously; he regarded them as a part of his *oeuvre*, and rightly so. Yet a large part of them can be seen from an entirely different perspective: as documents of a grand design that subordinated everything else to the will to make this *oeuvre* possible. The letters then appear as a tremendous network connecting and maintaining points of support and lines of retreat in a desperate battle.

It has been noted and often held against Rilke that he leaned so heavily in his correspondence upon the members of the German and the Austrian aristocracy—a decadent, obsolete, anachronistic society, we are told. Why so many countesses and baronesses, it has been asked, not seldom with a touch of indignation. Why, indeed? Was there no one else? Where, we might ask, were the wives of the German industrialists, of the big executives, of the bankers, the corporation lawyers, the directors of the famous medical institutes? Surely, nothing would have prevented them from extending a helping hand to a struggling poet. I can only speculate what it was that made some members of the nobility so much more responsive both to Rilke's distinction and to his needs than the rest of the affluent society. I suspect that there was still something alive of a tradition in which the aristocracy felt an obligation to sponsor the arts. Karl August of Sachsen-Weimar and Ludwig II of Bavaria are only the most prominent examples of this tradition; theater and music abound with illustrative instances. I also think that the education which the daughters of the aristocracy received had something to do with it. There was great emphasis upon literature, languages, music, the fine arts, and there was a lot of educational travel, again with the emphasis upon the arts. It was the kind of tradition in which the prince of Thurn und Taxis goes hunting somewhere in Bosnia, and the princess, in Duino or in Lautschin, sends for the Quartetto di Trieste or the Böhmische Streichquartett and has them play, sometimes for no one but herself.

Naturally, Rilke needed help, and he received help, but he was no parasite. It is perfectly true that he cultivated his relationships, but he did not crawl after friendship; it was offered to him. What is true in the case of the Princess Marie von Thurn und Taxis, who sought him out in Paris and invited him to her castles, is typical of all these encounters. Also, Rilke probably gave more than he received. And what he received was not just material support, which, after all, as far as one can tell from the correspondences, was not spectacular; he found an audience, readers and listeners who cared, who were responsive. They expressed interest, empathy, encouragement, for which Rilke was grateful. But the princess expressed the true relationship when she remarked in her *Memoirs* that Rilke's gratitude seemed inexplicable to her. "It was *we*," she writes, "only we who should have been grateful to *him*, from the bottom of our heart: for his mere existence."[5]

It would, however, be wrong to assume that Rilke depended primarily on patrons. At least from 1907 on he had in Anton Kippenberg a publisher who quickly grew into a friend and counselor and who tried to arrange Rilke's financial affairs in a manner that guaranteed him a certain measure of stability and security. That is to say, Kippenberg advanced him a certain sum on a monthly basis, with the understanding that these advances would eventually be balanced against Rilke's royalties. That Kippenberg's assistance was substantial can be concluded from the frequent expressions of gratitude in Rilke's letters to him, even though the selectivity of the edition deprives us of all specific information regarding finances. The editors themselves have stated that they omitted all communications referring to business and also all parts that deal with personal matters.[6] These deletions are disturbing, not so much because of the quantitative loss as such—apparently about one-third of the material— but because of the changed character of the whole.

How much there is missing can be glimpsed from a hitherto unknown letter that Rilke wrote to Kippenberg in October, 1915. It is published in the Schiller-Jahrbuch of 1974, and it is a very moving letter.[7] It concerns a fairly large sum of money; in fact, this was the only time in Rilke's life when he was rich, or thought he was. To his complete surprise, Rilke had received from an anonymous donor the sum of twenty thousand Austrian crowns. Actually, it came from Ludwig Wittgenstein, who was not yet a famous philosopher, but who had just inherited a substantial fortune and had decided to give part of it away to needy Austrian writers and artists. The First World War had just begun, and in the confusion of those uncertain days, the money was delivered not to Rilke but to Kippenberg instead. Kippenberg, very much concerned about Rilke's future "in uncertain times," decided that the twenty thousand crowns should be invested for him in "mündelsicheren Papieren" (something like triple A bonds) and that only the interest should be used. Rilke meekly went along with the plan; but, apparently regretting it, he wrote a letter of protest one year later. The gist of it is that he felt that for once in his life, as the owner of twenty thousand crowns, he should have been able to live accordingly; his life might have been different. As understandable as Kippenberg's parsimony is, Rilke's frustration is no less understandable. When we see how *Malte* reflects Rilke's fear during his Parisian years that "being poor and to perish meant almost the same," it is intriguing to imagine what the feeling of being rich and master of his life might have brought forward.[8] At any rate, letters like this were part of Rilke's existence, and this existence was somewhat different from the simplified and stylized picture that the *published* letters of Kippenberg and the equally selective six-volume collection of Rilke's letters give us.[9]

From these we gain the impression that Rilke corresponded with Kippenberg mainly about books and manuscripts, with his wife about Rodin, Cézanne, and his travels; that, half monk, half minstrel, he fixed his glance either upon God or the permanency of art; that he wrote to young poets about the exertions of poetry, to bereaved wives about the acceptance of death, and to his women friends about Bettina von Arnim and the beauty of nonpossessive love. When the readers of these editions later saw in Rilke's correspondence with Marie Taxis that the princess called him a "Don Juan," they must have been surprised because nothing in what they had read had prepared them for such a characterization. With the appearance of a few more unexpurgated editions of his letters, a more earthy Rilke will appear. Even now, we can clearly see that Rilke, in the pursuit of his strategy of life, deployed more circumspection and resourcefulness than he is usually credited with, and that he was not quite as helpless and inept in practical matters as the Rilke legend paints him.

Among these practical yet absolutely vital matters, Rilke's most stubborn problem was shelter. As uncertain as he must have been at times of his ability to provide a roof over his head, the problem was more difficult than that. Nor was it comfort or elegance he was after; here his tastes were as simple as in food. What he constantly searched for was something much harder to obtain: complete solitude.

Rilke was apparently unable to work at his writing without prolonged periods of absolute concentration. He was easily disturbed and distracted; a casual conversation was enough to wreck a day for him. We may be inclined to deplore this as an unfortunate quirk of his nature, some sort of supersensitivity unique to him, but a remark that Goethe once made in a letter to Schiller should give us pause. "I have again experienced," Goethe wrote, "that I can only work in absolute solitude, and that not only conversation, but even the mere domestic presence of dear and beloved persons completely diverts my creative well-springs."[10] It is quite a startling observation, made by someone who would appear to us so much more robust than Rilke.

As grateful as Rilke was to the wealthy landowners who opened their estates and castles to him, he usually declined their invitations, while at the same time trying to keep them open in case of future emergencies. For these castles, in spite of their rural seclusion, had severe drawbacks: they had owners, families, and often a turbulent social life. Hence, the innumerable diplomatic letters, written around the theme: not now, but perhaps later. Some of Rilke's hosts, however, were selfless enough to remove themselves during his presence. These places, then, became the perfect refuges. Among them belong Duino, where Rilke stayed alone from October, 1911, to May, 1912, and wrote the first two poems of *Duino Elegies* and fragments of the others; Schloß Berg am Irchel in 1920; and, above all, Muzot, the tower in the Valais which Werner Reinhart in Winterthur first rented and then bought for his use. There Rilke finished the *Elegies* and wrote *Die Sonette an Orpheus* and more than two hundred poems and fragments.

Solitude, however, is more than a secluded place. It is a human condition. Throughout his life, Rilke never tired of elaborating on this theme. He wrote long letters to the young poet Franz Xaver Kappus on the "one thing that is needed: solitude," and in a letter to an acquaintance he defined a good marriage as one "in which each appoints the other guardian of his solitude," for "*togetherness* between two people is an impossibility."[11] He tried to impress it on Clara that "*everyone* must be able to find in his *work* the center of his life," and it is clear what he was attempting to fend off with such a remark.[12] Speaking of Rodin, he wrote to Clara, with significant approval: "It is all so clear, so clear. The great men have all let their lives become overgrown like an old road and have carried everything into their art. Their lives are stunted like an organ they no longer need."[13] And to Lou Andreas-Salomé: "O Lou, in a poem that I bring off there is much more reality than in any relationship or affection that I feel."[14] All these are statements Rilke made when he was still fairly young, when he was about to find himself.

There is an old saying: "Hell is not to get what one wants." And then the phrase stops for a moment, as if to correct itself, and goes on: "No. Hell is to *get* what one wants." Well, Rilke got what he wanted. But when he looked at it carefully, it was not the solitude he had wanted and needed, it was isolation. On the one hand, he praises Duino while he has it all to himself as a "generous sanctuary," a "great, uninterrupted, protected piece of being all-by-oneself"; yet practically in the same breath he writes to Lou that it holds him "a little like a prisoner."[15] He finds himself behind a "tightly locked door," and this time he does not speak of Duino, nor is it Duino from which he has "no window upon the world"; he is speaking of his life, a life in which he feels "like someone who has surrounded himself on all four sides by very high walls."[16]

This theme pervades both Rilke's letters and his works. It generates all the countless images, metaphors, and symbols, the things enclosed and encircled which signify or can signify isolation, such as house, garden and park, tower and island, the mirror and its mythical figure, Narcissus —a Narcissus, moreover, who is not enamored of his image but horrified that he is surrounded by mirrors, that his view upon the world is blocked, and that wherever he looks, he sees ultimately nothing but his own reflection. And there are cage and prison and the prisoner; there is the panther, turning in circles behind the bars of his cage:

10

Ihm ist als ob es tausend Stäbe gäbe
und hinter tausend Stäben keine Welt.[17]

The analogy to the artist is obvious. Living in isolation in order to do his work, he must pay the penalty imposed upon such isolation: the separation from ordinary life. From this stems the conflict that arises over and over in Rilke's life: "die alte Feindschaft zwischen dem Leben und der großen Arbeit," as he puts it in *Requiem für eine Freundin*.[18]

Rilke is very conscious of this dilemma: "Ultimately," he writes to Marie Taxis, "it is always this one . . . irreconcilable conflict between life and work which I endure in ever new infernal modifications and which I almost do not survive."[19] He knows that not every artist experiences this same conflict, and he discusses and analyzes the reasons why he is hit so hard by it. Actually, however, it is a rather frequent theme in the literature around 1900; the names of Ibsen, Hauptmann, Hofmannsthal, Thomas and Heinrich Mann come easily to mind, even if we do not want to go back as far as Goethe's *Tasso*. The favorite *Gestalt* in which "life" appears in the literature of the epoch is "woman," and if Rilke had needed a literary model, Ibsen's *When We Dead Awaken* could have served very well. But his own life was all he needed. Erich Simenauer has shown the pattern that Rilke's affairs with women invariably followed, and he takes Rilke's letters to Mimi Romanelli as his sample.[20] They begin with enraptured and bewitching words of love, and one has to have sharp ears to detect, in the midst of the intoxicated language of Rilke's very first letter, the one telltale word, "solitude," followed by the statement that all who love him help him to support it. This is quickly covered with more words and more letters of fascinated admiration; but when Mimi later, in some serious crisis, needs support and comfort, Rilke suddenly has little to say. He explains—in gentle words, of course—that what strength he has must go into his work, and he begins to withdraw. Simenauer wonders why, after the separation, the correspondence still went on for almost two years. The answer is: because it was a correspondence. For letters had a twofold function in Rilke's life: they avoided contact and, paradoxically, they established or maintained it, yet always from a safe distance. It is well known how sternly Rilke reprimanded Goethe for his feeble response to the tempestuous advances of Bettina von Arnim, whom Rilke admired so much as "eine der großen Liebenden." "*I*," he declares, and one expects something like, "*I* would have known how to love her." But no, what he says is: "I would have loved to answer her letters."[21]

11

What was true in the case of Mimi Romanelli is true for all of Rilke's love affairs (with the exception of Lou): as soon as the danger of attachment became evident, he withdrew. This is just as apparent in the letters to Magda von Hattingberg where the final disappointment was perhaps greatest, as in the letters to Baladine Klossowska where his involvement was perhaps most intense. For this very reason, however, his attempt to recapture his solitude was perhaps the most obstinate.

Rilke used to speak with almost nostalgic tones of the complete solitude of the years in Paris when he wrote *Malte*, a solitude so extreme that over the years he saw hardly eight people. He spoke with despair of the years 1912–1922, when, famous by then and not insensitive to the temptations of fame, he found himself unable to create the solitude he needed in order to complete the *Duino Elegies*. In 1921 he finally became convinced that he would not finish them and wrote a kind of reckoning in which he tried to face without excuses what he considered the most severe failure of his life. It is a document which he called *Das Testament* and which has only recently been published. It consists of a strangely detached, highly stylized, autobiographical introduction, written in the third person, and some fragments and drafts of letters directed to Baladine Klossowska.

It is not always easy to read other people's love letters without a grain of cynicism, or at least a certain unconcerned equanimity; however, in the case of Rilke and Merline, it is difficult to avoid the word "tragic." Rilke, having found after years of distraction the refuge of Schloß Berg, had great hopes of finishing the *Elegies* there within the six months of seclusion granted him. When he yielded to a new love, he did it with the hope, so often frustrated in the past, that it might be possible to reconcile the irreconcilable, and that he would find in the person of Merline a tie with the world which he desired no less than he desired his solitude. Or, as he put it in the terms of his key metaphors: he expected of his beloved "that she be a window, opening into the expanded cosmic space of existence [not a mirror]."[22]

At the same time, he knew the danger—that he might wreck what mattered most to him. What he feared happened. Something else increased his feeling of guilt, something he had likewise foreseen; that he would raise expectations of a permanent bond which he could not fulfill, and that he would be unable to give the happiness he wished to give. Merline, on the other hand, felt guilty too, because she knew that by clinging to Rilke she would divert him from the one great task of his life. Both suffered. They speak frankly about all this in their letters, without reproach, except self-reproach, and with tenderness and great mutual understanding. Hofmannsthal, speaking of human relationships, once remarked that he tried to see a relationship as a whole, a unit in its own right: "The relationship between two human beings is something very distinct, it is an individuum, a delicate, but organic structure."[23] It is a beautiful remark that reveals the secret of great correspondences, and in this sense, Rilke's correspondence with Merline may very well be his most beautiful correspondence. As to the *Duino Elegies*: Rilke, as we know, did, after all, finish the poems the following year, at Muzot, the "refuge" which Merline had helped to find and make habitable for him.[24]

NOTES

This essay appeared previously in *Boston University Journal* 2 (1976): 14–21, and is reprinted here, in an edited version, by permission of the publisher.

1. Gerald Chapple, "Aus Rudolf Kassners Reisebriefen an Lili Schalk," *Neue Zürcher Zeitung* 246 (September 9, 1973): 49. When I quote from German publications, the translations in English are my own.
2. *Rainer Maria Rilke—Marie von Thurn und Taxis, Briefwechsel* (Zürich: Niehans, 1951), I: 44; letter of June 2, 1911.
3. *Letters of Rainer Maria Rilke*, trans. Jane Bannard Greene and M. D. Herter Norton, 2 vols. (New York: Norton, 1945 and 1947), I: 47.
4. Gottfried Benn, *Gesammelte Werke*, ed. Dieter Wellershof (Wiesbaden: Limes, 1959/1961), IV: 15. See also Wolfgang Martens, *Lyrik kommerziell* (Munich: Fink, 1975).
5. Fürstin Marie von Thurn und Taxis-Hohenlohe, *Erinnerungen an Rilke* (Frankfurt am Main: Insel, 1966), p. 12. Italics mine.
6. Rainer Maria Rilke, *Briefe an seinen Verleger, 1906–1926*, ed. Ruth Sieber Rilke and Carl Sieber, 2 vols. (Wiesbaden: Insel, 1949), I: 11.
7. Joachim W. Storck, "Ein unbekannter Brief Rainer Maria Rilkes an Anton Kippenberg," *Jahrbuch der Deutschen Schillergesellschaft* 18 (1974): 23–36.
8. *Rainer Maria Rilke—Lou Andreas-Salomé, Briefwechsel*, ed. Ernst Pfeiffer (Zürich: Niehans, 1952), p. 48; letter of June 30, 1903.
9. As to the latter, cf. E. M. Butler's scathing critique in her *Rainer Maria Rilke* (New York: Cambridge University Press, 1941), pp. 7–9.
10. *Briefwechsel zwischen Schiller und Goethe*, ed. Hans Gerhard Gräf and Albert Leitzmann, 3 vols. (Leipzig: Insel, 1912), I: 445.
11. The letter to Kappus is from *Briefe an einen jungen Dichter* (Leipzig: Insel,

n.d.), p. 31; letter of December 23, 1903. The second letter quoted may be found in *Letters,* I: 57; letter to Emanuel von Bodman, August 17, 1901.

12. Ibid., I: 105; letter of April 8, 1903 (italics mine).

13. Ibid., I: 83; letter of September 5, 1902.

14. Ibid., I: 121; letter of August 8, 1903.

15. The first quotation is from *Briefwechsel mit Lou,* p. 282; letter of December 19, 1912. See *Briefe* (Leipzig: Insel, 1933), IV: 211, for the second quotation, in a letter to Alfred Walter von Heymel, February 27, 1912. Last, see *Briefwechsel mit Lou,* p. 250; letter of December 28, 1911.

16. *Briefe,* IV: 343; letter to Tora Holmström, February 13, 1914. Ibid., p. 175; letter to Annette Kolb, June 23, 1912. Ibid., p. 154; letter to Julie Freifrau von Nordeck zur Rabenau, January 2, 1912.

17. "Der Panther," *Sämtliche Werke,* ed. Ernst Zinn (Frankfurt am Main: Insel, 1955), I: 505.

18. Ibid., p. 655f.

19. *Briefwechsel Taxis,* II: 639; letter of February 2, 1921.

20. Simenauer, *Rainer Maria Rilke* (Bern: Haupt, 1953), p. 265ff.

21. *Briefe,* IV: 47; letter to Clara Rilke, September 4, 1908.

22. *Das Testament,* ed. Ernst Zinn (Frankfurt am Main: Insel, 1975), p. 24.

23. *Hugo von Hofmannsthal—Ottonie Gräfin Degenfeld, Briefwechsel,* ed. Marie Therese Miller-Degenfeld (Frankfurt am Main: Fischer, 1974), p. 20.

24. *Briefe aus Muzot* (Wiesbaden: Insel, 1936), p. 25; letter to Nora Purtscher-Wydenbruck, August 17, 1921.

2

Rilke: Nirvana or Creation

WALTER KAUFMANN

Rilke was one of the greatest poets of all time. One might suppose that we are still too close to Rilke to judge him. After all, he was younger than Bertrand Russell, who died fairly recently, in 1970. Still, even in ordinary times a hundredth birthday anniversary should provide enough perspective, and in the more than half century that has passed since Rilke's death the world has changed so much that we can judge his poetry with some assurance.

Rilke has his detractors, however, and I am willing to make two concessions to them. First, many of Rilke's poems are not very good at all. That would seem to be true of almost all poets who have left a very large body of work, and it is mean-spirited to crow about their failures. Poets have to be judged by their best works, and in German only Goethe has given us as many first-rate poems as Rilke has.

Secondly, I should admit that, apart from his poetry, Rilke does not come across as an exemplary human being the way Goethe and Heine or Nietzsche and Freud do. This is not to say that some people may not find Rilke more attractive than the others and less problematic. The point is rather that, apart from his poetry, Rilke does not confront us as a representative figure of almost mythical stature. Although his only major prose work, *Malte Laurids Brigge* (1910), was a great and revolutionary work, any claim that he does would have to be based on Rilke's letters. They fill many volumes, and some of the letters are very beautiful. Yet the person who emerges from these volumes is weak, frequently precious, and disconcertingly lacking in humor.

Many of his poems are also marred by affectations, and even some of the best narrowly miss self-parody. But they do miss it. This distinction between Rilke as a human being and his poems may suggest that my approach is narrowly aesthetic. Yet the point is not at all that the poems are beautiful quite apart from any human reality that may find expression in them. On the contrary, Rilke's finest poems have a human dimension that needs to be felt but is often ignored.

Poetry has become an object of study—especially, graduate study— and difficult poems are attracting disproportionate attention. The kind of difficulty that attracts interpreters and is taught and written about most is all too often the kind that calls for erudition. In line with the cult of quantity and size that is so notable in other fields, too, long poems are often overrated, while short poems are appreciated insufficiently. In the following remarks I shall ignore Rilke's Duino elegies (1923), which are relatively long and have elicited a large body of exegesis. They strike me as uneven and might even be accounted a noble failure if, at the last moment, after Rilke had already considered the work completed, he had not written one more poem and substituted it for the original fifth elegy. Even now, the second, third, and fourth, and then again the sixth and seventh elegies do not brook comparison with the first and the fifth, the eighth and the ninth. To understand the *Elegies*, moreover, nothing is more helpful than to understand Rilke's short poems, to which, incidentally, they often allude.

What makes many of Rilke's short poems difficult—so much so that they are probably not often understood—is that they deal with experiences that many readers do not seem to recognize. The range of the best of them is rather limited. They are variations on a single theme that is, however, as significant as any theme can be. It is the choice between two modes of existence that might be called intensity and peace—the creative life that involves suffering and Nirvana, Eros and Thanatos. The same choice is expressed in the words of Moses: Choose life or death this day. It cannot be proved which choice is better, and a poet's business is not with proofs or arguments. He can try to explore experiences and show us what they are like. This is what Rilke did superbly.

Despite the occasionally disturbing artificiality of his style, Rilke's variations on his central theme are not contrived. They spring from a profound need and are anything but random variations. When they are considered chronologically, we begin to understand Rilke's development as a poet and a human being.

16

II

Compared to Goethe, not to speak of Rimbaud, Rilke matured late. Much of his early verse was poor. But with the appearance of the two volumes of his *Neue Gedichte* (1907–1908), he emerged as one of the major poets of the twentieth century. These "new poems" have often been called *Ding Gedichte*, but the best of them are not about *things*; they are about human experiences and revolve again and again around the central choice mentioned.

Unfortunately, Rilke is not so well known that one only needs to mention the titles of the most relevant poems; one has to quote at least a few poems. I shall limit myself almost entirely to poems that are readily available in a bilingual edition.[1] All of the translations are mine. The English versions aim to capture Rilke's tone as well as his meaning, the tone being part of his meaning.

A critic once cited Rilke's "Love Song" (in *Neue Gedichte*) as an example of Rilke's alleged subversion of our traditional values. In this poem "lovers seek separation, not union," he said, implying that this involved a Nietzschean revaluation of all values. Erich Heller made a major contribution to our understanding of Rilke by noting some of the important affinities between Rilke and Nietzsche.[2] Twenty years have passed since I responded and developed this suggestion in a very different, almost diametrically opposite way.[3] There is no need here to return to Rilke's crucial relationship to Nietzsche; but the claim that Rilke's "Love Song" inverts our traditional values misses not only the point of this one poem but Rilke's central concern with the alternative of Nirvana and intensity.

> Liebes-Lied
>
> Wie soll ich meine Seele halten, daß
> sie nicht an deine rührt? Wie soll ich sie
> hinheben über dich zu andern Dingen?
> Ach gerne möcht ich sie bei irgendwas
> Verlorenem im Dunkel unterbringen
> an einer fremden stillen Stelle, die
> nicht weiterschwingt, wenn deine Tiefen schwingen.
> Doch alles, was uns anrührt, dich und mich,
> nimmt uns zusammen wie ein Bogenstrich,
> der aus zwei Saiten eine Stimme zieht.
> Auf welches Instrument sind wir gespannt?
> Und welcher Geiger hat uns in der Hand?
> O süßes Lied.

Love Song

How could I keep my soul so that it might
not touch on yours? How could I elevate
it over you to reach to other things?
Oh, I would like to hide it out of sight
with something lost in endless darkenings,
in some remote, still place, so desolate
it does not sing whenever your depth sings.
Yet all that touches us, myself and you,
takes us together like a violin bow
that draws a single voice out of two strings.
Upon what instrument have we been strung?
And who is playing with us in his hand?
Sweet is the song.

What the poet seeks is peace. But he is far from deaf to the beauty that can come of lack of peace, of an intensity that is scarcely endurable. "Sweet is the song." The experience of love as a source of suffering is by no means new, although it has been emphasized far less in the West than in Buddhism. The Buddha became peace incarnate and taught that love and attachment breed suffering. The first volume of *Neue Gedichte* contains two poems entitled "Buddha," and the second volume yet another with the title "Buddha in the Glory" (two of the three are included in *Twenty-five German Poets*). In his longing for peace, Rilke returned to the Buddha again and again.

Perhaps none of Rilke's poems is more famous than his evocation of a caged panther in the Paris zoo. Many readers would agree that this is a perfect poem, and that it would be silly to suggest that Rilke's poems are designed merely to make a point. But the mistake made much more often in reading Rilke is to overlook that many of his poems also explore a particular experience and raise questions. The panther in his cage has found peace; but is peace really desirable? We are thrown back upon our central theme.

"Orpheus. Eurydice. Hermes" is a very much longer poem, but no less beautiful than "The Panther"; and it deals with the same alternative. The great poet, the unequaled master of the sweet song, descends to the underworld to bring back from the dead his wife:

Die So-geliebte, daß aus einer Leier
mehr Klage kam als je aus Klagefrauen;
daß eine Welt aus Klage ward, in der
alles noch einmal da war. . . .

The one so loved that from a single lyre
wails came surpassing any wailing women;
that out of wails a world arose in which
all things were there again. . . .

But Eurydice has found peace. Hermes accompanies the poet, and on the way back walks with Eurydice. Rilke's poem describes the ascent. Rilke accepts the tradition that if the poet looks back even once, his wife must return to the realm of death. The poem is woven around the contrast between the poet's intensity of which his art is born and the total peace of Eurydice. Orpheus

> . . . stumm und ungeduldig von sich aussah.
> Ohne zu kauen fraß sein Schritt den Weg
> in großen Bissen. . . .

> . . . looked ahead in silence and impatience.
> His paces, without chewing, gulped the way
> in outsized swallows. . . .

Eurydice

> . . . ging an jenes Gottes Hand,
> den Schritt beschränkt von langen Leichenbändern,
> unsicher, sanft und ohne Ungeduld.

> . . . walked at the hand of this great god,
> her striding straitened by the grave's long wraps,
> uncertain, soft, and void of all impatience.

She has found peace, and anyone who brought her back into this world would not do her a favor. Rilke's evocation of the other world in which —I still hear Marian Anderson singing those words in a spiritual—"all is peace" has never been surpassed. Though long, the poem is not too long; it sustains its mood and central contrast without flagging and ends beautifully.

Even so, those who come to Rilke with entirely different experiences and problems often miss his theme. Robert Lowell, for example, says in the introduction to his *Imitations* that "in poetry tone is of course everything. I have been reckless with literal meaning, and labored hard to get the tone." Yet his version of the Orpheus poem ends:

> . . . the reproachful god of messengers
> looking round, pushed off again.
> His caduceus was like a shotgun on his shoulder.

Rilke's poem ends by repeating two lines used earlier to describe Eurydice's ascent, which are equally appropriate to her descent:

mit trauervollem Blick der Gott der Botschaft
sich schweigend wandte, der Gestalt zu folgen,
die schon zurückging dieses selben Weges,
den Schritt beschränkt von langen Leichenbändern,
unsicher, sanft und ohne Ungeduld.

with sorrow in his eyes, the god of message
turned silently to follow back the form
that even then returned this very way,
her striding straitened by the grave's long wraps,
uncertain, soft, and void of all impatience.

In this poem peace is reaffirmed, but this is not Rilke's last word. He kept wrestling with the tension between creative, painful intensity and peace.

The Orpheus poem stands near the end of the first volume of *Neue Gedichte*. The second volume opens with "Archaïscher Torso Apollos." Here intensity is celebrated and desired. The challenge of the Greek torso is no longer that of the Buddha. Our lives are lacking in intensity. But intensity is nothing like busyness; it is embodied in a headless piece of stone. Still, the stone is not dead; it is glowing and introduces the imagery of burning into our theme.

As one turns the page from the "Archaïscher Torso" one encounters "Leda," a poem that invites comparison with one of the finest twentieth-century poems in the English language, William Butler Yeats's "Leda and the Swan," published fifteen years later, in 1923. Yeats's poem is violent, Leda is raped, and "The broken wall" brings to mind "the burning roof and tower / And Agamemnon dead." The terror of the girl's rape extends far beyond her, and as soon as "the brute blood of the air" has had his pleasure with her "the indifferent beak could let her drop"; as soon as the passion is spent, it is all over and the poem ends.

Rilke's version of the same myth is as different as can be. It is devoid of violence. Even where that may seem to be called for by the story, Rilke chooses to dispense with it, and nothing could be more alien to his tone and temper than a "shotgun" in the last line of "Orpheus. Eurydice. Hermes." Rilke is soft to a fault. But in "Leda," as in the Orpheus poem and in all of his best verse, the softness is no fault. His "Leda" ends:

. . . Er kam nieder
und halsend durch die immer schwächre Hand
ließ sich der Gott in die Geliebte los.
Dann erst empfand er glücklich sein Gefieder
und wurde wirklich Schwan in ihrem Schooß.

. . . He came down, smooth and white,
and sliding his neck through her weakening hand,
he loosed his godhead in her loveliness—
then only felt his feathers' full delight
and truly became swan in her caress.

In Rilke's poem the real climax comes after the sexual climax, after the passion is spent. The most intense experience is discovered to be compatible with peace.

III

Two years later Rilke published *Malte Laurids Brigge*, and another two years later, in 1912, he began his elegies but found himself unable to finish them. The World War did not tempt him to compromise himself as so many others did by writing patriotic trash. He was devastated and fell silent. Only the fourth elegy, which is not one of the better ones, was written during the war, in 1915.

On the last day of January, 1922, the ice finally broke and Rilke's soul was set free again. Perhaps no other poet has ever experienced such a storm of inspiration. In February Rilke was able to complete his *Duino Elegies*, writing the fifth, seventh, and eighth from scratch, and composing much of the ninth as well; and between the second and fifth of February he also wrote the twenty-six *Sonnets to Orpheus* of Part One, while the twenty-nine of Part Two were written between February 15 and 23.

The short poems Rilke wrote during this period are easily as remarkable as his *Elegies*. In fact, the elegies were begun in 1912 and could be offered as a unit, although the material written in February, 1922, is generally far superior to the earlier parts. In the short poems, however, Rilke found an altogether new voice that differs sharply from his earlier poems. While the *Sonnets to Orpheus* were the last volume of German poems Rilke himself published, he wrote other short poems in more or less the same voice until about two weeks before he died. The late short poems bring to mind some of the verse of the old Goethe, even as the *Elegies* brings to mind Nietzsche's "Dionysus Dithyrambs"; but Rilke's style, especially in the short poems, is quite distinctive. Rather oddly, Gottfried Benn (1886–1956), whose early poems—for example, *Morgue* and "Man and Woman Walk Through the Cancer Ward" (both 1912) —were about as different from Rilke's as poetry can be, imitated Rilke's later voice in his own later poems, beginning in the late thirties. Actually, Rilke was probably in the back of Benn's mind from the beginning. Rilke used the title "Morgue" for a poem in his *Neue Gedichte*, and Benn surely felt that this subject called for an altogether different style. But his late verse is plainly derivative from Rilke's, which was revolutionary.

Although Rilke found a new tone, his central theme remains unchanged. To show this one could cite a very large number of poems, but it will suffice here to consider a very few, beginning with the poem that marks the breakthrough to the final period. Rilke wrote it into a collection of his early verse, as a dedication for Nanny Wunderly-Volkart, whom he called Nike. The poem (datelined Muzot, the last day of January, 1922) was published posthumously.

> Solang du Selbstgeworfnes fängst, ist alles
> Geschicklichkeit und läßlicher Gewinn-;
> erst wenn du plötzlich Fänger wirst des Balles,
> den eine ewige Mit-Spielerin
> dir zuwarf, deiner Mitte, in genau
> gekonntem Schwung, in einem jener Bögen
> aus Gottes großem Brücken-Bau:
> erst dann ist Fangen-Können ein Vermögen,-
> nicht deines, einer Welt. Und wenn du gar
> zurückzuwerfen Kraft und Mut besäßest
> nein, wunderbarer: Mut und Kraft vergäßest
> und schon geworfen hättest. . . . (wie das Jahr
> die Vögel wirft, die Wandervogelschwärme,
> die eine ältre einer jungen Wärme
> hinüberschleudert über Meere-) erst
> in diesem Wagnis spielst du gültig mit.
> Erleichterst dir den Wurf nicht mehr; erschwerst
> dir ihn nicht mehr. Aus deinen Händen tritt
> das Meteor und rast in seine Räume. . . .[4]

> As long as you are catching *your* throws, all
> is skill and trivial gain. Only when you
> have suddenly caught in your hands the ball
> that an eternal female partner threw
> right at your core in a trajectory

that is an arch in God's vast edifice—
then is ability to catch, a glory—
not yours, a world's. And if you should possess
the strength and daring to return the shot—
no, still more wonderful, if you forgot
daring and strength and had already hurled
the ball—as an old year throws swarms
of migratory birds across the world
that aging warmth tosses to youthful warmth—
then only, in such risks, your playing matters.
Now you no longer try for easy prizes,
nor do you strain for what is hard and flatters
your prowess. Out of your hands rises
the meteor and speeds into its spaces. . . .

As so often in Rilke's late short poems, the syntax and thought are complex and so different from what most readers expect to find in poetry that his verse may seem inaccessible. But the theme we have traced here provides an entry. Forget daring and strength, forget yourself, cease straining, be ready. And suddenly the ball may be yours, and you no longer think, plan, or exert yourself:

. . . Out of your hands rises
the meteor and speeds into its spaces.

What meteor? The poem. It is no longer *your* poem, your work, but a cosmic explosion—a spark that nature struck from you, but suddenly it is not some small spark but something vast that leaves your hands and stuns large numbers of people whom you never knew.

Rilke had lived with the symbol of the ball for a long time. We encounter it, for example, in one of the finest poems in his early volume, *Das Buch der Bilder* (1902), in "The Song of the Idiot":

Ah was ist das für ein schöner Ball;
rot und rund wie ein Überall,
Gut, daß ihr ihn erschuft
Ob der wohl kommt wenn man ruft?

Look at that ball, isn't it fair—
red and round as an everywhere.
Good you created the ball.
Whether it comes when we call?

Only an idiot would think that it does, and Rilke had long learned to his sorrow how it does not come by being summoned or craved. But when it did come, he was ready for it.

In *Sonnets to Orpheus* our theme remains central. In the third sonnet, "Ein Gott Vermags," it is particularly accessible. Of the many other sonnets in which this theme is developed, it will suffice to mention the twelfth of Part Two, which begins:

> Wolle die Wandlung. O sei für die Flamme begeistert,
> drin sich ein Ding dir entzieht, das mit Verwandlungen prunkt;
> jener entwerfende Geist, welcher das Irdische meistert,
> liebt in dem Schwung der Figur nichts wie den wendenden Punkt.

> Choose to be changed. Oh experience the rapture of fire
> in which a life is concealed, exulting in change as it burns;
> and the projecting spirit who is master of the entire
> earth loves the figure's flight less than the point where it turns.

Here the motif of burning is fused with the imagery of flight and conversion, and the poem ends:

> . . . Und die verwandelte Daphne
> will, seit sie Lorbeern fühlt, daß du dich wandelst in Wind.

> . . . And Daphne, since her transformation
> into a baytree, desires that you choose to be changed into wind.

Still, you must change your life and choose to be changed—but not into something in particular that you desire. Rather it is a matter of not locking yourself up, of not being rigid, of becoming fluid and squandering yourself. The last words of the two sonnets cited here are the same in the original German: *Wind.* The meaning of that image is spelled out in a dedicatory poem of 1924: having no hiding place; being shelterless, living dangerously without any preconceived goal.[5] In these late poems the fusion of peace and intensity is attained.

IV

Both the *Elegies* and the *Sonnets* were published in 1923, and at the end of the year Rilke wrote another dedication for "Nike" into a copy of the *Elegies*.[6] It may be possible to read this poem, especially in the German original, without even noticing the image that seems crucial to me. In German the poem ends:

> aber, statt daß es schwinde,
> steht es im Glühn der Erhörung
> singend und unversehrt.

This is surely an allusion to the story of Moses and the burning bush: "the bush was burning, yet was not consumed."

24

Für Nike
(Weihnachten 1923)
Alle die Stimmen der Bäche,
jeden Tropfen der Grotte,
bebend mit Armen voll Schwäche
geb ich sie wieder dem Gotte
und wir feiern den Kreis.
Jede Wendung der Winde
war mir Wink oder Schrecken;
jedes tiefe Entdecken
machte mich wieder zum Kinde-,
und ich fühlte: ich weiß.
Oh, ich weiß, ich begreife
Wesen und Wandel der Namen;
in dem Innern der Reife
ruht der ursprüngliche Samen,
nur unendlich vermehrt.
    Daß es ein Göttliches binde,
hebt sich das Wort zur Beschwörung,
aber, statt daß es schwinde,
steht es im Glühn der Erhörung
singend und unversehrt.

For Nike
(Christmas 1923)
All of the streams' countless voices,
every drop from the rock,
as the cycle rejoices,
to the god I give back,
trembling with weak arms, and glow.
Sudden breezes, though mild,
were for me omen or fright,
even profound insight
made me again a child—
and I felt that I know.
Oh, I know, I feel sure,
names and their nature and need;
inside of what is mature
rests the original seed,
only increased and illumed.
Hoping for something divine,
rises, to conjure, the word,
and it refuses to wane,

burning as it is heard,
singing and not consumed.

Line ten borders on self-parody: "und ich fühlte: ich weiß." Indeed, this poem was not written all at once. The first twelve lines had been completed in the first days of February, 1922, and the rest had been added just before Christmas 1923. To my mind the bulk of this poem is a prelude to the last two lines; and the whole poem may be seen as a prelude to the last entry in Rilke's last notebook, probably written in mid-December, 1926, about two weeks before Rilke died of leukemia on December 29.[7] Here his abandonment has become total; there is no hiding place, no shelter, no effort, no memories, as the poet burns to death, singing.

There are many poems about death, many kinds of death, not many poems about cancer, none like this. It was born of a lifelong exploration of one of the greatest themes with which a poet could deal: the tension between peace and intensity, between the serenity of the Buddha and the challenge of an archaic torso of Apollo. And when nature hurled leukemia at the poet, he was ready and responded:

> Komm du, du letzter, den ich anerkenne,
> heilloser Schmerz im leiblichen Geweb:
> wie ich im Geiste brannte, sieh, ich brenne
> in dir; das Holz hat lange widerstrebt,
> der Flamme, die du loderst, zuzustimmen,
> nun aber nähr' ich dich und brenn in dir.
> Mein hiesig Mildsein wird in deinem Grimmen
> ein Grimm der Hölle nicht von hier.
> Ganz rein, ganz planlos frei von Zukunft stieg
> ich auf des Leidens wirren Scheiterhaufen,
> so sicher nirgend Künftiges zu kaufen
> um dieses Herz, darin der Vorrat schwieg.
> Bin ich es noch, der da unkenntlich brennt?
> Erinnerungen reiß ich nicht herein.
> O Leben, Leben: Draußensein.
> Und ich in Lohe. Niemand der mich kennt.

There is much that a "new critic" could tell us about this poem while ignoring the fact that it was written by a dying man. Rilke's mannerism may even invite an excessively aesthetic approach. But I have tried to show that his last poem as well as the others cited here have a dimension too often ignored by Rilke's readers. In a book on *Tragedy and Philosophy* (1968) I called it the philosophical dimension. What is

26

needed is the discovery of the poet's experience of life as reflected in his works, which need to be seen as stages in a development. "Komm du, du letzter, den ich anerkenne" marks the end of a road. And one understands the poem better when one has followed this road.

> You are the last I recognize; return,
> pain beyond help that sears the body's cells:
> as I burnt in the spirit, see, I burn
> in you; the wood, that for so long rebels
> against the flame you kindle, comes of age;
> behold, I nourish you and burn in you.
> My earthly mildness changes in your rage
> into a rage of hell I never knew.   .
> Quite pure, quite planless, of all future free,
> I climbed the stake of suffering, resolute
> not to acquire what is still to be
> to clad this heart whose stores had become mute.
> Is it still I that burns there all alone?
> Unrecognizable? memories denied?
> O life, O life: being outside.
> And I in flames—no one is left—unknown.

NOTES

Revised versions of this essay have appeared in *The Times Literary Supplement*, London, December 5, 1975, and in *Life at the Limits: Photographs and Text*, by Walter Kaufmann (New York: Reader's Digest Press, distributed by McGraw-Hill, 1978). *Life at the Limits* is also included in *Man's Lot: A Trilogy: Photographs and Text*, by Walter Kaufmann, also published by Reader's Digest Press (1978). This fuller version includes my translations of "The Panther," "Archaic Torso of Apollo," and *Ein Gott Vermags*.

1. With three exceptions, "Nike," "For Nike," and "Komm du, du letzter . . . ," all of Rilke's verse cited here will be found in *Twenty-five German Poets: A Bilingual Collection*, ed. and trans. Walter Kaufmann, with an introduction (New York: Norton, 1975). The publisher's kind permission is acknowledged gratefully.

2. E. Heller, "Rilke and Nietzsche," in *The Disinherited Mind* (Cambridge: Bowes & Bowes, 1952).

3. "Nietzsche and Rilke" and "Art, Tradition, and Truth"—both published originally in 1955 and reprinted in *From Shakespeare to Existentialism* (Garden City, N.Y.: Doubleday, 1960).

27

4. *Sämtliche Werke* (Frankfurt am Main: Insel, 1956), II: 132; henceforth *SW*.

5. *SW*, II: 261, and *Twenty-five German Poets*, p. 249.

6. *SW*, II: 256–57.

7. *SW*, II: 511.

3

The Poet and the Lion of Toledo

HANS EGON HOLTHUSEN

To arouse enthusiasm about Rilke today is difficult. From the very beginning, and according to its own thematic nature, Rilke's poetry has been able to show its true contour only in the counterperspective of critical thought! When it came into existence, the poetry appeared as an exuberant celebration of itself: as a jubilant affirmation of "das Ganze" in the name of Orpheus, the divine singer; as an unqualified self-glorification of the "Apollonian principle," in the language of a great poet of the twenties. "Errichtet keinen Denkstein. Laßt die Rose / nur jedes Jahr zu seinen Gunsten blühn."[1] These words were once known by heart and were quoted again and again, and it was regarding these very times that one could say that "ein Gespräch über Bäume fast ein Ver-brechen war" because it implied a silence about so many crimes.[2] And he who made this bitter point was himself one of the great German poets of the century. Yet this would be no argument against the other, the only one who could possibly challenge his, Brecht's, position as the best poet of the age. "Nur im Raum der Rühmung darf die Klage / gehn, die Nymphe des geweinten Quells."[3] This was taken as the height of poetic accomplishment, as irrevocable as a verse of Horace. It has surely not declined in quality during the fifty years since Muzot, yet how is it that it has lost some of its power and sonority? This can clearly be explained by an enormously changed intellectual climate, the omnip-otent *Zeitgeist*. The *Zeitgeist*, if indeed it is still definable in mytho-logical terms, today sides with the punished faun Marsyas and against the executioner Apollo, against an arrogant, cruel, and "repressive" Apollo.

In what ways, then, does the poet of the *Duino Elegies* concern us

29

here today? The "secondary literature" has recently decided to focus on Rilke's political ideas. Thus, Egon Schwarz took a few of Rilke's statements of a naïvely pro-Mussolini attitude from the poet's correspondence with the young Italian countess Aurelia Gallerati-Scotti (*Lettres Milanaises*) and wrote a book under the title *Das verschluckte Schluchzen* (1972) about the "fascist" Rilke. Schwarz compiled many "reactionary," "inhumane," and allegedly "antisemitic" materials from the writings and letters of his victim. He discovered a direct connection between the Milan Letters and the "ideology" of the *Duineser Elegien*. As an example, he viewed the implied praise of simple "things" in the ninth elegy (such as "house," "bridge," "well," "gate," "jug," "fruit tree," "window") as a "flight into a precapitalistic past," a defense for "Blut und Boden."[4] An excellent presentation of the "antifascist" Rilke can be found in the catalog for the memorial exhibition of the German Literary Archives in the Schiller National Museum, on display in Marbach in 1975. Here we are presented, in great detail, not only with a leftist Rilke, linked to Rathenau and Masaryk, but also with an *extreme* leftist Rilke, almost a bolshevist, a bosom buddy of Kurt Eisner and Ernst Toller. It would appear that Rilke left Munich in the year 1919, for all practical purposes out of disgust at the White Terror. The *Milan Letters* are here disposed of in a few words as an excusable misinterpretation explainable by sickness and misunderstandings.

Both of these perspectives are deplorably misleading. Thus, it is high time to defend the *genus irritabile vatum* once and for all from the increasingly rude imputations of political pedantry. I do not know if an effort to find new access to Rilke in the present situation can succeed. Rilke himself recommended that his most particular opus, *Malte Laurids Brigge*, be read "against its current" ("gegen seinen Strom") or "against the grain" ("wider den Strich").[5] For him, *Malte* was something like a "methodic" experiment, and ergo it was—even after it had been finished—an open question between the reader and the author inasmuch as they can be seen as partners bound to each other by the text and being together on the road of "des longues études." Thus, one is not entirely at cross purposes with this poet when, as a literary critic, one follows a course that to some extent is "against him," which, nevertheless, does not underestimate his position and does not deny a very basic interest and sympathy. Much could be gained if such an effort merely succeeded in replacing the nonsense of false political suspicions and empty insinuations with a meaningful—although critical—argument.

True, Rilke was a favorite poet of the thirties, a favorite object of the prevailing method of Germanic studies, and a favorite model for the philosophical school of the day. I must add that, in my own case, the ideas of existentialist philosophy were a stimulus to my work as well as a great help to me in my struggle against the totalitarian ideology of the Nazi state. At the same time, the ideas of dialectic theology (and the concomitant reform attempts within the Roman Catholic church) appeared attractive. Thus, it is understandable why the theologically oriented books by Fritz Dehn (1934) and Romano Guardini (1941) found such a ready audience. Anyone who wishes to convince us today that the Rilke literature at that time was written primarily by "hagiographers," and, indeed, in such a tone "als habe dieser Dichter auf einem fremden Planeten gelebt und nicht unter uns auf einer von allen möglichen historischen Katastrophen . . . heimgesuchten Erde," just does not know the literature.[6] Egon Schwarz, for one, shows us in the first lines of his book that either he did not read those secondary works or that he did not understand them. After all, it was a question of *niveau*, intelligence, and sometimes almost a question of political ethics as to who was captivated by Rilke, and why, and under what circumstances.

I think of W. H. Auden, who, along with Stephen Spender and J. B. Leishman, was one of the most fervent admirers of Rilke in England, and who, for a time, was so much under Rilke's influence that many of his productions from that period sound almost like English translations from the *Neue Gedichte*. I think, above all, about a sonnet from Auden's 1938 cycle, *In War Times*. This poetic cycle is part of a book that Auden wrote, together with Christopher Isherwood, about a mutual trip to China, under the title *Journey to a War*. China was at that time entangled in a military conflict with Japan, and Auden knew what the importance of this Japanese aggression was, inasmuch as it was related to Franco's attack in Spain, and what it portended for the future of human civilization. No one knew better than this young international reporter from Oxford who at the time wanted his lyrical work understood as a type of poetic journalism. This sonnet is the poem of a passionate antifascist who was, at the same time, a passionate Rilke admirer, and who, surprisingly, linked the theme of resistance against the fascist enemy around the world to a motif from Rilke's biography. The name of the tower of Muzot is mentioned, and every reader of Rilke will immediately grasp the anecdotal detail from the poet's correspondence to which a reference is being made. The passage is a well-known one from a letter to Lou Andreas-Salomé, written on the evening of the eleventh of February, 1922, to notify her of the great event represented by the completion of the *Elegies*: "Ich bin hinausgegangen und habe das kleine Muzot, das mirs beschützt, das mirs, endlich, *gewährt* hat, gestreichelt wie ein großes altes Tier."[7] And here follows the text of Auden's poem:

> When all the apparatus of report
> Confirms the triumph of our enemies;
> Our bastion pierced, our army in retreat,
> Violence successful like a new disease,
>
> And Wrong a charmer everywhere invited;
> When we regret that we were ever born:
> Let us remember all who seemed deserted.
> Tonight in China let me think of one,
>
> Who through ten years of silence worked and waited,
> Until in Muzot all his powers spoke,
> And everything was given once for all:
>
> And with the gratitude of the Completed
> He went out in the winter night to stroke
> That little tower like a great animal.[8]

It is not the aesthetic quality of the elegies that is meant here but the moral energy, the solemn patience required to complete such an enormous undertaking as this cycle, which quite obviously was not to be accomplished according to Rodin's monastic law "Toujours travailler!" However, we should give a second thought to the fact that it was this particular case that had become a legend in Auden's poem: this "Dottore Serafico," this discoverer of the "bees of the invisible," who was related to the social reality of his time in the same way the imaginary unicorn, a favorite of his muse—"O dieses ist das Tier, das es nicht gibt"—was related to the ordinary reality of Brehm's "Tierleben." This should encourage us to reflect once more the antithesis between the "ethical" and the "aesthetic," a relationship of meaning that in recent times has been understood only in terms of a sharply exclusive "either / or," to recognize again the essential kinship of concepts, over and above the antithesis, the ever-possible *quid pro quo*.

With the Second World War behind us, the borders were open again; the international horizon *in artibus et litteris* was revived. In England, T. S. Eliot stood at the peak of his fame, and in Paris the existentialist left dominated the scene. How did the reputation of the hermit of

Muzot and his popularity, in the sense of his influence on others, fare? Rilke seemed then, twenty years after his death, an established "great" in world literature, his work a "modern classic." He shared this honor with an international aristocracy of authors who, often despite fundamental differences in themes, national traditions, and the requirements of their languages determined by historical usage, still were considered as more or less equal in rank: authors such as Joyce and Eliot, Proust and Valéry, Kafka and perhaps Thomas Mann. The series of names could be shortened or lengthened; one would perhaps have to include Garcia Lorca and Pablo Neruda and, from the last two decades on, probably Brecht, too. One could argue about Valéry, but one would probably be able to agree on the five or six most important names. Those great writers were the ones who were viewed as the decisive initiators of "modern" literature, literature that was experienced as "modern" and classified by means of international consensus. People were indebted to them for what was won and secured in the years 1910 through 1930 as the result of their "revolutionary" breakthrough accomplishments in literature, and, indeed, in notable cooperation with the great artists and thinkers from almost all other disciplines of human cultural endeavor: painting, architecture, music, etc.

I cite here a critical finding which at that time was overpoweringly clear to me, but which to many contemporaries must have remained a matter of complete indifference; for it has something very selective and, at the same time, something too succinct about it. It ignores the empirical diversity of the manifestations with which the scholarly world must be concerned. I speak of the idea of the modern "Ausdruckswelt" as an ensemble of artistic achievements of a "revolutionary" nature. At that time the topics being discussed by artists and others were so-called "changes in consciousness," matters concerning the history of ideas, definitions of the "situation." "Erkenne die Lage," said Gottfried Benn (around 1950), and he said it with the elegance and a sharpness in his tone typical of staff officers. Further, he stated, "Der Mensch steht ganz woanders als seine Syntax." Man was in need of protection and orientation. He had been driven, by means of a philosophical catastrophe, from a metaphysically secure home. He was a "disinherited mind" ("enterbter Geist") and an "unsheltered man" ("unbehauster Mensch"). Both are definitions that have been articulated in view of figures such as Rilke and Kafka and have appeared as titles of volumes of essays which at that time were able to arouse a certain amount of interest. Both phrases (or titles) reveal how much even here the European tradition—those "three thousand years" apostrophized by Goethe—was honored as a normative criterion. Tradition and "revolutionary" development were related to each other as point is to counterpoint. Thus, a kind of *avant-garde* traditionalism was the watchword of the day. The great human and artistic verification of this apparently paradoxical formula was T. S. Eliot.

Muttering from the ranks of the veterans? Why not, if something can be demonstrated by the old stories, something that can be of use in clarifying the current attitude towards a problem? Even traditionalists without a home ("unbehauste Traditionalisten") have their difficulties with each other. Thus, at that time a difference of opinion (one which I am tempted to view as exemplary) became a matter of public record between Erich Heller, the author of *Enterbter Geist*, and me (I was responsible for *Der unbehauste Mensch*). By means of our difference of opinion, the problematical aspect of Rilke was touched upon and even, one might say, described in somewhat shocking terms. To make a long story short: I had maintained that some of Rilke's most characteristic ideas were "mistaken"; for example, the idea of one's own death ("der eigene Tod"), the idea of nonpossessive love, and the idea of the "Weltinnenraum," within which the border between immanent and transcendent reality is denied.[9] This was certainly a rather unscholarly position. I think I was very much under the influence of Rudolf Kassner who later, in a brilliant foreword to Rilke's correspondence with Marie von Thurn und Taxis, himself characterized the Rilkean "doctrine" flatly as a false doctrine, as a "fallacy," a fallacy that could have been the "basis of a wonderful poetical work" ("Grund, Unterlage einer wundervollen Dichtung").[10] In my discussion I proceeded from a Christian-existentialist point of view and operated on the basis of a method that polarized the poet-reader relationship. It was a method that in many respects was more interested in essayistic maneuvers than in philological detail work. At least one could say about the method that it represented the exact opposite of what the American critic Cleanth Brooks once called the "heresy of the paraphrase."[11]

It is possible that the sort of thing that can be accepted in a piece of great prose by Kassner must be viewed as unacceptable in a straightforward literary-critical discussion. In any case, it was Erich Heller's opinion that one could not permit me to get by with such an amateurish argumentation. He admonished me vigorously, but at the same time he let the question stand; for the question of "poetry and belief" had definitely belonged in England to the old standbys of literary discussion since the early essays of T. S. Eliot. Heller wrote: "If the ideas [that is, Rilke's] were all humbug, or if, as Herr Holthusen suggests in his book on Rilke, they were all 'wrong,' in the sense of contradicting that 'intuitive logic' which tells us what is a true and what is a false picture of man, then the poetry would have little chance of being what he believes it to be: *great* poetry."[12]

Even today I am seized by a sort of philosophical attack of shivers whenever I think about this "intuitive logic." But then my position was strengthened because T. S. Eliot himself bestowed on us the honor of intervening in our dispute in the context of his Goethe speech in Hamburg of May, 1955. Eliot had been challenged in the most pointed manner in Heller's article, which dealt primarily with him, and it was, therefore, not surprising that he took my side and voted against Heller. Today I tend to believe that Heller probably was more right than wrong *vis-à-vis* Eliot. At that time I viewed Eliot's expressed opinion as the intervention of a *deus ex machina*, whereby it was certainly less important for whom he decided than that he considered our line of questioning valid, indeed, that he expressly identified with it.

Ten years after Eliot's speech in Hamburg, a critical symposium took place in Berlin, a symposium dedicated simultaneously to Rilke and Thomas Mann that revealed an extremely far-reaching change in the intellectual climate. I remember a quite drastic formulation from one of the newspaper accounts that summed up the results of the discussion. Rilke was compared to a fish about to be cooked: head and tail had to be thrown in the garbage; only the middle was edible. Both the early and the late Rilke were rejected in favor of the middle Rilke, the author of the *Neue Gedichte* and *Malte* (or at least of certain passages of *Malte*). It was a call for a realistic Rilke, a Rilke whose image could be reconciled with certain conceptions of literature stressing realism.

It is possible that this gathering of critics in Berlin was dominated by strongly Marx-oriented people. Nevertheless, the voice of the symposium expressed a view held not only in the camp of the leftist critics but also by its opponents, a view held by dissenters of all persuasions, by practically all of the partners in the critical discussion: a general, unavoidable, and probably also irreversible new orientation in matters relating to Rilke. Let us not speak at this moment of the all-encompassing change in the intellectual climate that has been apparent in the previous twenty years. Let us, instead, call to mind something quite simple and elementary: the pure passage of time, historically lived time. The Russian theoretician Viktor Šklovskij, one of the leading intellects of the formalistic school, once suggested, in order to explain the phenomenon of literary development (not a specific development, but development in general), the concept of a "dialectical self-generation of new forms."[13] By means of the concept he expressed an insight that, in my opinion, cannot be overestimated. Let us modify Šklovskij's definition just slightly and apply it to our topic. The history of the response to literature ("Rezeptionsgeschichte") can be explained in a new way as a continuous "dialectical self-generation of new judgments." Stated concretely and rather like a postulate: an extremely manneristic, masterly artist such as Rilke, whose language became ever more refined and extravagant, an artist like this *had* to meet sooner or later with critical reserve, displeasure, skepticism, finally even with opposition. One of the first among Rilke's early admirers to put such a reaction into words was W. H. Auden. As early as 1956, in his inaugural lecture as a professor of poetics at Oxford entitled "Making, Knowing and Judging," we find a declaration that, even though polite, is still rather crushing: "Boredom does not necessarily imply disapproval; I still think Rilke a great poet, though I cannot read him any more."[14] I would not cite this passage by Auden if I did not know how many Rilke readers of my generation—often very hesitantly—came to a similar conclusion. How am I to relate such a conclusion to Robert Musil's famous opinion, expressed in 1927, that was once so evident to all of us: "This great lyric poet did nothing other than to make the German poem perfect" ("Dieser grosse Lyriker hat nichts getan, als dass er das deutsche Gedicht zum ersten Male vollkommen gemacht hat")?[15] What is a "perfection" that is not immune to the influence of time, which robs a work of its magic and its value? Could it be possible that Musil had set perfection on a par with boundless virtuosity and technical mastery of the highest degree? Could it, on the other hand, also be conceivable that the quality that Auden believed made Rilke a "great poet" was hidden behind his virtuosity and only needed to be expressed in a new way?

I ask myself which quote from the teeming quodlibet of available Rilke materials would be suitable in order to demonstrate what I mean but what I still have not made abundantly clear. I decide instinctively for the second stanza of one of the several "Narcissus" poems which originated in April, 1913. Let us attempt to disregard all that we already know about the topology of the narcissistic image, about its role as protagonist in the late-symbolistic poetry, in works by George, Valéry, and others, about its significance for the understanding of the thematic constellations in works by the later Rilke. Let us concentrate, instead, with a regained sense of innocence, on the text:

> Er liebte, was ihm ausging, wieder ein
> und war nicht mehr im offnen Wind enthalten
> und schloß entzückt den Umkreis der Gestalten
> und hob sich auf und konnte nicht mehr sein.
> He loved back what had been in him before,
> reconquered what the open wind had captured,
> short-circuited perception, and, enraptured,
> cancelled himself, and could exist no more.[16]

The stanza is unbelievably accomplished; it is elegant, subtle, modish, at the same time of an unreserved artistic radicality. Its thematic constellation is highly distinguished; its form is perfect if not "ravishing"; but is it beautiful? Is it as beautiful as, for example, Goethe's "An den Mond," Mörike's "Laß o Welt o laß mich sein"? Doesn't one have the feeling that something is missing in these verses, keeping them from being entirely beautiful, an indispensable vitamin, an essence that is not soluble in the sheer virtuosity of the versification? Is something suppressed and kept from us? The language, one could say, is alone with itself. Whoever wishes to go a step further could say that the language sleeps with itself. That is an intriguing, somehow shocking and strange finding. If my feeling for language does not deceive me, this diagnosis may be deduced directly from the wording of the stanza, and, indeed, from the first line: "Er liebte, was ihm ausging, wieder ein. . . ." I will not repeat at the moment my earlier thesis on the "falsity" of the idea of nonpossessive love. I maintain that this line presents itself as an offense against the sense of linguistic "tact." What Rilke intended to be real precision and "genuine accomplishment" ("reines Leisten") looks a bit strange in printed form. It is linguistically untenable, distorted to the point of grotesqueness, involuntarily funny, and a bit embarrassing, a bit—obscene. "Er liebte, was ihm ausging, wieder ein. . . ." I am not speaking here about the phenomenon of the "Stilblüte," which in the works of bad or inexperienced writers is not uncommon and which occasionally crops up even in the works of great authors: for example, Schiller's "Milch der frommen Denkungsart." What I have in mind is a tendency toward linguistic errors originating in Rilke's fundamental conception of "Weltinnenraum" and revealing a disjointed relationship between interior and exterior, between a subjective lyrical "I," which proliferates rapidly, and a "non-I," which is enervated and disembodied to the point of unreality. Ever since my student days I have cherished the following example, found in one of the famous letters from and about Toledo addressed to the Princess Thurn und Taxis in the fall of 1912. There Rilke attempts to portray the impression of the magnificence, the elemental quality, and the echoes of Genesis that this city made on him, certainly not without assistance from El Greco's great painting. In the process, it occurs to him: "Aber draußen auch wieder, kaum hundert Schritt vor dieser unübertrefflichen Stadt, müßte es denkbar sein, auf einem der unverheimlichten Wege einem Löwen zu begegnen und ihn sich durch etwas Unwillkürliches in der Haltung zu verpflichten."[17]

Now, this lion that one is supposed to obligate to oneself there on a Spanish highway in the year 1912 by means of some instinctual behavior, this lion is not to be compared with Rilke's unicorn, "das Tier, das es nicht gibt." This is not even possible as a creature of the imagination because the language, which possesses its own sense of reality, does not permit him to exist.

There are worse things, one might maintain, than a small comical lapse in the zeal of reporting about a great travel experience. God knows, there are, and we'll find an abundance of them in Rilke's poetry. In the "Ode an Bellman" (from the year 1915), for example, we find an incredibly unsuccessful variation, miscarried to the point of parody, on one of Rilke's own cardinal themes, the affirmation of suffering for the sake of the "whole":

> Da schau, dort hustet einer, doch was tuts,
> ist nicht der Husten beinah schön, im Schwunge?
> Was kümmert uns die Lunge!
> Das Leben ist ein Ding des Übermuts.
> Und wenn er stürbe. Sterben ist so echt. . . .

> Look, someone's coughing. Yet, in his distress,
> has he not reached a kind of rhythmic beauty?
> Lungs can't claim all our duty.
> Life always was a piece of wantonness.
> Suppose he died. Why, dying is so true. . . .[18]

Or we find, in a letter-poem to the young Viennese woman Erika Mitterer, a two-line mishap with unavoidably ambiguous overtones:

> Ob ich regnen kann, ich weiss es nicht,
> über dir, du sanfteste der Matten . . .

I wonder if I can rain (I don't know)
on you, the softest of meadows.[19]

Perhaps it would not be entirely senseless, apropos of Rilke, to discuss the concept of a highly gifted tastelessness. As an example of Rilke's tastelessness, one could cite the famous infamous passage about the "Telephone Christ," into which one calls continuously, "Hey, who's there?", and no one answers (in the letter from Ronda of December 17, 1912).[20] In addition, there would be the fatal *Sieben Gedichte* from the late fall of 1915, in which the resurrections, the ascensions, and the burials of the human phallus are celebrated, with a consciously blasphemous mix-up of the spheres.[21] The poems are a nightmare of tastelessness, which Rilke, to be sure, never published, but which he also did not destroy. And so on it goes. If I were to suggest to someone the dissertation topic "The Grotesque in Rilke's Poetry," I would recommend that the doctoral candidate vigorously systematize the wealth of material and that he, above all, not overlook the role that the conscious and often skillfully inserted stylistic element "grotesque characterization" plays in Rilke's work. A famous example would be the Puritan church from the tenth elegy, the "fertig gekaufte, reinlich und zu und enttäuscht wie ein Postamt am Sonntag."[22]

"Nirgends, Geliebte, wird Welt sein als innen," goes the famous line from the seventh elegy.[23] How often and endlessly has that line been interpreted: as the central and key thought of a poetic evaluation by Rilke of his contemporary world and as the guiding principle of a nearly systematic doctrine of individual existence and cosmic reality as Rilke developed it in his two great poetic cycles of the year 1922. Erich Heller, in his essay entitled "Die Reise der Kunst ins Innere" (1965), linked up the Rilkean idea of a continuous and consistent transformation of the "visible" world into "Weltinnenraum" by means of the human powers of perception to a thesis from Hegel's aesthetics. According to Hegel's thesis, art is bound, on its fateful one-way trip through the ages, to become the expression of the "pure inwardness of human subjectivity" ("der reinen Innerlichkeit der menschlichen Subjektivität") in its last, i.e., its "romantic" phase. Heller sees in Rilke's late works a literal fulfillment of a Hegelian prophecy. Hegel is here elevated to the position of a binding authority against whose philosophical oracle there is no appeal.[24] Heller's interpretation has always given me somewhat uneasy feelings. It has something fatalistic about it, almost defeatist. From Hegel's director's chair it is declared that all romantic art is an art "post artem." The end-stage art described here seems to be a last gesture of leave-taking as a human soul departs from the external world—with an adoring side-glance upon the fourth elegy, which again and again has proved to be particularly challenging to this excellent scholar. I ask myself if one should register opposition to such a boldly speculative maneuver, opposition, that is, to the peculiar kind of fatalism implied by it. After all, the poet of the *Duino Elegies*, inasmuch as he can be interpreted as the voice of the "pure inwardness of human subjectivity," is kind of *ex cathedra* approved and canonized, as it were, and the end of art is confirmed forever in the name of Hegel. I ask myself how I can argue against this poet in view of the pathological deficiencies of his verse as well as the curiously idiosyncratic "perfection" that Musil had in mind. I find my argument in the writings of a rather well-known contemporary of Hegel who was also his peer, though in matters of romantic art not quite in agreement with him. I find it in Goethe's formula of "die Wahrheit des Realen."[25] We see at first glance that, *vis-à-vis* this formula, the lion of Toledo will be difficult to defend.

Why, however, at the second-to-the-last moment should I still involve the old bigwig of Weimar, by whom one can, as is well known, prove anything? Because there is something very crucial and decisively important about Rilke's relationship to Goethe. One has to think it over most carefully in order to understand Rilke's peculiar position in the history of German literature. In linking Rilke with Goethe, I am making the assumption that Goethe in a sense represented the very wholeness of German literature as its overwhelming *Pontifex maximus*, and he does so to a degree such as could scarcely be said of another author in any other literature of our cultural orbit. By saying this I do not wish to idolize him, but only to emphasize that strangely comprehensive, all but all-embracing quality of his achievement with its profound and long-range effects as far as the development of the German language is concerned. There was something "cosmic" in the universal character of his *oeuvre*, or, let's say, rather something like an "objective correlative" to the awareness of a cosmic wholeness within which one could feel "at home." I would like to call it the "ecumenical" quality of his nature, in the original Greek sense of "world inhabited by human beings." No one has defined the ecumenical dimension more appropriately than Herman Grimm, one of the great Goethe scholars of the nineteenth century, when he, in the introduction to his Berlin lectures (1874) on

Goethe, asserted, with a bold but obvious comparison from the world of the natural sciences: ". . . that Goethe affected the intellectual atmosphere of Germany like a tellurian event which raised our climatic temperature by so and so many degrees. If something like that were to happen a new vegetation, a different form of agriculture and, thereby, a new basis for our entire existence would result."[26] Here one is reminded in a charmingly casual way of the agriculturally based etymology of the word "culture" (from *colere*). It is well known that Goethe was not exactly a kindred spirit of Rilke, for whom he had significance only in his later life, if at all. I remember the often quoted letter of the thirty-six year old Rilke to a young lady who had called his attention to the "Harzreise im Winter": "What will you think of me when you read that I didn't know those great lines of classical moderation until last evening. . . . I must tell you that only now, gradually and under all kinds of precautions, do I gain admiration for Goethe; to be sure, where it does occur, it is immediately the very greatest, most absolute, admiration." It is true that Rilke was enthusiastic about the Gustgen letters; he read the *Campagne in Frankreich* and *Die italienische Reise*; but all of this was something like "make-up work" and does not appear very significant.

Let us now add to our thoughts on the relationship (or rather non-relationship) of Rilke and Goethe, the following circumstances of Rilke's life: his growing up in a linguistic diaspora, in the environment of Prague, which he perceived very strongly as the literary "provinces"; then his life-long aversion to identifying himself with the German world and to settling in Germany; and his life-long lack of a geographic home, a situation he insisted on and strongly maintained. It even may be said that the various (extra-German) elective homelands, as epoch-making as they were at any given time for his artistic development, above all Russia, Paris, and the Valais, in different ways again express his essential homelessness. Let us imagine a poet who prefers to live in a foreign-language environment in order to keep his own language more or less exclusive as a luxury-dialect, a dialect spared from the everyday world and intended only for artistic purposes. One day—the scene is Paris—the need to hunt up a German equivalent to the French word "palme" (inner surface of the hand) seizes him suddenly like a ravenous hunger; he leaves his cave, rides through the entire city in order to seek out his friend André Gide. In this situation, Gide alone can help, for he is—so cultivated was this generation—the owner of a copy of Grimm's German dictionary. If we now summarize these impressions and also recall the unmistakable lyrical idiom of the hermit from the Rue de Varenne (from Muzot, etc.), always with the concept of the "ecumenical" in the background as a point of reference, then we have before us a phenomenon for which I can find no other word but this: "exterritorial." Rilke's art was created between languages, between peoples, to a certain degree even—when I think of the range of motifs in the *Neue Gedichte*—between the arts.

No other poet of the late-symbolistic generation deviated so far from Goethe and the literary community—neither Hofmannsthal nor George, and not even Benn. No one went further in the alchemy of the conversion from spoken speech into art-and-nothing-but-art, no one drove sheer virtuosity so far. Therefore, he could appear to Robert Musil to be the greatest lyric poet since the Middle Ages. On the other hand, Auden does not mention Rilke in his poem "Thanksgiving," where, shortly before his death, he paid tribute to those authors from the English and world literature to whom he was especially indebted. Horace, Brecht, Yeats, Kierkegaard, and Goethe appear—Goethe, strange to say, as a natural scientist:

Goethe, devoted to stones
Who guessed—he never could prove it—
Newton led Science astray.[27]

Rilke is not mentioned any more. It seems to me, however, that since Auden was not only a person of breathtaking intelligence but also of all non-German men of letters whom I knew the one who loved the German language most and knew German literature best, his ever-increasing admiration for Goethe in the later years of his life is a fact of considerable importance. I cannot help relating it to his earlier respect for Rilke. In a foreword to an English translation of Goethe's *Italian Journey*, Auden made a number of perceptive remarks, including the following: "He [Goethe] always refused to separate the beautiful from the necessary, for he was convinced that one cannot really appreciate the beauty of anything without understanding what made it possible and how it came into being. To Goethe, a man who looks at a beautiful cloud without knowing, or wishing to know, any meteorology, at a landscape without knowing any geology, at a plant without studying its structure and way of growth, at the human body without studying anatomy, is imprisoning himself in that aesthetic subjectivity which he deplored as the besetting sin of the writers of his time."[28]

Here we have a defense for the "Wahrheit des Realen," from which beauty is not to isolate itself. It is a defense for the whole realm of man and nature as conceived by Goethe, of earth and heaven, primeval stone and artistic creation. It is the judgment of a hardened, unbending "realist" who also once went through a period of Marxism without suffering lasting damage. I read this passage involuntarily as a critical reply to a passage from Rilke's second elegy, which I once admired deeply:

Frühe Geglückte, ihr Verwöhnten der Schöpfung,
Höhenzüge, morgenrötliche Grate
aller Erschaffung,—Pollen der blühenden Gottheit,
Gelenke des Lichtes, Gänge, Treppen, Throne
Räume aus Wesen, Schilde aus Wonne, Tumulte
stürmisch entzückten Gefühls und plötzlich, einzeln,
Spiegel: die die entströmte eigene Schönheit
wiederschöpfen zurück in das eigene Antlitz.

Early successes, Creation's pampered darlings,
ranges, summits, dawn-red ridges
of all beginning,—pollen of blossoming godhead,
hinges of light, corridors, stairways, thrones,
spaces of being, shields of felicity, tumults
of stormily-rapturous feeling, and suddenly, separate,
mirrors, drawing up their own
outstreamed beauty into their faces again.[29]

Here the beautiful is obviously no longer linked to the necessary; it has become autonomous in an extravagant way, highly narcissistic in character, only concerned with itself, charmed by itself, blissfully void of any world. So, too, the linguistic texture of these verses which seem to be a perfectly adequate rendering of that celestial vision: white on white, splendor on top of splendor, an excessive supply of ö- and ü-sounds, a hyperbolic style reminiscent of Quirinus Kuhlmann: "O überweißes Weiß. . . ." I know that these verses, compared to others of their sort, are unsurpassed, but I read them today without significant personal feelings of sympathy, with cold admiration.

In conclusion, I wish to cite still another short Rilke poem that doesn't play in heaven and not even above the tree line, "Ausgesetzt auf den Bergen des Herzens" (once a favorite poem of the generation of the 1930s), one that leads us back down into the valley, into the world inhabited by human beings. It is no more than a six-line sigh in the form of a poem, unrhymed, parlando, a soft, composed witness of solidarity with one's fellow-creatures. It should remind us that beyond the reach of this critical attempt there is still much to discover in Rilke's poetry, about which we can become genuinely enthusiastic:

> Immer wieder, ob wir der Liebe Landschaft auch kennen
> und den kleinen Kirchhof mit seinen klagenden Namen
> und die furchtbar verschweigende Schlucht, in welcher die andern
> enden: immer wieder gehn wir zu zweien hinaus
> unter die alten Bäume, lagern uns immer wieder
> zwischen die Blumen, gegenüber dem Himmel.

> Time and again, however well we know the landscape of love,
> and the little church-yard with lamenting names,
> and the frightfully silent ravine wherein all the others
> end: time and again we go out two together,
> under the old trees, making our couch once more
> between the flowers, face to face with the sky.[30]

NOTES

Virginia Miller prepared the translation of Professor Holthusen's German manuscript. This essay appeared previously in German, entitled "Der Dichter und der Löwe von Toledo," in Hans Egon Holthusen, *Kreiselkompaß* (Munich: Piper Verlag, 1976), pp. 138–60. Reprinted by permission of the publisher.

1. R. M. Rilke, *Sämtliche Werke* (Frankfurt am Main: Insel, 1955), I: 733; henceforth *SW*. ("Set up no stone to his memory. Just let the rose / bloom each year for his sake.") *Sonnets to Orpheus*, trans. M. D. Herter Norton (New York: Norton, 1962), p. 25.

2. Bertolt Brecht, "An die Nachgeborenen." In this poem Brecht writes that "a conversation about trees was almost a crime."

3. *SW*, I: 735. ("Only in the realm of praising may Lament / go, nymph of the weeping spring.") Trans. Norton, p. 31.

4. Egon Schwarz, *Das verschluckte Schluchzen* (Frankfurt am Main: Athenäum, 1972), p. 103.

5. R. M. Rilke, *Briefe aus den Jahren, 1914–1921* (Leipzig: Insel, 1937), p. 241, and *Rainer Maria Rilke et Merline, Correspondence*, ed. Dieter Bassermann (Zürich: Niehans, 1954), p. 25.

6. Schwarz, p. 1.

7. *Rainer Maria Rilke—Lou Andreas-Salomé, Briefwechsel*, ed. E. Pfeiffer (Zürich: Niehans, 1952), p. 464.

8. *The Collected Poetry of W. H. Auden* (New York: Random House, 1945), p. 331.

9. H. E. Holthusen, *R. M. Rilke: A Study of His Later Poetry*, trans. J. P. Stern (Cambridge: Bowes & Bowes, 1952), pp. 42–43.

10. *Briefwechsel mit Lou*, p. xxxvii.

11. Cleanth Brooks, *The Well Wrought Urn* (New York: Harcourt, 1947), p. 192.

12. Erich Heller, *The Disinherited Mind: Essays in Modern German Literature and Thought* (New York: Farrar, Straus & Cudahy, 1957), p. 156.

13. Quoted from Boris Eichenbaum, *Aufsätze zur Theorie und Geschichte der Literatur: Aus dem Russischen übersetzt von Alexander Kaempfe* (Frankfurt am Main: Suhrkamp, 1965), p. 47.

14. W. H. Auden, *The Dyer's Hand and Other Essays* (New York: Random House, 1962), p. 51.

15. Cf. H. E. Holthusen, *Rainer Maria Rilke in Selbstzeugnissen und Bilddokumenten* (Hamburg: Rowohlt, 1958), p. 167.

16. *SW*, II: 56. Trans. J. B. Leishman, in R. M. Rilke, *Poems, 1906–1926* (New York: Norton, 1957), p. 145.

17. R. M. Rilke, *Briefe aus den Jahren, 1907–1914*, ed. Ruth Sieber-Rilke and Carl Sieber (Leipzig: Insel, 1939), p. 259.

18. *SW*, II: 101. Trans. Leishman, p. 212.

19. *SW*, II: 300.

20. *Briefe aus den Jahren, 1907–1914*, p. 270.

21. *SW*, II: 435–38.

22. *SW*, II: 721–22.

23. *SW*, I: 711.

24. Erich Heller, *Die Reise der Kunst ins Innere* (Frankfurt am Main: Suhrkamp, 1966).

25. Conversation with Eckermann on December 25, 1825.

26. Herman Grimm, *Goethe: Vorlesungen* (Berlin: Hertz, 1887), pp. 1–2.

27. "Thanksgiving," in *Thank You, Fog: Last Poems by W. H. Auden* (New York: Random House, 1974), pp. 36–37.

28. J. W. Goethe, *Italian Journey (1786–1788)*, trans. W. H. Auden and Elizabeth Mayer (New York: Schocken, 1968), p. xvi.

29. *SW*, I: 689. Trans. J. B. Leishman and Stephen Spender, in R. M. Rilke, *Duino Elegies* (New York: Norton, 1967), p. 29.

30. *SW*, II: 95. Trans. Leishman, p. 205.

4

Rilke and Eliot

STEPHEN SPENDER

I

Rilke's *Duino Elegies* and Eliot's *Four Quartets* have it in common that whilst in both poems the poetry realizes in its language the aims of symbolism and the aesthetic movement at the end of the last century, this language of apparently pure poetry merges with meanings which are religious. The poetry itself is, one might say, not the only goal of the poems: or, perhaps one should say there is a goal beyond the one of pure poetry—religious vision. I don't mean that these poems fail to provide deep aesthetic satisfaction. But the aesthetic merges into the religious significance. In these poems Rilke and Eliot are both using the aesthetic tradition in order to convey their religious sense of life.

For the purposes of what I am saying it is important at the outset to illustrate this. So let me begin by citing an example of Rilke's symbolism in a passage which, read in part, seems symbolist poetry; but which, reading on, one sees to go beyond the symbolist to the religious vision.

In the ninth elegy, Rilke writes:

Sind wir vielleicht hier, um zu sagen: Haus,
Brücke, Brunnen, Tor, Krug, Obstbaum, Fenster,-
höchstens: Säule, Turm.

Are we, perhaps, here just for saying: House,
Bridge, Fountain, Gate. Jug, Fruit tree, Window,—
possibly: Pillar, Tower?[1]

Read so far and one might think that experience and ideas, which are the material of the poem, lead to these symbols, which are mysterious ends-in-themselves, as in a poem of Mallarmé. The German words are: "Haus, Brücke, Brunnen, Tor, Krug, Obstbaum, Fenster," and, "höchstens: Säule, Turm." By themselves these words seem to be *termini*, points of arrival rather than departure, symbols of pure poetry, mysterious ends-in-themselves. However, read further and one discovers that these symbols are not ends, but beginnings, starting off points. Where I have used the word "beginnings" Rilke uses the word "threshold." "Threshold" means the point at which things symbolized press forward into consciousness and attain their being and their significance, which is religious as well as poetic. Rilke views this realization of consciousness of nature, the past, God, as the supreme task of man. The task is to make the forces outside him become conscious through him. Poetry is a means, though not the only one, by which this can be achieved. But it is supreme in being the use of language in which all transformations become imagined and explicit. After the evocation of the symbols "Pillar" and "Tower" in the passage I have quoted, it continues:

> . . . aber zu *sagen*, verstehs,
> oh zu sagen so, wie selber die Dinge niemals
> innig meinten zu sein. Ist nicht die heimliche List
> dieser verschwiegenen Erde, wenn sie die Liebenden drängt,
> daß sich in ihrem Gefühl jedes und jedes entzückt?
> Schwelle. . . .

> . . . but for *saying*, remember,
> oh, for such saying as never the things themselves
> hoped so intensely to be. Is not the secret purpose
> of this sly Earth, in urging a pair of lovers,
> just to make everything leap with ecstasy in them?
> Threshold. . . .

The poetic symbol then is not an ultimate, a verbal sign in which a great many experiences, associations, sounds, odors, color, dissolve into the poetic word. Something has to be said, self-realization is fulfilled through the symbolism. Nor—I should hasten to add—is the symbol simply a sign which stands for some identifiable object outside itself. "Jug" does not stand just for a vessel that will hold liquid nor does it stand for something for which it is identifiably metaphorical, such as the pleasures of the senses symbolized by the jug of wine in Fitzgerald's version of the quatrain of Omar Khayyám. It retains its mystery, the evocativeness and effulgence of the word within the context of the poem. But while doing this it is a point at which the things symbolized spring into consciousness.

For Rilke, the symbol is a point at which things become transformed into what he calls "invisibility":

> Erde, ist es nicht dies, was du willst: unsichtbar
> in uns erstehn?-Ist es dein Traum nicht,
> einmal unsichtbar zu sein?-Erde! unsichtbar!
> Was, wenn Verwandlung nicht, ist dein drängender Auftrag?

> Earth, is it not just this that you want: to arise
> invisibly in us? Is it not your dream
> to be one day invisible? Earth? invisible!
> What is your urgent command, if not transformation?

The poets are the vehicles of consciousness. Rilke conceives of it as their task to bring what is symbolized by things into consciousness; that is, to make them achieve invisibility.

Rilke has a highly selective view of those who are capable of the task of transforming earth—that is, the material of living—into the invisible: a task which the angels perform with consuming ideal energy:

> . . . und gesetzt selbst, es nähme
> einer mich plötzlich ans Herz: ich verginge von seinem
> stärkeren Dasein. Denn das Schöne ist nichts
> als des Schrecklichen Anfang, den wir noch grade ertragen,
> und wir bewundern es so, weil es gelassen verschmäht,
> uns zu zerstören.

> . . . if one of them suddenly
> pressed me against his heart, I should fade in the strength of his
> stronger existence. For Beauty's nothing
> but beginning of Terror we're still just able to bear
> and why we adore it so is because it serenely disdains
> to destroy us.

Men and women who have the greatest ability to transform the visible into the invisible are those whose lives are consecrated in heroism, prayer, suffering, or death: lovers at certain moments of mutual ecstasy, but still more those who have remained faithful to an unrequited love, heroes absorbed into the energy of their own action, the newly dead, saints. They do this through becoming their state of being. The poet realizes in language their existing. He recognizes them and enshrines them in his poetry. The angels have no existence independent of his power to imagine forces so incomparably greater than his. The poet has to suffer, imagine the angels who are only a magnified, reflected image of his own making and transforming. In this concept of the task of the poet, Rilke is close to Keats in *The Fall of Hyperion* where the poet is portrayed as having to bear the burden of the real world in its wholeness, which he transforms through imagination into language. In Keats's poem, corresponding to Rilke's angels who are perpetually transforming the material of life into burning spiritual energy, is Moneta, the priestess of the temple, the stern instructress who tells the poet that a poet who is only a dreamer is less than nothing. The true poets are "those to whom the miseries of the world / Are misery and will not let them rest." Moneta herself represents the ideal functioning of great poetic imagination. Keats writes of Moneta as Rilke might have written of the angels:

And yet I had a terror of her robes
And chiefly of the veils, that from her brow
Hung pale, and curtained her in mysteries
That made my heart too small to hold its blood.

The poet then is looked on as an intermediary between angel or priestess and his poetry. But angel or priestess are of course his own supreme fiction. Thus for Keats and Rilke the endured or suffered world is potential poetry in which that world discovers a higher reality. This is their humanist religion. Fundamentally, there is no separateness of poetry from religion in their minds. The two are fused in the projected ideal figures of Keats's Moneta, Rilke's angels.

II

But Eliot insists on the separation of poetry from religion, although at certain points the two overlap. Eliot's earliest held view of the relation of the content of ideas or emotions or experiences which go into a poem and the poem itself was that these were simply material to be transformed into the "language rich and strange" which was the poetry and which became something quite separate from the content. He argued in essay after essay of his early criticism that poets do not express philosophies or emotions in their poetry. They need not necessarily believe the views that they put into their poetry: views which are only there because the poet sees how he can make poetry out of them. Thus Dante might have written *The Divine Comedy* not because he accepted the philosophy of Thomas Aquinas but because it provided him with material out of which he could make his masterpiece. He need not have believed in the philosophy of Aquinas at all.

When Eliot became converted to Christianity, the idea that a poet who expressed Christian views in his poetry need not necessarily be a Christian lost its appeal for him. He even conceded that Dante perhaps after all did believe in the philosophy of *The Divine Comedy*. Indeed he now found himself wondering how much a reader could understand Dante without entering into his beliefs. Yet he still insisted that the language of poetry was not the same as that of religion. He thought that the language of religion was that of dogmatically stated truth and as such it was much more important than poetry. However, the language of poetry sometimes overlaps with that of religion, that of religion with poetry. Nevertheless, even when this happens in *Four Quartets*, it is still very much Eliot's concern that poetic truth and religious truth should not be regarded as one. Hence he maintains throughout *Four Quartets* a three-sided debate between poetry considered as pure poetry, poetry which overlaps with the language of religion, and religion which is not poetry but dogma and literal truth. The meeting place of dogmatic truth and poetic truth is in the word considered as poetry and the Word (with upper case *W*) considered as God, the Word made Flesh. Both are seen in the aspect of their own special truth. There is the truth attained and then lost again in the struggle of the poet to use language with precision, and the truth that is the Word of God incarnate which is sacred doctrinal truth sometimes expressed in language indistinguishable from poetry. At times, poetry is the only language in which revelation can speak, but that does not make religion poetry.

> Words strain,
> Crack and sometimes break, under the burden,
> Under the tension, slip, slide, perish,
> Decay with imprecision, will not stay in place,
> Will not stay still. Shrieking voices
> Scolding, mocking, or merely chattering,
> Always assail them. The Word in the desert
> Is most attacked by voices of temptation,
> The crying shadow in the funeral dance,
> The loud lament of the disconsolate chimera.[2]

There is a transition then from the word which is poetry to the Word which is God.

Eliot does not abandon altogether the aim of pure poetry. But he is striving here towards something else, something which shifts between the philosophy or belief out of which he makes poetry, and language in which the belief is more important than the poetry. Yet the distinction between language as poetry and language as belief is obstinately maintained. He dismisses a lyrical passage reminiscent of Mallarmé with the words:

> A periphrastic study in the worn-out poetical fashion,
> Leaving one still with the intolerable wrestle
> With words and meanings. The poetry does not matter.

The poetry does not matter, but the dismissal of it is itself an artistic poetic device, of a kind employed by Beethoven—and Eliot is, I think, deeply influenced by Beethoven. In the last movement of the Choral Symphony, the themes of the first three movements are played for a few bars by the orchestra and then dismissed, until the theme of the finale is introduced in which the words of Schiller's *Ode of Joy* are used in order that Beethoven may inject into the music the statement of world-brotherhood in which he himself believes. The Word finds words.

III

So the *Duino Elegies* and *Four Quartets* mark a stage in the development of the work of both their authors when they have come to believe in certain ideas that are more important to them than the poetry. Although they do not abandon their idea that poetry is "autotelic," nevertheless both poems, as it were, reverberate with a theme which is beyond the poetry. Some system of values is constantly being referred to which lies outside the poetry, but upon which the poetry is nourished. The symbol is no longer an end in itself, the poetry is no longer self-sufficient; it is a point of departure to the expression of supernatural values.

These values are different in the work of each poet and attached to entirely different and opposed metaphysical systems. The most obvious difference is that Rilke's supernatural world, in which the angels are occupied in attaining total imaginative consciousness of the world which they tower over, is thought up by Rilke. Eliot's supernatural world claims objective validity in that it is guaranteed by the beliefs of generations of people, it draws on a vast external structure of ideas postulated by philosophers and theologians, and has its habitations in churches, educational systems, and many other human institutions. It is the tradition in its supernatural aspect. All the same, it has to be believed in as literally true, where Rilke is only aesthetically true.

Rilke's angels are projections of his own subjective consciousness. It is not suggested that anyone ever saw one of them or attempted to shoot it down. The obvious parallel here to Rilke's systematization of creatures of his imagination is the system of esoteric symbols of W. B. Yeats in *A Vision*. Yeats sometimes referred to these spirits, mentors, and advisers as though they really existed and as though one of them had, indeed, dictated *A Vision* to him; and sometimes, more modestly, as a storehouse of symbols and metaphors that he could conveniently draw upon in writing his poetry. He does appear to have occasionally, partly, or intermittently believed in these emanations. They have a kind of switched on and off reality, not so glowing and intense as that of the familiar spirits in Blake's poetry, but of that order of being independent of the poet's subjective life.

The angels become convincing if one regards them neither as real nor as inventions but as symbols idealizing human functions that are supremely important, like Coleridge's idea of the imagination as a function of poetic genius which stands close to the eternal I AM of the Creator. The angels express the idea that for human beings to deal with their situation all the material that makes life significant has to be brought into consciousness.

The angels express the ideas of a function, a task of consciousness. The prodigiousness of their performance equals the immensity of the task, which in turn equals that of the material. In his imagery of the angels Rilke seems to be holding out an impossible goal and then criticizing human beings for not attaining it. But before asking whether this does not make impossible demands on humanity (by setting up as standards of comparison with it superhuman beings called angels) we might picture to ourselves that task which is of people reading in a library. In shut volumes on the shelves, row upon row, are nothing less than the spirits of the dead. Consider now: a few people sit reading and writing at tables, transforming through their intelligence these spirits of the dead so that they enter into and become a living part of contemporary life. But most readers and most scholars do this in a mechanical way, throwing the dead material upon the living world like ashes. It is only the scholar who contains what one might call a spark of the Rilkean angelic power and energy who is able to transform that past so that it exists as luminous contemporary life.

Everyone who is, say, a considerable scientist, or artist, or lover, or man of action, projects a kind of shadow-image—or perhaps most exactly a halo-image—around him of the vocation which, as task, he intermittently fulfills. Wherever there is true vocation we see the person who is called dwarfed under the shadow of the ideally fulfillable, but in reality only partially fulfilled, task. The very word "vocation" suggests Rilke's word equals threshold.

Humanity itself is dwarflike against the background of the immense unfulfilled tasks of consciousness. In his letter of November 13, 1925, to his Polish translator, Rilke explains this functioning of the angels which is conceived of as the ideal task of human consciousness. (He employs here the word "transitoriness," by which he means, I take it, events about which we have emotions which take place within, and are swept away by the passage of time.)

> Transitoriness is everywhere plunging into a profound Being. And therefore all the forms of the here and now are not merely to be used in a time-limited way, but, so far as we can, instated within those superior significances in which we share. Not though, in the Christian sense . . . but, in a purely terrestrial, deeply terrestrial, blissfully terrestrial consciousness, to instate what is here seen and touched within the wider, within the widest orbit—that is what is required. Nothing within a Beyond, whose shadow darkens the earth, but within a whole, within the Whole.

This interesting passage concludes:

> The "Angel" of the Elegies has nothing to do with the angel of the Christian heaven. . . . The Angel of the Elegies is the creature in whom that transformation of the visible into the invisible we are performing already appears completed. . . . The Angel of the Elegies is the being who vouches for the recognition of a higher degree of reality in the invisible.—Therefore "terrible" to us, because we, its lovers and transformers, still cling to the visible.—All the worlds of the universe are plunging into the invisible as into their next-deepest reality; some stars have an immediate waxing and waning in the infinite consciousness of the Angels,—others are dependent on beings that slowly and laboriously transform them, in whose terrors and raptures they attain their next invisible realization.[3]

IV

If I look at the angels from the point of view which Eliot adopted when he looked at the humanism of Irving Babbitt, I am bound to say that they appear to be the humanist writ large and reflected in a magnifying mirror. Humanism quintessentializes from past civilization certain examples of virtue and high achievement in thought, art, and noble behavior, isolates them from the religious beliefs that perhaps provided the context that made such achievements possible, just as Rilke extracts and isolates his angels from Christianity.

This process is ultimately subjective in its view of the poet whose task of consciousness is so pressing because it carries the burden of imagining the universe.

Eliot, needless to say, is Rilke's opposite, in being as little as possible subjective. The whole emphasis in Eliot's work is on objectivity. It might be argued that Eliot and Rilke have it in common that they both aim at making individual consciousness the vehicle of tradition, the past, nature, and God. Nevertheless, there is a complete difference of emphasis in them. For Rilke the task of human consciousness is so urgent because nothing, not even God, can become conscious except through the subjective individual who indeed is asked not just to be a transmitter of what is outside him and coming into existence through him, but to aspire to its state of transcending itself through his being; hence the heroes, hence the lovers, and hence the failure of most of us consciously to exist. "For we, when we feel evaporate; oh, we / breathe ourselves out and away."

But for Eliot consciousness is objective spiritual truth, the supernatural outside the individual who can only partake of it by the diminution of whatever in him expresses self. Even before his religious conversion we can sense Eliot feeling that the tradition, the past, enclosed in the great monuments of art, forms a communion of the dead to which the living can only add something by taking measure of its greater reality and entering into its objectivity. In *Four Quartets* the supernatural is viewed as objective, outside time. Through discipline, prayer, and self-denial, the individual may gain an awareness of union with the eternal. But this experience is not of the self, indeed it is of what is objectively valid beyond the self and can only be attained through repudiation of the self.

Eliot and Rilke are both concerned with what Eliot called the "final facts," the nature of love. But for Eliot these are forces external to man, though nevertheless essential to his being. In Eliot's system the individual enters through suffering into the impersonality that is external to himself. With Rilke nature and the divine achieve their significance through being transformed by subjective human experience into language. In the *Duino Elegies* there is no difference between the language that is poetry and that which is religious.

The attitudes of Rilke and Eliot can be contrasted by comparing in the *Elegies* and the *Quartets* the image of the man praying. For Eliot he is someone who deprives himself almost of his own being and enters into the objectivity outside himself. For Rilke he is a man who becomes in his innermost being that self which prayer makes him aware of:

> Voices, voices. Hearken, my heart, as only
> saints once hearkened: so that the giant call
> lifted them off the ground; they, though, impossibles,
> went on kneeling and paid no heed,
> such was their hearkening. Not that you could hear God's
> voice, by a long way. But hark to the suspiration,
> the uninterrupted news that grows out of silence.
> Rustling towards you now from those youthfully dead.

In the *Duino Elegies* Rilke set up a picture of life in which everything external to it acquires significance through entering into that wholeness which is the individual imagination. The angels represent the supremest realization of this transforming task, an ideal which is of course impossible to the poet. Heroes and lovers and the youthful dead represent at moments approximations to this aim, which corresponds in Rilke's universe of transcendent self-awareness, to the point of intersection of that consciousness which exists in time with the timeless, in Eliot.

Rilke enlarges our conception of the great task of comprehension, which is consciousness. However, since consciousness is everything, there is little room left in his view of the world for ordinary people or for those who only have glimpses of awareness—in Eliot's system: "The moment in the draughty church at smokefall."

Rilke, believing thus that it is the task of consciousness to transform the visible into invisible inner life, regards it as a grave defect of our human condition that we are constantly distracted from this task. On the one hand (in the seventh elegy):

> Nirgends, Geliebte, wird Welt sein, als innen. Unser
> Leben geht hin mit Verwandlung. Und immer geringer
> schwindet das Außen.

> Nowhere, beloved, can world exist but within. Our
> Life passes in transformation. And, ever diminishing,
> outwardness vanishes.

But, on the other hand:

> Ja, wo noch eins übersteht,
> ein einst gebetetes Ding, ein gedientes, geknietes—,
> hält es sich, so wie es ist, schon ins Unsichtbare hin.
> Viele gewahrens nicht mehr, doch ohne den Vorteil,
> daß sie's nun innerlich baun, mit Pfeilern und Statuen, größer!

Nay, even where one thing survives,
one single thing once prayed or tended or knelt to,
it's started to reach, as it is, into invisibleness.
Many perceive it no more, but neglect the advantage
of building it grandlier now, with pillars and statues, *within*.

But for Eliot consciousness goes on in the mind of God independently of human beings, and it is only through grace and discipline that man can enter into this objective existence.

Proust, in the midst of describing, in *Time Regained*, a great social occasion, makes one of his asides, to point out that "even a man of genius, from whom we expect, gathered as though round a turning table, to learn the secret of the infinite, utters only these words—the same that had just issued from the lips of Bloch—'Take care of my top hat.'" This indicates a limitation apparent even in men of the most intense inner life, men of learning, imagination and genius, which is undeniable. If we consider the *Duino Elegies* as "criticism of life" in the Arnoldian sense, then on the negative side, Rilke criticizes life for the inability of us who live it, to attain an ideal of total consciousness—of turning externalities into *within*ness. It is this ideal which the angels represent and which heroes, lovers, saints, the newly dead, aspire towards their concentration on their own emotional and spiritual states of being. Rilke's philosophy is, as I have pointed out, ultimately humanist since he divides life into on the one hand that which is to be apprehended and transformed—nature, the earth, the dead, tradition, etc.—and on the other those whose task it is to achieve this transformation of these things outside them into their own inner life. Rilke believes that in the past the traditional pieties of living made it more possible than it is today for men to undertake tasks of transformation. Today the whole world of commercialism, acquisitiveness, advertising, etc., presents a picture of a materialism incapable of such transformation.

In his very illuminating essay "Rilke and Nietzsche" (in *The Disinherited Mind*), Erich Heller states the aims for future humanity which are the positive position from which Rilke makes his negative criticism of humanity, and he connects them with Nietzsche's concept of the Superman. Heller points out that both Nietzsche and Rilke aimed at showing

> . . . that the traditional modes of thought and feeling, in so far as they were determined, or decisively modified, by Christian transcendental beliefs . . . had been rendered invalid by the end of the religion; to replace

them; to overcome the great spiritual depression, caused by the death of God, through new and even greater powers of glory and praise; to adjust, indeed to revolutionize, thought and feeling in accordance with the reality of a world of absolute immanence; and to achieve this without any loss of spiritual grandeur.[4]

And Heller quotes an entry made into a notebook by Rilke at the time when he was reading *Zarathustra*, in which he writes: "He who no longer finds what is great in God will find it nowhere—he must deny or create it."

Eliot's position is the opposite of all this because he felt the modern situation which demanded that man should identify his own consciousness of the past with the God who had died put too great a strain on human nature: even on that of exceptional beings. Also it implied too much contempt of ordinary human beings who were incapable of transferring values once backed by God to some kind of humanist bank. Just as Rilke's vision was of the possibility of man realizing within his own subjective consciousness those values and those mysteries which in the past had been regarded as being outside and beyond humanity, so Eliot's derived from his vivid sense of the limits of the subjective personality. Despair of the ability of human beings to replace supernatural values with their own human ones forced him back onto the vision of supernatural values, of objective forces moving in eternity. Yet with Rilke as with Eliot, both their attitudes arose from reaction to a common despair at what Nietzsche saw as the death of God. They reacted though, in opposite directions, extremes of subjective being and of belief in objective values.

These opposites result in different attitudes. The *Duino Elegies* and the *Four Quartets* belong to opposing worlds. But they derive from that common despair, and therefore have affinities on the level of the deepest seriousness.

For Rilke the "final facts" are the visible reality which has to be transformed into the invisible: a process only achieved by his angels. This is a task of imagining and expressing in language. Inevitably the poet is the priest of such a task. The angels terrify him with the realization of its immensity. The function of poetry is the realization of the task of transformation. There is a feeling in this work of Rilke being imprisoned in poetry: the earth, the past, reality, each is potential poetry and the poet turns it into poetry. True that certain kinds of human behavior of heroes, lovers, etc., are viewed as the type of the visible yearning towards invisible significance, and exist therefore on the level of being which precedes poetry; but who is to recognize this except the poet, and how is it to be realized except through poetry? Thirdly, since immanence—the attaining of significance of the visible by transformation into the invisible—is the theme of the *Duino Elegies*, ordinary people have a place there only as those who fail—being unconscious that there is such an attempt to be made:

> Each torpid turn of the world has such disinherited children,
> those to whom former has ceased, next hasn't come, to belong.

The human world of the *Duino Elegies* is divided into those—the poet—who see what is significant and turn it into poetry, those whose lives are significant and therefore subjects for poems, and the disinherited children.

With Eliot the "final facts" are the supernatural, objectively true, incredibly believed in claims of Christianity. To say that God has to be created by the efforts of man would be simply a denial of the existence of God and of an objectively existing world of supernatural values outside subjective humanity. Religious language is the language of revelation. To treat the language of poetry as that of religion would be to regard religion as poetic symbols and metaphors for the human condition in a world without God.

It follows from this that whatever may be the function of poetry, it is not to become a substitute for religion or for the language of divine revelation. The word of poetry has a very small *w* compared with the infinitely large *W* of the Word made flesh. The function of poetry then is to do only with poetry, and with language. Poetry may be regarded as a kind of game, in which poets are occupied in making poems out of their given material of ideas, experiences, feelings. The responsibility of poets is towards language: purifying "the dialect of the tribe," keeping its meanings precise so that it retains its connections with the language as spoken by the dead, also making it receptive to extensions and modifications, the results of living in the modern world, while resisting the vulgarization, commercialization, and other forms of corruption of it which occur in these circumstances.

According to this view, the seriousness of poetry lies in the poet's realization that it is not serious: this realization opens a door onto what is serious—the Word beyond the word. "The poetry does not matter"—but the realization that it does not do so occurs when the language of poetry coincides with that of religion. And this releases a spring which opens a door onto the language of truth that does matter.

The *Duino Elegies* implies a world in which every other significance in order to attain its meaning within a higher wholeness has to enter into the imagination which is poetry. This leads involuntarily and inescapably to a certain arrogance of poetry, or of great poetry, that which approaches most closely to the function of the angels. It also leads, as we have seen, to a certain disdain for ordinary people, the "disinherited children" who are incapable either of creating significance or behaving significantly. The opposite of this involuntary arrogance of poetry in Rilke, is, in Eliot, humility. The view of life in *Four Quartets* is not that ordinary men and women should achieve states of existence like those of lovers, heroes, saints, the newly dead, etc., as happens with Rilke, but that each according to the limits of his capacities should recognize the objective existence of the supernatural outside himself.

I am not here trying to argue that the philosophy of either Rilke or Eliot, out of which each makes his poetry, is superior to the other. These are perhaps the two greatest long poems of the century. What should interest us is that poems, equally great, could be written from such opposite points of view: Rilke's making such tremendous demands on the subjective consciousness of the individual, Eliot's postulating its near-annihilation in order that it may enter into the objectivity of the supernatural outside itself.

I have not argued here that the philosophy contained in the poetry is immaterial to the merits of the poetry, and that all that matters is that the poet should have transformed the philosophy into poetry. I think that in both these great poems the beliefs of the poets about life are communicated. Moreover, these beliefs, being so different, go far to explain why the poems themselves are so utterly different. They qualify and modify the world communicated by the poetry. I think too that each poem centers on a great and important truth, though the truths conveyed by both poems are opposites, and that the reader's appreciation of the poetry is enhanced by his reception of the communicated truth. Lastly, I think that although these truths are opposite, there is one point at which they meet.

The truth that the *Duino Elegies* rests on is that the meaning of life consists of our consciousness of significance which we create for ourselves. Even if we fail to find a meaning the very search for one, as well as the refusal to be satisfied with a life that is one of purely material achievement or of routine, already has meaning. The meaning of life is the search for a meaning; without this search, life is meaningless. Shelley made the criticism of the modern world in his *Defence of Poetry* that our knowledge has outstripped our capacity to digest it, and that "we must imagine that which we know." Of all Shelley's idealizations this is the one which least has an air of unreality. On the contrary it strikes one as literally true and that our peculiar modern sense of being lost comes from our not having fulfilled this task of imagining. Rilke's truth in its negative aspect rests on the tragic inadequacy of humanity to attain consciousness in its situation as the sole consciousness in the universe. On the positive side his poem provides us with an extraordinary vision of what such consciousness might be.

Eliot's poem is also concerned with consciousness. But it rests on the idea that consciousness does exist partly as the result of the accumulated history of civilization, partly because there is God. Even before he became a Christian, Eliot was acutely aware of the objective reality, the accumulation of all the monuments of civilization as a vast quantitative and qualitative achievement, to which the contemporary individual—poet or scholar—could only relate himself by deprivation of self-consciousness so as to enter into that objectivity. It is at this point that one can say that the opposites of Rilke and Eliot meet. They meet in the conviction that the visible demands to be transformed into the invisible. Rilke, however, regarded this as a purely human task, though one incapable of achievement and therefore projected onto his ideal figures of the angels—themselves perhaps forerunners—as Erich Heller suggests—of a Nietzschean superhumanity. Eliot viewing life in the light of eternity did not make demands on the individual that he must always stand under the reproach of not being able to exceed his own capacities, nor did he judge the whole of humanity by the standard of comparative success or failure in attaining consciousness. Consciousness was the objective reality of supernatural values.

NOTES

1. For this and other revised quotations from the *Duino Elegies*, see Rainer Maria Rilke, *Duino Elegies*, trans. J. B. Leishman and Stephen Spender (New York: Norton, 1967).

2. For references to Eliot's *Four Quartets*, see T. S. Eliot, *The Complete Poems and Plays, 1909–1950* (New York: Harcourt, 1958), pp. 117–45.
3. Cf. *Letters of Rainer Maria Rilke, 1910–1926*, trans. J. B. Greene and M. D. Herter Norton (New York: Norton, 1969), pp. 374–75.
4. Erich Heller, *The Disinherited Mind* (New York: Meridian, 1959), p. 160.

5

Rilke and Ponge:
L'Objet c'est la Poétique

WALTER A. STRAUSS

I

By linking the names of Rainer Maria Rilke and Francis Ponge, I am proposing an examination and a contrast of two significant phases in the development of the modern *Dinggedicht* (thing-poem, object-poem);[1] the first phase, approximately 1906 to 1926, reached its apogee in Rilke, from the *Neue Gedichte* onward to the end of Rilke's life, and climaxed by the *Duino Elegies* and the *Orpheus Sonnets*; the second phase is the entire output of Francis Ponge (born 1899), reaching from about 1920 to the present moment, climaxed by the collection *Le parti pris des choses* and extending to *Le Grand Recueil* of the early sixties and beyond. The dates indicate that the poetic activity of both poets overlaps slightly: Rilke died in 1926; Ponge's writings begin around 1919; yet it must be added that these early pieces attracted practically no attention until the publication of *Le parti pris des choses* in 1942. Nor is there any point in speaking about "influence": I have never been able to find a single reference to Rilke in Ponge's writings. In view of the fact that the French poet's reflections on poetics are rather copious, this phenomenon is tantalizing enough all by itself. Ponge does tend to restrict his remarks almost exclusively to French poets; whether he simply has not read Rilke, or whether he is reluctant to use foreign poets as illustrations for his arguments, remains a moot point. But the aim of the present paper is really not to establish influence, or even affinity, but to contrast the utilization of *things* in poetry as understood by Rilke in the first quarter of this century with the fortune of "les choses" in the years immediately preceding and following the Second World War. It seems to me that such an investigation might succeed in establishing a frame of reference for distinguishing, on the one hand, between a mode of creation that is principally characterized by a Symbolist approach to the image and to language, and, on the other hand, a newer mode of creation that has as yet no adequate designation, but which might well be termed a new "Sachlichkeit," or "Dinglichkeit," or better: a new materialism. At the same time, Ponge's poetics raises all sorts of questions of a cosmological and epistemological nature, and therefore serves as a suggestive and eloquent contrast to the poetry emerging out of Symbolism, a poetry which, as a matter of fact, contains some of the germs of this more recent *poétique*. To put it somewhat differently: our problem will be to distinguish between two kinds of transubstantiation. These reflections consequently involve certain considerations about poetry and its relation to the world, and its interdependence with thought, as well as considerations about the radical centrality of language in any poetry of the present moment, as well as of the future. ("Cet avenir sera matérialiste"—"That future will be materialistic," Rimbaud had proclaimed in his famous "Lettre du voyant.")

I shall begin with a somewhat succinct summary of Rilke's position, as I see it, and then proceed in a more leisurely fashion to Ponge's object-centeredness and its implications.

II

Rilke's career is marked by three nodal points, which pinpoint definite advances in his growth as an artist: points at which various loosely connected strands in his perception of the world and in his grasp of the exigencies of his art tend to coalesce. These nodal points are also geographical landmarks; their names are Paris, Duino, and Chateau de Muzot in Valais. Between them lie periods of crisis and torment, but also of patient fallowness and slow maturation. In Paris the crucial events are Rodin and Cézanne: the discovery of sculptured and painted *things*, which resulted in the first harvest of a new poetry—principally, the *Neue Gedichte*—and issuing in the self-questioning, anguished crisis of *Malte Laurids Brigge*. The second high-water mark is, of course, the Castle of Duino, where the fully-ripened vision is at last sketched out and the beginnings of the *magnum opus* committed to paper. Then follows another period of incertitude and torment, finally resolved and surmounted in Muzot by the completion of the *Elegies*, the *Orpheus Sonnets*, and the mellow yield of the final years.

The Paris experience, then, is the first acid test. "In Paris Rilke learned to see objectively," one critic observes, echoing Rilke's own "Ich lerne sehen" ("I am learning how to see") in *Malte*.[2] Contact with Auguste Rodin and with his work provides the first extensive immersion into a world of man-made objects; and, in a profounder sense, a new contemplation of the artifacts of the Symbolist imagination. Thus the experience of Rodin's art draws Rilke into the magic circles of Baudelaire's and Verlaine's poetry and into an intensification and concentration of his own poetic practice. First of all comes the discovery of *things*. Rilke opens his lecture on Rodin of 1907 with a revealing remark: "But, since I am trying to survey the subject before me, I am persuaded that I must not speak to you about human beings but about things" (*SW*, V: 208).[3] There follows a eulogy on things: "Try to remember whether there was anything that was closer, more familiar and more necessary to you than a thing like that. . . . You seldom realize that even now you still have a need of things which, like those things in your childhood, await your confidence, your love, your dedication" (*SW*, V: 209). Rilke is already stressing the familiarity of certain objects and the inward bonds and resonances that things offer us; the link to childhood is here particularly significant, as it is for his great contemporary, Marcel Proust. Many of these perceptions will be more fully and firmly articulated in the *Duino Elegies*. At the same time, Rilke is also beginning to define the new spatial dimensions of his poetry:

> But let us consider for a moment whether all that we have before us and become aware of and explain and interpret—whether all that is not surface? And that which we call spirit and soul and love: is not all that a mild change upon the small surface of a face close by? And he who wants to give this to us, formed, must he not restrict himself to what is tangible, what corresponds to his means, to the form which he can grasp and feel? And whoever might be enabled to see all forms, and to render them, would he not (almost without knowing it) render all that is spiritual also?
> [*SW*, V: 212]

All these questions culminate in a declarative paragraph that asserts the primacy of artistic craftsmanship upon the surface of things:

> There is but one single surface, mobile and modified in a thousand ways. In this thought one could for one moment think the entire world, and it

was simply entrusted to the hands of him who had this thought. For whether something can become a life does not depend on great ideas but upon the question whether you create from them a handiwork, something that partakes of everyday living, something that endures next to you until the end. [*SW*, V: 213]

The tribute is meant for Rodin, but it is also a gloss on Rilke's poetry of those years—the second part of the *Neue Gedichte* bears the dedication "à mon grand ami Auguste Rodin"—and of the years still ahead. Rilke, in defining the artist's task as a transmutation of surfaces into enduring form, is here appropriating the significant tenets of Symbolist poetics as practiced by Baudelaire, Verlaine, and Mallarmé But there is, nevertheless, a more decidedly "romantic" strain in Rilke, when he summarizes Rodin's work in a lyrical peroration that sounds as though it had been noted down by Malte Laurids Brigge:

Perhaps the secret of this master was that he was so full of loving that nothing could resist him. His desire was so long and passionate and unbroken that all things yielded to him: natural things and all the mysterious things of all times in which the human yearned to be nature. [*SW*, V: 216]

By means of an immense arch he lifted his world over us and placed it into nature. [*SW*, V: 242]

The yearning to obliterate the distinction between art and nature, though it can be glimpsed as a remnant of the Romantic legacy in Baudelaire, is subjected by the French poet to hierarchical dissociation: art is greater than nature, because nature is irretrievably fallen, whereas art has become the modern mode of redemption. Rilke is free from this dualism: things are not only before us and with us and serve as signposts toward an inward spirituality which is not merely metaphorical (that is, verbal), but they are—and will become in his later poetry—the occasions for a transformation of self and world. In this sense Rilke's conception of things remains fully grounded in metaphor and metamorphosis. "Du mußt dein Leben ändern"—"You must change your life"—is the message of the "Archaic Torso of Apollo." We shall have occasion to note that in Francis Ponge "les choses" no longer have a message to communicate; all that is left is an *impulsion* reaching from objects to language, and from language to objects.

The model of Rodin's art, as we have noted, was decisive in Rilke's progression from the *Buch der Bilder* (*Book of Images*) of 1900–1903 to the *Neue Gedichte* (*New Poems*) of 1906–1908 (concomitant with the activity on *Malte*, which is equally important). Nevertheless, the Rodin sculptures are not sufficient to account for the direction that Rilke's mind was taking in those years. Here Cézanne, many of whose paintings the poet studied assiduously in the retrospective exhibit held in the Salon d'Automne of 1907 (exactly one year after the painter's death), plays an important role. Herman Meyer notes that "in Cézanne's art Rilke found a more precise realization than in Rodin's of his own objectivizing intention."[4] If we view this middle phase of Rilke's development as a concerted and intensive effort to achieve a fusion of "seeing" and "saying"—of projecting the poetic object-image in such a way that the resulting object-poem becomes, so to speak, self-sufficient and autonomous, without the intrusion of "meaning" from the outside—we conclude that Rodin's work had simply showed him the way. Rodin's sculptures, after all, are strongly emblematic: *Le penseur, L'éternel printemps, Le baiser, La cathédrale*, and so forth (note the definite articles!)—these works of art call for certain associations from the outside: they ask the spectator, for example, to establish a metaphorical association between the two folded hands and a cathedral. Rilke was evidently searching for something more self-contained in his poetic articulation, such as is splendidly demonstrated in certain poems from the *Neue Gedichte*—most of them well known—such as "Der Panther," "Die Flamingos," "Römische Fontäne," the two hortensia poems, and "Archaïscher Torso Apollos." In these poems, the inward perspective of things, which was to become the focal center of his later poetry, has already been successfully achieved. It should be added, however, that these poems do invite interpretation, but from the *inside*, from the *données* of the poetic statement. This practice is, in many ways, no different from the one espoused by the French poets from Baudelaire to Valéry, a number of whom Rilke was certainly studying at this time. But Cézanne's art offered a more radical challenge: here, in the landscapes and particularly in the still-life paintings, the painter proposed an art of still, harmonious, and totally integrated relationships that were not lost to the inquisitive and perceptive eyes of the poet. On October 10 he writes to Clara Rilke: "Today again I spent two hours looking at individual pictures; in some way I feel that this is useful to me" (*Br*, I: 193). His first impression was reminiscent of Rodin: "Generally speaking, he is often reminiscent of Rodin in his statements" (*Br*, I: 190–1). But most of the remarks go beyond Rodin's lesson; perhaps the comparative "*schauender*" ("more contemplatively") in this letter of October 18 is a clue: "I was only convinced that there are personal inner reasons that place me more contemplatively in front of pictures that perhaps only a little while ago I would have passed with casual interest, without returning to them with greater excitement and anticipation" (*Br*, I: 205). Thus, Rilke praises Cézanne for going beyond Chardin in representing fruit on the kitchen table: "In Cézanne their edibility actually ceases, they have become so real as things ["dinghaft wirklich"], so simply unconsumable in their obstinate presence" (*Br*, I: 187). *Dinghaft* . . . thingified, *chosifié* . . . a truly Rilkean adjective casting its spell over the Aix-en-Provence landscape! It should be noted, in this connection, that Rilke characteristically rendered Cézanne's term "réalisation" into "Dingwerdung," which is not exactly correct as a translation but unimpeachable as an act of poetic appropriation.[5] On the last day of the salon, Rilke goes back to look at *The Lady in the Red Fauteuil* and concludes "It is as if each area knew of all the other areas" (*Br*, I: 217; letter of October 22).[6] That observation is a kind of preview of "Archaïscher Torso Apollos," written during the following summer. Moreover, after showing that every part of the torso is integrated, Rilke says: "denn da ist keine Stelle, die dich nicht sieht" ("for there is no area that does not see you"); and this is, after all, very typically Rilkean: the statue *looks* at the beholder and in effect says to him "Du mußt dein Leben ändern"—which, of course, makes the poem hortatory and emblematic. In fact this striving for pure *Dinghaftigkeit* still lies in the future for Rilke, as yet hidden in the gales of Duino and in the tranquillity of Muzot. The problem is, I think, indirectly articulated in a letter of October 13:

> Today I spent time again with his [Cézanne's] pictures; strange—the kind of environment they produce. Without looking at any particular one and standing between the two rooms, you feel their presence fusing into an immense reality. . . . You also notice increasingly how necessary it was to transcend even love; after all, it is natural to love each one of these things while doing it; but if you show it, you do it less well; you *judge*, instead of *saying* it. You stop being impartial; and the best part, the love, remains extraneous to the work, it does not go into it but is left out, untransmuted: in this way atmospheric painting (which is in no way superior to painting substances) came into being. It was like painting "I love this thing here," instead of painting "here it is." Expecting everyone to see whether I loved it. That is not shown at all, and some may even declare that love didn't have anything to do with it. All that love has been consumed without residue in the art of making. This consumption of love in anonymous toil, from which such pure things are born—perhaps no one has ever done it as successfully as that old man; his diffident and crabbed inner nature supported him. [*Br*, I: 199–200]

68

The quest for love surmounted is, after all, the same that informs Rilke's version of the Parable of the Prodigal Son at the end of *Malte*, and in many respects, the entire book; the quest for anonymous creativity is the hallmark of the orphic poet that fully came into being only at Duino.

In the *Elegies*, then, Rilke discovers the appeal of *things* to the poet and the poet's responsibility toward them. Near the beginning of the first elegy the poet asks the pointed question, "Ach, wen vermögen / wir denn zu brauchen?"—"Alas, whom are we, after all, able to make use of?" and, after declaring that animate beings—angels, human beings, animals—have ceased to be spiritually, poetically, of use to us, because we are "nicht sehr verläßlich zu Haus . . . in der gedeuteten Welt"—"not very reliably at home . . . in the interpreted world" (lines 9–10, 12–13), Rilke inevitably turns to "things":

> Es bleibt uns vielleicht
> irgend ein Baum an dem Abhang, daß wir ihn täglich
> wiedersähen; es bleibt uns die Straße von gestern
> und das verzogene Treusein einer Gewohnheit,
> der es bei uns gefiel, und so blieb sie und ging nicht. [13–17]

> There remains to us perhaps some tree on a slope, one that we might see day after day; there remains to us yesterday's street and the spoiled loyalty of a habit who enjoyed being with us, and therefore it stayed and did not leave.

This sequence of "things" is revealing, since it shows an important difference between Rilke's and Ponge's stance toward things: here we have a natural object, a man-made object, and a pattern of human behavior characterized by its quality of being (being loyal, like a spoiled household pet); note: not "Treue," but the substantivized "Treu*sein*." That is to say, the possibility of a familiar *dialogue* with inanimate things is always *given* in Rilke's world. Over against the "interpreted world" of public existence, an existence in which we feel alienated (from authentic being, to use an existentialist phrase), there remains this pregnant silence of things which invites the poet to enter into communion with them. As the eighth elegy argues, at the beginning of our lives there is "das Offene" ("the open, open-ness"), which reason and interpretation close off as we grow older. The recovery of this openness makes possible, in the ninth elegy, the poetic communion of man with objects and proclaims the task of poet as the "saying" of things. Referring to the poet's obligation to the angel, Rilke writes:

Sag ihm die Dinge . . .
Zeig ihm, wie glücklich ein Ding sein kann, wie schuldlos und unser,
wie selbst das klagende Lied rein zur Gestalt sich entschließt,
dient als ein Ding, oder stirbt in ein Ding—, und jenseits
selig der Geige entgeht. Und diese, von Hingang
lebenden Dinge verstehn, daß du sie rühmst; vergänglich,
traun sie ein Rettendes uns, den Vergänglichsten, zu. [58, 60–65]

Say the things to him . . . Show him how blissful a thing can be, how
free from guilt, and how very much it can be our own; how even the song
of lament can disclose itself pure into form, how it serves as a thing, or dies
into a thing—, and blissfully emanates beyond, out of the violin. And these
things, which live on perdition, understand that you praise them; though
transitory, they entrust a rescuing power to us, who are the most transitory of all.

What appears to be a modern vindication of animism is in effect a deeply
felt plea to awaken the silent voice of things in their relatedness to man,
to break out of the prison-house of interpretation into the openness of
mutuality with objects. The instrumentality of this liberation is poetic
articulation: saying and naming. The objects become involved in a cycle
of transmutation: matter—breath, or spirit—linguistic creation, which
spiritualizes and eternalizes this matter and restores to it an integrity that
it would have irretrievably lost if it had not been for the act of grace
provided by human articulation. Such is the program of the *Orpheus
Sonnets*, in which the reconciler Orpheus functions as the patron saint
and inspirer of this transubstantiation. And since those sonnets are not
only demonstrative but also exemplary and hortatory, we need not be
surprised at the questions they raise and at the solutions they propose.
For example, the remarkable anemone poem, number five of the second
Orpheus sequence:

Blumenmuskel, der der Anemone
Wiesenmorgen nach und nach erschließt,
bis in ihren Schooß das polyphone
Licht der lauten Himmel sich ergießt,

in den stillen Blütenstern gespannter
Muskel des unendlichen Empfangs,
manchmal *so* von Fülle übermannter,
daß der Ruhewink des Untergangs

kaum vermag die weitzurückgeschnellten
Blätterränder dir zurückzugeben:
du, Entschluß und Kraft von *wie*viel Welten!

Wir, Gewaltsamen, wir währen länger.
Aber *wann*, in welchem aller Leben,
sind wir endlich offen und Empfänger?

Flower-muscle, which discloses the morning meadow by and by for the
    anemone, until the polyphonic light of the resounding skies showers
    into its womb,
muscle of the infinite receptivity tensed in the tranquil star-blossom, some-
    times *so* overpowered by fullness that the tranquil beckoning of sunset
is hardly able to return to you the petal-borders flung far back: you, de-
    termination and force of *how many* worlds!
We violent ones, we endure longer. But *when*, in which one of all lives,
    are we finally open and receivers?

The poetic imagery in the sonnet happily unites the male and female
components into an androgynous unit: the "muscular" energy and the
receptive "womb-like" energy; the interplay of visual and auditory sensation; and the progression within the sonorous spectrum from low vowels
to high; the simultaneity of the two energies encapsulated in the unusual
word "weitzurückgeschnellten." And in the final tercet, the word "Kraft"
has been debased into "Gewalt" and has been brought to bear upon our
present-day dilemma, upon the misdirection of our energies, precisely in
order to dramatize our lack of openness and receptivity. In this way the
late poems of Rilke are even more urgently invitations to action—to self-
transformation—more intricate, more subtle, and more accomplished
than the *Neue Gedichte*, which anticipates them.

III

Francis Ponge's earliest texts go back to his twentieth year. Approximately at the time when Rilke was bringing his triumphant vision of the
Duino Elegies and the *Orpheus Sonnets* and the final poems to its full
conclusion, Ponge was laying the foundations of his own *poétique*. In a
brief text written in 1919 and entitled "La promenade dans nos serres"—
"Walking in Our Greenhouses" (*TP*, 145–46) he begins with a poetic
exordium that, except for its characteristic stress on rhetoric, runs parallel
to Rilke's concerns:[7]

O word-draperies, assemblage of literary art, o shrubbery, o plurals, flower-
beds of colored vowels, decoration of lines, shadows of the mute e, masterful
consonant-links, architectures, flourishes of points and short signs, help me!
help a man who no longer knows how to dance, who no longer knows the
secret of gestures, and who no longer has the courage or the knowledge of
direct expression by means of movement.

But he continues in a rather different vein:

> Divine necessity of imperfection, divine presence of the imperfect of vice
> and death in writing, offer me your help too. May the *impropriety* of terms
> give rise to a new induction of the human among signs that have already
> become too detached from the human, signs that are too desiccated, too
> pretentious, too pompous.

And he concludes with a call for a rhetoric of nonsignification:

> O human traces at arm's length, o original sounds, monuments of art's in-
> fancy, barely imperceptible physical modifications, CHARACTERS, mys-
> terious objects perceptible by only two senses and nevertheless more real,
> more congenial than signs—I want to bring you closer to substance itself
> and take you away from quality. I want people to like you for your own
> sake rather than for your meaning. To raise you at last to a nobler status
> than that of simple designations.

This simultaneous animadversion to the *substance* of objects and to the
attribution of *all* the resources of language, conceived in the framework
of nonsignification without, however, abandoning the poetic impetus toward glorification, marks the point of departure of Ponge's work as a
poet and measures his increasing distance from the mystical propensities
of the Symbolists and of Rilke. At the beginning of Ponge's road toward
creation, there stands a resolute commitment to things—the "parti pris
des choses" ("taking the side of things")—doubled by an equally intense
dedication to the possibilities of language, what Ponge first calls "la rage
de l'expression" ("the rage of expression") and subsequently more modestly labels "compte tenu des mots" ("taking account of words").

The point of view of things has its closest parallel in the work of
contemporary painting; in this instance, it is less the canvases of Cézanne
that provide the model, as they did for Rilke, but one of Cézanne's most
illustrious heirs, namely Georges Braque. Despite Ponge's great admiration for Cézanne and Picasso, Braque is actually the great signpost.
Rather than to the vast architectonic compositions of Cézanne, the dramatic and restless creative omnivorousness of Picasso, Ponge is drawn to
the more measured and homely discipline of Braque. The apotheosis of
the still-life, the calm and lyrical surfaces of Braque's interiors—the décor
of rooms with their walls, ceilings and floors, the tables and *guéridons,*
the tablecloths and the fruit, the vases and pitchers—all these things provide suggestive parallels to Ponge's prose-poems. It is true that the work
of Braque would certainly not have been the same without Chardin and
Cézanne, both intensely admired by Rilke as well as Ponge. Yet the

achievement of Braque, it seems to me, lies finally in the mastery of the grammar of painting within the deliberately confined frame of the canvas: the full control of color and shape in the service of the organization of a restricted pictorial space. It is interesting to note that Rilke's admiration for contemporary painting did not go much beyond Cézanne; though he admired greatly the earlier work of Picasso (the fifth elegy is eloquent proof of the fact), he appears to have been uneasy about Picasso's cubist breakthrough as well as about Paul Klee's "distortions." There is, as far as I know, no comment on Rilke's part about Braque's work—that in itself is symptomatic. But it does indicate another point of differentiation between Rilke and Ponge: both poets are strongly drawn to the visual arts during their entire lifetime; Rilke shunned Cubism and Expressionism as "subcutaneous painting," whereas Ponge correctly grasped Cubism for what it was: the liberation of the two-dimensional canvas, the autonomy of pictorial structure, and the recoil from externally imposed "meaning."

Yet the parallel between Braque and Ponge is still closer. Braque's *Notebooks* contain a wealth of aphoristic statements, whose forcefulness was not lost on Ponge.[8] Here are some samples:

> All is sleep around us. Reality is only revealed in the illumination of a ray of poetry. [97]

> The rose gives a form to the void, and music gives a form to silence. [48]

> To define a thing is to replace it with its definition. [35]

> For me, it is no longer a question of metaphor, but of metamorphosis. [99]

> The painter thinks in forms and colors. The object is his poetics. [11]

Place these alongside Ponge's own aphorisms of 1924, and the basic parallel becomes evident:

> The poet must never propose a thought but an object, that is to say that he must make even a thought strike the pose of an object.

> The poem is an object of enjoyment proposed to man, made and set down especially for him. That intent must not be short-changed by the poet. [*TP*, 148–49, "Natare piscem doces"]

As a matter of fact, the affinity and friendship of poet and painter are evident from a number of collaborations, notably Braque's illustrations for Ponge's *Cinq sapates* and Ponge's various essays and *témoignages* in behalf of Braque. Could one not say that, just as for Braque painting is the creation of a geometric (cubic, if one prefers) space inhabited by the objects of man's sight, touch, and contemplation, so Ponge's poems create a verbal and grammatical space inhabited by these same objects?

In this connection let us consider the contrast between Rilke's affectionate handling of the word "Krug" ("pitcher")—admittedly one of his favorite words, one of his privileged *things*—and Ponge's poem "La cruche" (*GR:P*, 105–8). It begins like this:

> Pas d'autre mot qui sonne comme une cruche. Grâce à cet U qui s'ouvre en son milieu, cruche est plus creux que creux et l'est à sa façon. C'est un creux entouré d'une terre fragile: rugueuse et fêlable à merci.

> There is no other word that sounds like "cruche." Thanks to that U which opens up in the middle, "cruche" is more cupped than a cup and after its own fashion. It is something cupped and surrounded by fragile earth: rough and brittle at will. [Translator's note: the word-play in the original involves the similarities of sounds between *cruche*, "pitcher," and *creux*, "hollow."]

This is really a sort of phenomenological bracketing of the object, in such a way that it becomes immediately the occasion for the play of sonorities, and subsequently generates more and more extravagant verbal divagations:

> Elle n'a pas les formes emphatiques, l'emphase des amphores. C'est un simple vase, un peu compliqué par une anse; une panse renflée; un col large—et souvent le bec un peu camus des canards.

> It does not have the emphatic forms, the emphasis of amphoras. It is just a simple vase, a bit complicated by a handle; a bloated belly; a wide neck—and often the somewhat flattened bill of ducks.

These verbal operations do not place the pitcher in a Rilkean "contour of feeling," but in a context of playful articulation, which animates the facets of the objects in such a way as to choreograph their own independent motion, rather than their ballet within us and with us. The poet here acts as a *souffleur* rather than a *maître de danse*. Ponge concludes, fabulously, "Car tout ce que je viens de dire de la cruche, ne pourrait-on le dire, aussi bien des *paroles*?" ("What I've just said of the pitcher, could that not be said of *words* as well?")

Here is yet another comparison between Rilke and Ponge. In the summer of 1924 and spring of 1926 Rilke wrote eleven short poems in French on the subject of "Les fenêtres"; in every instance the window is assimilated to the human feeling that it evokes: the "inward" reality of the window (as the ninth elegy has proposed) merges with the inward reality of the poet who contemplates it.

N'es-tu pas notre géométrie,
fenêtre, très simple forme
qui sans effort circonscris
notre vie énorme? [*GW*, II: 548 and 587]

Are you not our geometry,
window, very simple shape,
you who without effort circumscribe
our enormous life?

and

Fenêtre, toi, ô mesure d'attente,
tant de fois remplie,
quand une vie se verse et s'impatiente
vers une autre vie. [*GW*, II: 549 and 588]

Window, o you measure of waiting,
so often filled,
when a life pours forth and becomes impatient
toward another life.

and

Assiette verticale qui nous sert
la pitance qui nous poursuit,
et la trop douce nuit
et le jour, souvent trop amer. [*GW*, II: 549]

Vertical plate which dishes up to us
the pittance that pursues us,
both the too-gentle night
and the day, often too bitter.

These are the beginnings for three of the poems; they show the rapid and intensive humanization of the metaphors with which the quatrains open. As Rilke had declared in a poem written in 1914, "Werk des Gesichts" ("work of seeing") has by now fully been converted into "Herzwerk" ("work of the heart"):[9] these windows are quickly "translated" into Rilke's innerspace. In a poem of the French *Vergers* series, the poet asks the question:

On arrange et on compose
les mots de tant de façons,
mais comment arriverait-on
à égaler une rose? [*GW*, II: 551]

You arrange and you compose
words in so many ways,

but how could you reach the point
of equaling a rose?

It is this word "égaler" that strikes me as typical of the Rilkean aspiration—and therefore very un-Pongean; Ponge wants merely to *name* the window, to nominate it for poetic office, not to establish a verbal equality, or even equivalence: for him, the order of things and the order of words do not fully coalesce; the thing remains for him, to some extent, a plaything, a display (or "objeu," as he calls it later). Accordingly, his piece "La fenêtre" ("The Window") (elaborated between 1929 and 1953) is subdivided into "Variations avant thème" (!), "Poème," and "Paraphrase et poésie" in an amusing adaptation of baroque musical and poetic terminology. The "pre-theme" variations begin preludically with conceits reminiscent of poets like John Donne or, more relevantly, the French *libertin* poets of the early seventeenth century:

Harem nombreux du jour
Humiliant tribut
Niches au ciel vouées
à raison d'un millier par rues.

O préposées aux cieux
avec vos tabliers.
Bleues contusions
Ecchymoses.

Fantômes immobiliers.

. . .

Par le propre maçon
porte aux ruines ouverte. [GR:P, 41, 43]

Numerous harem of daylight
humiliating tribute
Niches dedicated to the sky
Because there are a thousand of them along the streets.

O sky-waitresses
with your aprons.
Blue contusions
Black-and-blue spots.

Real-estate phantoms, not movable

. . .

By your own mason
Door opened upon ruins.

The "blue contusion" image gives rise to another image which moves across a pun (a punch!) to the following image:

O punchs!
O ponches!
Ponches dont jour et nuit
flamboie la barbe bleue! [*GR:P*, 42]

O punches!
O punch-bowls!
Punches from which day and night
blazes the blue beard!

In the "Poème" the color blue becomes dominant and serves to correlate the profusion of images inventoried in haiku or aphoristic form in the "Variations."

OH BLEUS PAR TOUT LE CORPS DES BASTIONS AUX CIEUX
TRACES DES HORIONS DE L'AZUR CURIEUX
DE TOUTE HABITATION TU INTERROMPS LE MUR
PAR LE PROPRE MAÇON PORTE AUX RUINES OUVERTE
CONJOINTE SOUS UN VOILE AUX ROIS EXTÉRIEURS
PAGE DE POÉSIE MAIS NON QUE JE LE VEUILLE

. . . .

PONCHES DONT JOUR ET NUIT FLAMBOIE LA BARBE BLEUE
LA CLARTÉ DU DEHORS M'ASSOMME ET ME DÉTRUIT [*GR:P*, 45][10]

OH BLUE ALONG THE ENTIRE BODY OF BASTIONS AGAINST
    THE SKY
EVIDENCE OF BLOWS BY THE CURIOUS BLUE SKY
YOU BREAK UP THE WALL OF EVERY DWELLING
BY YOUR OWN MASON DOOR OPENED UPON RUINS
CONJOINED UNDER A VEIL TO OUTSIDE KINGS
PAGE OF POETRY BUT AGAINST MY BETTER WISHES

. . . .

PUNCHES FROM WHICH DAY AND NIGHT BLAZES THE BLUE
    BEARD
THE BRIGHTNESS FROM THE OUTSIDE OVERWHELMS AND
    DESTROYS ME

The profusion of images bears witness to the Surrealist conception of poetry; but the organization is tighter than that of the Surrealists, generally speaking: the Braquean blue color "governs" the poem; the linguistic play "horions" whisks us out of the expected window-perspective of horizons and shoves us into a boxing-match replete with chin-contusions, the whole mixture being finally stirred into a flaming punch-bowl; then there is a return to the Black-and-Blue-Beard, violence now evoking eroticism (the harem has by this time been transposed into veils —no longer merely curtains—serving as off-limits signs on the kings' own property), and the whole thing winds up in a burst of Matisse-Braque *clarté*.

"Page de poésie mais non que je le veuille" stands in the center of the poem. Ponge, with his interior mock-signature "Ponches," seems to be implying, "Yes, the window is poetic, but that's not why I am writing about it. I am writing about it because it is endlessly fascinating." The word "poésie," in contrast to "poème," has something ultimate about it. And, as a matter of fact, the "Poésie" that concludes "La fenêtre" is rather pale and abstract by comparison:

LA FENÊTRE
DE TOUT SON CORPS
RIMANT AVEC ÊTRE
MONTRE LE JOUR. [*GR:P*, 47]
    WINDOW-FENÊTRE
WITH ITS WHOLE BODY
RHYMING WITH "ÊTRE"
SHOWS THE DAY [LIGHT].

That is not altogether surprising. For a creative personality so fully dedicated to *objective* (in both senses of the word) poetry, the French tradition—the European tradition—of rhymed and metrical poetry, *poésie*, was bound to create a dilemma. In his critical and self-critical writings Ponge occasionally raises the question "Am I a poet?" and tends to circumvent any straightforward answer. He is right, of course; it matters very little how his work is finally classified, since it is manifestly *poetic* (that is, it relies exclusively on metaphoric and linguistic correlations) and rests soundly on a *poétique* (that is, on a perception of the subject to be treated and a method of treatment).

The earliest—and inevitable—shape that Ponge's work takes is that of the "Proême." The term is the poet's own coinage, obviously a conflation of "prose" and "poème," and it thereby asserts its own right of eminent domain on the ground prepared by Baudelaire, Rimbaud, Claudel, and many others: the *poème en prose*. This new and intermediate mode of poetic articulation attempts to strike a balance between the discursive and the lyrical. Yet I would not want to rule out a secondary significance of "proême"—lyrical introduction, overture. All of Ponge's poems are openings into the phenomenal world, preparations for seeing and saying, too modest (or too wise?) ever to claim closure or ultimacy. As a matter of fact, this multiplicity of perspectives, this loving concern for the multifacetedness, the tantalizing variety, of things becomes a method of perpetual groping, or probing of the *thing*. The *Ding an sich*, Kant insisted, was unknowable. Ponge would agree, but he would surely add that it was eminently probe-able (that is, probable) and indefinitely nameable. So that the sum total of Ponge's work will constitute (and already does) not a new *De rerum natura* but (as Ponge himself frequently suggested) a *De rerum varietate*.

The early brief pieces in the collections *Proêmes* and *Le parti pris des choses* tend to converge upon aphoristic or emblematic formulations; most of them are celebrations of the things themselves and of the poetic act of dressing them in linguistic garb. Thus, they exist side by side, without any particular order. Yet the fundamental impulse toward a more cohesive cosmology, implicit already in the conjunction of things and words, keeps asserting itself; some of the longer prose-poems toward the end of the collection, notably "Notes pour un coquillage" ("Notes Toward a Shell"), "Faune et flore," "Végétation," and particularly "Le galet" ("The Pebble") point toward a cosmogony (rather than a cosmology) of matter and of language. "Le galet" begins, modestly enough, with the disarming statement "Le galet n'est pas une chose facile à bien définir" ("The pebble is not an easy thing to define clearly") (*TP*, 104)— and there follows a long geological disquisition on rocks. Toward the end of this paleolithic survey, Ponge tells us:

> Si maintenant je veux avec plus d'attention examiner l'un des types particuliers de la pierre, la perfection de sa forme, le fait que je peux le saisir et le retrouver dans ma main, me font choisir le galet.
>
> Aussi bien, le galet est-il exactement la pierre à l'époque où commence pour elle l'âge de la personne, de l'individu, c'est-à-dire de la parole. [*TP*, 111]
>
> If now I want to give more attention to examining one of the particular types of the stone, the perfection of its shape and the fact that I can pick it up and hold it in my hand cause me to choose the pebble.
>
> Moreover the pebble is exactly the stone at the period at which the age of the person, of the individual, begins; that is to say, the age of speech.

Thus the archaeology of things opens the way to language, which, of course, has its own archaeology: etymology. Just as the naturalists have provided us with the paleontology of the created world, so the etymological dictionary—Littré—becomes the indispensable tool of poetic creation. Ponge's workshop is a veritable Republic of Littré marshaled by a dogged "rage de l'expression." Ponge would like to accomplish for all objects what he undertakes to do for the shrimp in "La crevette dans tous ses états" ("The Shrimp in All Its States") (*GR:P*, 13–38); and although even in any individual instance this ambition turns out to be unattainable, he always accentuates the joy and the excitement of this patient labor— never the frustration. Erich Heller called Rilke the "Saint Francis of the Will to Power";[11] might we not call Ponge the Francis of the will to expression?

In the later poetry the "rage de l'expression" becomes attenuated to "compte tenu des mots." As Ponge gains greater security and mastery over his materials and method, the individual prose-poems in "Pièces" (as they are now called) often become more elaborate, more comprehensive. The fauna and flora of his world become more diversified; nor must we forget man-made things. Here are some characteristic titles to place beside the mollusk, stone, orange, and candle of *Le parti pris des choses*: after 1942 we have prose-poems on the lizard, the spider (twice), the goat; there are potatoes and asparagus and even a very tall glass of water (sixty pages!); for something more earthy, "La terre" ("The earth") and "Le pré" ("The Meadow"), and also "Ode inachevée à la boue" ("Unfinished Ode to Mud"); as for man-made objects, let me mention a factory chimney, a window-shutter, and most particularly a cake of soap; nor would I want to leave out two long, fascinating items called "Texte sur l'électricité" ("Text on Electricity") and "Le soleil placé en abîme" ("The Sun in Depth"). It is easy enough to see that this collection is much larger, much more "objective" than Rilke's more modest and homely inventory. Ponge, moreover, takes a certain pleasure in writing an extensive discourse-meditation-*proême* on a topic as banal and expendable as a cake of soap; the book—well over a hundred pages—is almost a kind of impertinence, a *défi*. He justifies the choice of soap by pointing out that such objects have become, for us, virtually "natural objects"; that is to say, we take them for granted: "We have come to consider these objects as natural objects, as objects which are due to us from nature without the least effort on our part, unless that of paying for them (not much)" (*S*, 122). But that is not all; with singular pride he concludes that "the real *makers* (and not merely contemplators) of these objects are the writers, the poets" (*S*, 125)[12]—which makes the poet the *homo faber* par excellence.

Ponge's work has become diversified in another way since *Le parti pris des choses*. The three new volumes of his work that came out in 1961 under the general title *Le grand recueil* are divided into "Lyres"—writings on painting and sculpture—paralleling Ponge's own work with the pen; "Méthodes"—containing his reflections on the art and methodology of his poetry; and "Pièces"—the prose-poems themselves. Thus, as in virtually all poets since Baudelaire, the critic acts as *Doppelgänger* to the poet: either as a self-critic or as an artist in quest of his poetics. In Ponge's case we also have several striking examples of the method that produces a particular piece of work. As in the case of a number of great painters, from Vermeer and Velásquez to Matisse and Braque, we are admitted to the *atelier*. Beginning with the volume *La rage de l'expression* of 1952, Ponge invites us to see him at work: how he observes the object in nature (the mimosa or the carnation, for instance), notes down details and impressions, then looks up in Littré's dictionary a long list of words that have cropped up during this investigative process; and then we can witness and delight in a kind of copulation between the thing and the words—". . . writing: like the orgasm of a being or, say, of a structure . . ." (*S*, 127). Two of the more recent instances are the very extensive documentations of the making of "Le savon" ("soap") and of "Le pré," the latter handsomely adorned by reproductions of a wide variety of paintings.

Of Ponge's discourses on method I should like to extract several important passages. One of the key essays, entitled (in English) "My creative method," begins with the poet's distrust of ideas—"ideas are not my strong point" (*GR:M*, 9)[13]—and his trust and pleasure in *things*, precisely because they do not demand his consent ("agrément"), because they do not need it. (Note once more how far we have come from Rilke's "Ach, wen vermögen wir denn zu brauchen . . ." and his predilection for the word "consentir" in his French poems.)[14] But because of this "otherness" of things, things become the poet's *pretext*: "Their variety constructs me, and might make it possible for me to exist in that very silence. Like the spot around which they exist" (*GR:M*, 12).

Ponge's solution, at least poetically, appears to be an attempt to establish a *modus vivendi* between mute matter and expressive materials by coexistence and (re)conciliation—in contrast to Rilke (and Mallarmé), who are intent upon spiritualizing (internalizing) matter. "What I shall attempt will be on the order of definition—description—work of liberation" (*GR:M*, 14), followed by the act of "placing the chosen object at the center of the world," a description of the object *ex nihilo* so that it can be recognized, executed in such a way that each object is grasped by and in a theoretical form appropriate to it (*GR:M*, 33–36). The instruments indispensable to this process are the encyclopedia and the dictionary (Larousse and Littré). The crucial declaration is the following:

> All in all, this is the real point: TAKING THE SIDE OF THINGS *equals* TAKING ACCOUNT OF WORDS.
> Certain texts will have a larger dose of (1) in their alloy, others a larger dose of (2). [*GR:M*, 19]

The function of poetry becomes that of the reconciliation of man and world:

> To nourish man's mind by putting him (or it) in touch with the cosmos. All that is needed is to scale down our pretention of dominating nature and to raise up our pretention of being physically a part of it, so that the reconciliation can take place. [*GR:M*, 197, "Le monde muet est notre seule patrie"—"The Silent World Is Our Only Homeland"]

But this is to be accomplished not within the context of the time-honored notions of beauty; as a matter of fact, the following declaration has a strong component of rebellion and intransigence:

> Our intention is definitely not to write a BEAUTIFUL text, a beautiful page, a beautiful book. No! Quite simply, we won't allow ourselves to be DEFEATED by (1) what is beautiful or interesting in Nature or, for that matter, in the least object. Moreover, we have no sense of any hierarchy of things to say; (2) we won't allow ourselves to be defeated by language. We keep trying. . . . [*GR:M*, 198–99]

Thus, "the silent world is our only homeland" (*GR:M*, 199), and

> . . . the work of art derives all its virtue from its resemblance to as well as its difference from natural objects. Where does its resemblance come from? From the fact that it is also made of matter. But its difference?— From expressive matter, or matter made expressive for the occasion. What does expressive mean? It kindles the intelligence (but it must extinguish it right away). But what are expressive materials? Those which already mean something: the languages. The only question is to see to it that they don't so much carry meaning as FUNCTION. [*GR:M*, 193, "Le murmure"—"The Murmur"]

It is obvious from the foregoing that Ponge resolutely aligns himself with a modern esthetic that stresses expressivity, function, and structure, instead of beauty and meaning. The principal modes of this poet's activity are observation, nomination, and, above all, the fabrication of the poem: *écriture*. But, lest we get sidetracked by the serious and cosmogonic features of Ponge's *poétique*, let us not forget the joy of making, the *réjouissance, le plaisir poétique*, which is always a concomitant of Ponge's creative work. The convergence of object, poetic pleasure, and language itself is synthesized in Ponge's coinage "objeu," first used in "Le soleil placé en abîme" and defined as "verbal functioning, without any laudatory or pejorative coefficient" (*GR:P*, 166). In retrospect, all of his poetic works are "objeux," and the more recent pieces highlight the "jeu" even more than the earlier ones. Here is a representative example, "Le lézard" ("The Lizard") (*GR:P*, 94–99). The common lizard, by its rapidly darting movement, by its smallness, by virtue of its closeness to the ground, and because of its metaphorical transposability makes a virtually ideal poetic object/subject for Ponge. Hence, "Le lézard" is a kind of allegorical "objeu" that brings out the entire apparatus of the poet's lizardry. The text begins with a playful "prehistory" that alludes in passing to metal-work and concludes with a pun on "saurien":

> Lorsque le mur de la préhistoire se lézarde, ce mur de fond de jardin (c'est le jardin des générations présentes, celui du père et du fils),—il en sort un petit animal formidablement dessiné, comme un dragon chinois, brusque mais inoffensif chacun le sait et ça le rend bien sympathique. Un chef-d'oeuvre de la bijouterie préhistorique, d'un métal entre le bronze vert et le vif-argent, dont le ventre seul est fluide, se renfle comme la goutte de mercure. Chic! Un reptile à pattes! Est-ce un progrès ou une dégénérescence? Personne, petit sot, n'en sait rien. Petit saurien.
>
> When the wall of pre-history cracks, this back garden wall (the garden of the present generations, of the father and the son),—a little animal of formidable design comes out, like a Chinese dragon, brisk and inoffensive, as everyone knows, and that makes it very nice to have around. A masterpiece of prehistoric jewelry, made of a metal between green-bronze and quicksilver, whose belly alone is fluid, swells up like the drop of mercury. Cute! A reptile with feet! Progress or degeneration? No one knows, little fool, so how'd I know? little dinosaur.

After fixing these observations by a metaphor ("Ce petit poignard qui traverse notre esprit en se tortillant d'une façon assez baroque, dérisoirement"—"that little dagger which enters our mind by twisting in a rather baroque manner, ludicrously"), Ponge stops ("lets change our point of view") and starts off in a more rigidly *verbal* direction: "Le LÉZARD dans le monde des mots n'a pas pour rien ce *zède* ou *zèle* tortillard, et pas pour rien sa désinence en *ard*, comme fuyard, flemmard, musard, pendard, hagard" ("The LIZARD in the world of words does not have that twisty *z* or *zeal*, nor does it have that ending in -*ard* for nothing, like laggard, haggard, niggard"). Ideographic equation of thing and word.

Other images follow to describe the lizard in motion: "petite locomotive haut-le-pied" ("little runaway engine"), "petit train d'allégations hâtives" ("little train of hasty thoughts"), finally "gamme chromatique" ("chromatic scale"), "arpège" ("arpeggio"). Next, we get the lizard at rest: "poignard" ("dagger"), "petit bibelot ovipare" ("little oviparous knick-knack'); finally, the heraldic comparison with the dragon. By this time the poet has reached a point of vantage from which the entire field of visual and verbal exploration can be compounded (necessitating once more a neologism), and the lizard can make his full-fledged appearance:

> Le LÉZARD suppose donc un ouvrage de maçonnerie, ou quelque rocher par sa blancheur qui s'en approche. Fort éclairé et chaud.
> Et une faille de cette surface, par où elle communique avec la (parlons bref) préhistoire . . . D'où le lézard *s'alcive** (obligé d'inventer ce mot).

* *s'alcive*: combination of *alcyon* ("halcyon") with *alcide* ("tough guy," cf. Hercules-Alcides) and *arrive*.

> Et voici donc, car l'on ne saurait trop préciser ces choses, voici les conditions nécessaires et suffisantes . . . , pratiquement voici comment disposer les choses pour qu'à coup sûr apparaisse un lézard.

> The LIZARD then presupposes a work of masonry, or some rock by its whiteness which comes close. Brightly lit and warm.
> And a crevice in that surface, whereby it keeps in touch with (let's speak curtly) prehistory, from which the lizard *alcives* (obliged to invent this word).
> And so—for you can't make these things too clear—here are the necessary and sufficient conditions . . . , for practical purposes here is how things must be arranged, so that a lizard might appear for sure.

This is capped off by the emblematic conclusion heralding the poem and, by way of the poem, the Pongean conjugation of matter and mind:

> A quoi ressemble plus cette surface éclatante de la roche ou du môle de maçonnerie que j'évoquais tout à l'heure, qu'à une page,—par un violent désir d'observation (à y inscrire) éclairée et chauffée à blanc? Et voici donc dès lors comment transmuer les choses:
> Telles conditions se trouvant réunies:
> Page par un violent désir d'observation à y inscrire éclairée et chauffée à blanc. Faille par où elle communique avec l'ombre et la fraîcheur qui sont à l'intérieur de l'esprit. Qu'un mot par surcroît s'y pose, ou plusieurs mots. Sur cette page, par cette faille, ne pourra sortir qu'un . . . (aussitôt gobant tous précédents mots) . . . un petit train de pensées grises,— lequel circule ventre à terre et rentre volontiers dans les tunnels de l'esprit.

> What is it that looks most like that shining surface of the rock or the pier

of masonry that I referred to a moment ago, if not a page—brightly lit and at white heat (to be written upon) from a violent desire for observation. And so here is how to transmute things:

The following conditions being fulfilled:

Page by a violent desire for observation to write upon it, brightly lit and at white heat. Crevice whereby it remains in contact with the shade and the cool that are inside the mind. In addition, let a word, or several words, sit down on it. On this page, by this crevice, only one word will come out (it will immediately gobble up all the preceding ones) . . . a little train of gray thoughts—which runs about, belly to the ground, and is glad to go back into the tunnels of the mind.

Allegory of the white page (but not quite an echo of Mallarmé!), allegory of the crack in the wall, allegory of the communication of matter and mind, light and shade, fable of the poet as lizard. And, of course by demonstration, as wizard. The metamorphosis is greater than the metaphor: we are back in the company of Mallarmé, Braque, and Rilke.

IV

The differences between the two poets are striking enough. But, without talking about influence—there appears to be none whatsoever— we can see that a new *poétique*, a new epistemology, and a new conception of man are at stake, in Rilke as well as in Ponge, who represent two distinct and important *moments* in the drama of modern European consciousness. The common ground in both poets, as I have been at pains to emphasize, is their single-minded reliance on *things*. In an essay on Bachelard, Robert Champigny, with a fine flair for aphorism, said "For poetry does not name things; it things names."[15] And Wallace Stevens asserts that "a poet's words are of things that do not exist without the words."[16]

Why are things so important in modern literature? Is it that the novelists' increasing preoccupation with "les choses," especially after Balzac and Flaubert, has invaded the sacred domain of poetry? Is it an admission of a gradually fading interest in human and social realities and even in philosophical inquiry? Is it evidence of the progressive reification that an industrial and commodity-oriented society has inflicted on our minds? The answer to all these questions may be partly in the affirmative; yet the object-centeredness of modern poetry has more deepseated causes. The concern with things on the part of the modern poets (and by extension, the painters, as well as most novelists), amounts to an earnest, sometimes desperate, attempt to vindicate this world and its objects in the face of a loss of transcendent reference. This process of disinheritance has been persuasively documented and analyzed by Erich Heller. All the major poets from Hölderlin and Blake onward, and particularly since Baudelaire, have made a heroic effort either to shore up the ruins of a collapsing order, or to seek meaning and order—the possibility of meaning and order—by new constructs and new visions. Thus Baudelaire conferred a new "esthetic dignity" (to use Erich Auerbach's memorable phrase) upon certain objects that have become the receptacles and agents of human feeling so intensely that they have become integrated, so to speak, into the imaginative and passionate compass of human experience. It was Mallarmé, after Baudelaire, who most acutely realized the extraordinary burden that language would have to bear in articulating the nexus of object and meaning, in such a way that the polyvalence of impressions could be rendered into a compact and scintillating whole, which would yield its own meaning from within. If meaning was no longer available from the outside, then the work of art would have to create its own order of discourse; and this result could be attained only by the most painstaking manipulation of all the aspects of the poetic *verbe*. Rilke, who does not seem to have known Mallarmé's poetry particularly well—although his contact with Rodin and his friendship with Valéry certainly provided him with some awareness of Mallarmé's impact on poetry and the arts—came to write the kind of poetry, in the *Duino Elegies* and the *Orpheus Sonnets*, that attains a verbal intensity and a cosmological range that Mallarmé, that supreme *poète savant*, aspired to, and in part attained, in his more rigorously severe and more intellectually playful way. In a way, Rilke's closer affinities are to Proust, rather than to Mallarmé. In Proust the object serves as the focal point of contemplation that releases the mainsprings of creative expression and, in some special and exalted instances, the object becomes the repository of a sensation and of an authentic inner reality that transforms and renews the self.

With Ponge the poetics of things has changed; the remnants of animism and anthropomorphism that are still in evidence from Baudelaire to Rilke have vanished; we have moved from *correspondances* to *témoignage*, from epiphany to coexistence. Ponge's poetic activity parallels the shifts in painting that occurred shortly after Cézanne's death. One might also mention the gestures of the Surrealists in their rebellious stance toward language, their cult of the image, and their insistence upon the power of the arts to renew mankind. But Ponge, despite his contact with the Surrealists in his younger years, always remains closer to the painters, and especially to Georges Braque; that is to say, he steers clear of the "inwardness" of writers like Rilke and Proust, and of the intellectuality of Valéry. Nor would Ponge be able or willing to say (as Rilke did) that he "strayed upon the other side of Nature" or that "the taste of the Creation was in his being" ("Erlebnis"—"Experience," 1913) (*SW*, VI: 1038 and 1041). Essentially he remains, like Théophile Gautier (whom he otherwise resembles very little), "a man for whom the outer world exists."[17] His delineation of *his* subject matter at an early stage of his development (the decision to make *things* his poetic province) and the concomitant awareness that the phenomenological viewing of things necessitates a linguistic, or "metalogical," discipline—this conjunction of subject matter and method has remained steadfast throughout his career, having undergone a certain refinement and a growing mastery over the past fifty-five years. It is altogether characteristic of Ponge, who is a poet of deliberate self-limitation—for him, "to define" means literally "to enclose within boundaries," similar to the canvas-frame of Braque—that he should choose for his major models the confined and disciplined poetry of Malherbe, the smaller-scaled keyboard works of Bach and Rameau (not the vast structures of the former and not the operas of the latter), the poetry of La Fontaine, the pictures of Chardin, and the more restricted and modest visual universe of Braque (over against Picasso). But a universe it is by now, full of objects perceived by a most inquisitive eye and verbalized by a keen and playful intelligence. A finite universe, accepted as such, celebrated as such. What remains inexhaustible in this *De varietate rerum* are precisely the varieties of perception, the endless possibilities of alternating current flowing between words and things, the never-ending circuit of reconciliation of man and world in which this current operates. And within this field of material and verbal forces the possibility of a more humble cosmology is also given. The true materialist is the believer, said Braque,[18] and Ponge, in his way, said it too: ". . . the veneration of matter: what can be more worthy of the mind than that?" (*GR:P*, 104, "La terre"—"The Earth"). A remarkable short text, written in 1963, probes further into the question:

A LA RÊVEUSE MATIÈRE

Probablement, tout et tous—et nous-mêmes—ne sommes que des rêves immédiats de la divine Matière:

Les produits textuels de sa prodigieuse imagination.

Et ainsi, en un sens, pourrait-on dire que la nature entière, y compris les hommes, n'est qu'une écriture d'un certain genre; une écriture *non-significative*, du fait qu'elle ne se réfère à aucun système de signification; qu'il s'agit d'un univers indéfini: à proprement parler *immense*, sans mesures.

Tandis que le monde des paroles est un univers fini.

Mais du fait qu'il est composé de ces objects très particuliers et particulièrement émouvants, les sons significatifs et articulés dont nous sommes capables, qui nous servent *à la fois* à nommer les objets de la nature et à exprimer nos sentiments,

Sans doute suffit-il de *nommer* quoi que ce soit—d'une certaine manière—pour exprimer tout de l'homme et, du même coup, glorifier la matière, exemple pour l'écriture et providence de l'esprit. [*NR*, 177]

TO DREAMING MATTER

Probably all things and all beings, including ourselves, are but immediate dreams of divine Matter:

The textual products of its prodigious imagination.

And thus, in a sense, it could be said that all of nature, including men, is but a scripture of a certain kind; a *non-significant* scripture, because of the fact that it does not refer to any system of signification; what it amounts to is an indefinite universe: properly speaking, an *immense*, measureless, universe.

Whereas the world of speech is a finite universe.

Yet because of the fact that it is composed of these very particular and particularly thrilling objects, the significant and articulated sounds of which we are capable, which can be used *at the same time* to name the objects in nature and to express our feelings,

No doubt it is enough to *name* anything whatsoever—in a certain way—in order to express all of man and, simultaneously, to glorify matter, as a lesson in writing and as a providence of the mind.

A curious text, reversing in some ways the medieval view of the world as a book, and yet in another way substituting its own *scripture* for the old Book of Signs. Here we have two entities: an indefinite world of things, and a finite world of speech. The act of naming is here the energy that *voices* nature and at the same time articulates the human being in a continuous burst of glorification. Like Mallarmé, like Rilke, like Claudel, like Saint-John Perse, Ponge is a poet of celebration. There is even the suggestion of a mystique here: is everything that has material substance perhaps ("probablement") striving to become spirit, trying to transform its "muteness" into *parole*: *caro* (or better: *materia*) *verbum facta est*, the Creation reversed by having matter generate, or release, its own latent spirit through the human *logos*? Ponge has not elaborated this notion further, but his more recent work gives evidence of a more intensive preoccupation with this topic.

So this new "nominalisme foncier" that Philippe Sollers speaks of is more complex than would appear at first glance.[19] Sartre observed quite rightly in his perceptive but also somewhat perverse essay on Ponge that a true materialist would never have written *Le parti pris des choses*, "because he will rely on Science, and Science demands *a priori* a radical externality, that is to say, the dissolution of all individuality."[20] That is perhaps true, but it is beside the point, since Ponge is evidently not even pretending to be "scientific" (that is, logical) but metalogical; he transforms the discourse of cognition to articulation, scripture ("écriture"). "Our soul is transitive," says Ponge (*NR*, 145). Sartre is intransitive. Ponge's interest resides almost exclusively in the world of things. His phenomenology is "poetic," as he labels it once;[21] that is to say, it is not cognitive, like Husserl's. Are we not, in the case of Ponge's poetics, closer to the later Heidegger than to Husserl? Heidegger said in his *Der Ursprung des Kunstwerkes*: "Wo keine Sprache west, wie im Sein von Stein, Pflanze und Tier, da ist auch keine Offenheit des Seienden und demzufolge auch keine solche des Nichtseienden und des Leeren" ("Where no language dwells, as for example in the being of the stone, plant and animal, there is no openness of being and consequently no openness of non-being and of the void").[22] This statement reads like an ontological gloss on Rilke; it would not be incorrect, in my view, to equate Rilke's and Heidegger's "Offenheit" ("openness") with Ponge's transitiveness. Moreover, Susan Sontag's perceptions in her essay "The Aesthetics of Silence" concerning "the benign nominalism proposed by Rilke (and proposed and practiced by Francis Ponge)" are entirely on target, especially when she continues, "Rilke and Ponge . . . assume that if there are states of false (language-clogged) consciousness, there are also authentic states of consciousness—which it's the function of art to promote."[23] Still, there is a difference between the two poets relative to the act of naming. Rilke does want to eternalize this act; Ponge remains loyal to a nominalism that needs to be qualified as "semantic," rather than "significative." "If Ponge seems to freeze human signification, it is in order, quite on the contrary, to liberate it, but by situating it lower down, in a realm deprived of the freedom even of having meaning, until Ponge came along, and which he is the first to re-annex to humanism," writes Jean-Pierre Richard,[24] and, in a way, this might constitute a reply to Sartre.

And although this poetry is concerned primarily with seeing and making, it also embodies thought. It is true that Ponge does not relish philosophy or ideas, but he is a poet-thinker all the same, in the sense in which practically all poets since Hölderlin have been thinkers. In the absence of cogent philosophical and theological frameworks for thinking (all that we have had since Hegel, with very few exceptions, have been partial conceptualizations), the major poets of the nineteenth and twentieth centuries—those who have tried to propose a coherent vision of *their* world—have been compelled to assimilate their linguistic creation, their *parole*, to the exigencies of their thought. It is no different with Ponge. The initial bracketing of things and words, which defined his poetic terrain, has been implemented by a series of researches into the appearance of things and the malleability of words: the eye, the pen, the brain are in constant interplay with one another. The main difference is that the "progressive colonization of inwardness" (in Heller's phrase) that began with Hölderlin and Blake and culminated in Rilke has by now given way to an attempt to negotiate a reconciliation with the material world. Perhaps that is the only avenue left open, short of retreat into an inhuman and icy privacy. In the instances of both Rilke and Ponge, the last bastion of security has been the *thing*: what finally matters is matter itself. Rilke proclaimed in his fourth elegy

> Wir kennen den Kontur
> des Fühlens nicht, nur was ihn formt von außen. [17–18]

> We do not know the contour
> of feeling, only that which shapes it from the outside.

Perhaps no single quotation marks more decisively the distance between the two poets: for Ponge the external contour of feeling is all there is, and it is sufficient unto itself.

> gegenüber sein
> und nichts als das und immer gegenüber. [Eighth elegy, 33–34]

> to be vis-à-vis
> and nothing but that and always vis-à-vis.

Rilke rails against this dividedness, this duality, and calls for a reversal ("Umkehr"); he absorbed things into his "Weltinnenraum," Ponge leaves things intact in the "Weltraum." Rilke's first sonnet of the second Orpheus cycle celebrates this change of world-space by means of a breath-intake into "inner space" and makes it emblematic of the act of poetic creation:

Atmen, du unsichtbares Gedicht!
Immerfort um das eigne
Sein rein eingetauschter Weltraum. Gegengewicht,
in dem ich mich rhythmisch ereigne.

Einzige Welle, deren
allmähliches Meer ich bin;
sparsamstes du von allen möglichen Meeren, —
Raumgewinn.

Wie viele von diesen Stellen der Räume waren schon
innen in mir. Manche Winde
sind wie mein Sohn.

Erkennst du mich, Luft, du, voll noch einst meiniger Orte?
Du, einmal glatte Rinde,
Rundung und Blatt meiner Worte.

Breathing, o invisible poem!
Perpetually for its own
being purely exchanged world-space. Counterweight,
in which I come rhythmically into my own.

Single wave, whose
gradual sea I am;
thriftiest of all possible seas,—
gain of space.

How many of these parcels of space have already been
inside myself. Many winds
are like sons to me.

Do you recognize me, o air, so full yet of places once mine?
You, once smooth bark,
rounding-off and leaf of my words.

For Ponge, the corresponding term describing this process is not "einge-tauscht" ("exchanged"), but "intéressé," more modest and at the same time very precise: "interest" is that which is *between* (man and world, words and things). A passage from the meditations on the creation of the poem "Le pré" shows this eloquently enough:

> Why, though we are tempted to do so, aren't we going to *do without* those names, do without words, why aren't we going to decide *not* to give preference to, say, painting or music, or to any other *means* of expression?
>
> Well, from a love of difficulty, and also from the feeling (intuition) that naming is the key to everything—and that if *we are interested* in this difference between words and things, it is because as a matter of fact *we are involved* in the highest degree, that *we* are the ones whom this difference (the problem of this difference) concerns, that it is nothing less, in fact, than *our* business—our own existence, our own personality, our

own liberty, our own justification, our only *duty* (toward ourselves as well as toward society, toward each one of our brothers, toward the entire world, toward all of nature, toward the machinery, the universal operation, in which we participate). [*FP*, 26]

This profession of faith, like Rilke's in his ninth elegy, marks the most recent phase in man's quest to strengthen his bonds with the outside world; in both cases, though in very different ways, the coordinates within which this *entente cordiale* is to be graphed out are called Things and Names. It is as though both poets had heeded Zarathustra's exhortation: "Bleibt der Erde treu!" ("Remain loyal to the earth!").

NOTES

1. This topic has been studied by Kurt Oppert, "Das Dinggedicht: eine Kunstform bei Mörike, Meyer und Rilke," *Deutsche Vierteljahrsschrift für Literaturwissenschaft und Geistesgeschichte* (1926), pp. 747–83. The following study has also been helpful in the preparation of the present essay: N. M. Willard, "A Poetry of Things: Williams, Rilke, Ponge," *Comparative Literature* 17 (1965): 311–24.
2. H. F. Peters, *Rainer Maria Rilke: Masks and the Man* (New York: McGraw-Hill, 1960), p. 87.
3. The following abbreviations for Rilke's writings are used in the text: *SW—Sämtliche Werke,* 6 vols. (Frankfurt am Main: Insel, 1955–66); *Br—Briefe,* 2 vols. (Wiesbaden: Insel, 1950). The translations are my own unless otherwise noted.
4. Herman Meyer, *Zarte Empirie* (Stuttgart: Metzler, 1963), p. 264.
5. Ibid., p. 255.
6. This is surely the painting entitled *Madame Cézanne in a Red Armchair* (1877), now in the Bostom Museum of Fine Arts.
7. The following abbreviations for Ponge's works are used in the text: *TP—Tome premier,* 1965; *GR:M—Le grand recueil: Méthodes,* 1961, and *GR:P—Le grand recueil: Pièces,* 1961; *NR—Nouveau recueil,* 1967; *S—Le savon,* 1967—all published by Gallimard, Paris; and *FP—La fabrique du pré* (Geneva: Albert Skira, 1971). The translations are my own unless otherwise noted.
8. Georges Braque, *Illustrated Notebooks, 1917–55,* trans. Stanley Appelbaum (New York: Dover, 1971).
9. "Werk des Gesichts ist getan, / tue nun Herz-Werk" ("Wendung," June 20, 1914; *SW*, II: 83).
10. The suspension points are in the text.
11. Erich Heller, *The Disinherited Mind* (New York: Meridian, 1959), p. 131.

12. The two translations from "Le savon" are in *Soap*, trans. Lane Dunlop (London: Jonathan Cape, 1969), pp. 90, 93.
13. This is no doubt a barb thrown at Valéry, whose Monsieur Teste (a man of ideas of sorts) begins: "La bêtise n'est pas mon fort"—("Stupidity is not my strong point").
14. See my *Descent and Return* (Cambridge: Harvard University Press, 1971), pp. 216–17.
15. Robert Champigny, "Gaston Bachelard," in *Modern French Criticism: From Proust to Valéry,* ed. John K. Simon (Chicago: University of Chicago Press, 1972), p. 186.
16. Wallace Stevens, *The Necessary Angel* (New York: Random House, 1965), p. 32.
17. In *Entretiens de Francis Ponge avec Philippe Sollers*, p. 169, Ponge approvingly quotes this well-known sentence.
18. Quoted in Jean Leymarie, *Braque* (Cleveland: World, 1961), p. 116.
19. Philippe Sollers, *Francis Ponge* (Paris: Pierre Seghers, 1963), p. 41.
20. Jean-Paul Sartre, "L'homme et les choses," *Situations I* (Paris: Gallimard, 1947), p. 270n.
21. Letter to Bernard Groethuysen quoted in Sollers, *Francis Ponge*, p. 33n.
22. Martin Heidegger, *Der Ursprung des Kunstwerkes* (Stuttgart: Philipp Reclam, 1960), p. 84.
23. Susan Sontag, *Styles of Radical Will* (New York: Farrar, Straus & Cudahy, 1969), p. 25.
24. Jean-Pierre Richard, "Francis Ponge," *Onze études sur la poésie moderne* (Paris: Éditions du Seuil, 1964), p. 169.

6

Alienation and Transformation: Rilke's Poem "Der Schwan"

HERBERT LEHNERT

Among the novels which accompanied the economic recovery of the Federal Republic of Germany, venting uneasiness with it, is *Die Rote* by Alfred Andersch (1961). At the beginning of the novel, the red-headed woman of the title muses about her husband whom she has just left forever. Her contempt for him is nourished by the thought that he still reads Rilke secretly, even though he is afraid he would be considered ridiculous if it became known. This reference associates Rilke's poems with an obsequious social climber, a weakly aesthete who has adjusted himself to the emerging new wealth, and takes pride in a thin veneer of culture that has lost meaning. Yet Andersch himself had reported, in his autobiographical account *Die Kirschen der Freiheit*, how he had escaped into introversion, reading Rilke, after having been released from a concentration camp in 1933. He had been a member of a Communist youth organization. The same Rilke who had become an island and sanctuary for the young and frustrated revolutionary was used by the mature writer, no longer a Communist, as a symbol for a new, conservative, but ruthless bourgeoisie masking its materialism with empty aestheticism.

In Rilke's own biography there is a strange ambivalence between his adaptability to rich men and, especially, women, preferably members of the old aristocracy, and an independent, antisocial trait, a strange, neurotic restlessness, a fear to be tied down to anything and anyone. For a time, during World War I, he was even interested in leftist outsiders with whom he shared pacifist convictions, but he tended to be more antimodern, criticizing the capitalist world from a conservative viewpoint.[1]

There is no doubt that Rilke came from a bourgeois background, and that his life was sustained, his production supported, by educated bourgeois readers, including his publisher. Neither can there be any doubt that Rilke's poems may be used and have been used to sustain a withdrawal to the "inner cosmos" ("Weltinnenraum"). That they offer themselves for such a withdrawal, however, is due to what I call bourgeois alienation, which was prevalent in German literature in Rilke's times.

The alienation theme has a tradition in German literature. The first world-wide success of a German novel, Goethe's *Die Leiden des jungen Werthers* (1774/1787), begins it; Romanticism from Tieck's and Wackenroder's *Herzensergießungen eines kunstliebenden Klosterbruders* (1797), through E. T. A. Hoffmann's artist stories, and Richard Wagner's program of enveloping his audience in artistic rapture leads up to Thomas Mann's dichotomy of artist and burgher, to Rilke's works, and on to the Expressionists' revolt against the father. Romanticism and Wagner had their influences on Baudelaire and French Symbolism which, in turn, very strongly affected German literature.

When Rilke began his career, the antibourgeois feelings of young bourgeois writers amounted to alienation (Entfremdung) from the society to which they nevertheless belonged. This alienation is meant here in a descriptive sense and has two aspects: (1) the belief that bourgeois society exercises unbearable pressure on its members, especially its younger, sensitive ones, and (2) the feeling that the industrial mass society has debased authentic existence. Authenticity was oriented by a nostalgic view of preindustrial life.

Alienation in this sense is not identical with the Marxist concept which derives from the alienation of the product from the worker in nineteenth- and twentieth-century industry, combined with dehumanizing reification of man, the proletarian being forced to sell his labor-power. Yet I believe that alienation in the descriptive sense of social uneasiness fed by a Romantic tradition has a common root with Marxist alienation in the sense that both are oriented by a nostalgia seeking authenticity of life in premodern life-styles. While Marxism also affirmed progress through industrial objectivation, anarchist groups, which in Germany frequently were related to literary circles, were usually much closer to Romantic ideas. Artistic escape, imaginative models of a more authentic life, reformistic ideas, revolutionary utopias, criticism of bourgeois society from the left and from the right abounded in German literary circles, including bohemian ones, and the positions were much less fixed than they are now. Rilke's political ambivalence is to be seen on this background. The basis of this ambivalence is his bourgeois alienation, which also deeply affected his works as well as it affected his life.

Rilke described separation from his bourgeois family in a story written in 1898, two years after he left Prague in reality. The story remained untitled, and was not published until after Rilke's death. It is known by the name of the main character, Ewald Tragy, who represents the young Rilke. It even today produces a convincing effect, which can hardly be said of Rilke's other prose products before *Die Aufzeichnungen des Malte Laurids Brigge*. The reason for the young writer's separation from his family is his refusal to conform to the bourgeois life-style, and to view money and the opinions of others as factors determining his life: "I am my own lawmaker and King; there is no one over me, not even God. . . ." The pathos is mitigated by self-irony: "It would behoove me to stay here as everyone expects me, to be good and modest and to go on living one and the same miserable day time and again."[2]

This contrast between autocratic pretension and humble modesty characterized Rilke, who soon learned to conceal his autocratic trait. It is, however, always present in his persistent refusal to concede any control or authority over his artistic mission to others, individuals, or society as a whole. He stubbornly pursued the goal to liberate his artistic method of perception and expression from conventional ways, especially social conventions. Thus his strained relationship to society is alienation in the sense defined above. His artistic sensitivity was on the defense against bourgeois society, which he conceived of as conformistic. His art was to transform the conventional world into one with new laws that the artist was to give, producing them from his imagination. They are not real, must not be real. The artistic transformation thus becomes subject to inspiration; only in the act of artistic perception and expression the new truth can be found. This leaves the artist empty in real life. There is an amazing passage in *Ewald Tragy* near the ones just quoted in which the same young poet, capable of stressing his independence from all social or divine authority, can soberly and meekly say: "You should know that I tell lies very often, as I need them, upward ones and downward ones, I should be in the middle; but sometimes I think, there is nothing in between."[3]

Rilke's detachment from society led to his psychic wavering between artistic pride and desperate, alienated feeling of rootlessness. In his biography the attempts to establish substitute homelands in Russia or in Worpswede-Westerwede result from this insecurity, which was a condition for his production. He had left the family he established in Westerwede because of economic necessity, but he did not return because he feared to be trapped by a bourgeois way of life. Paris offered him a transient, anonymous existence, surrounding him with people speaking a language different from his mother tongue, yet with an aristocratic touch, in contrast to the language situation in his hometown, Prague. Rilke went to Paris to study Rodin, and it was also the city of Baudelaire and the French Symbolists.

The sentimental early style of Rilke changed in Paris. Even though occasional lapses occur, his *Neue Gedichte* and the fictional diary *Die Aufzeichnungen des Malte Laurids Brigge* mark the turning point in Rilke's work. In them Rilke transformed the theme of alienation from society into artistic form.

Malte, the author of his fictional diary, is a poet who understands the necessity of detachment from society for the production of art. He is exposed to mass civilization in the big city of Paris and tries, at the same time, to delve into his childhood in order to free the creative urge. But the decisive inspiration does not come. He writes: "Only one step and my deep misery would be bliss, but I cannot take this step. . . ."[4] The successful poem would be the transformation of the misery of alienation into art. This transformation is envisioned by Malte in terms of transcendence in the same passage: "The time of the second interpretation will dawn, and no word will remain upon the other, and every meaning will be dissolved like clouds, and descend like water."

The ambivalence of bourgeois alienation in *Aufzeichnungen des Malte Laurids Brigge* is apparent in Malte's uncanny interest in the outcasts of the big city. The poor and the old are useless, and therefore not bourgeois, alienated like Malte. Yet his upperclass education refuses to admit this resemblance. Another device to display ambivalent alienation is the motif of the family. Malte's childhood experiences are to show the difference between adult conventionality and the child's imaginative world, open for playful transformation. The price for living in the world of fantasy includes threats from unknown sources and inexplicable fears. Malte's revision of the parable of the Prodigal Son is about the son's withdrawal from family love. It is Rilke's version of Thomas Mann's *Tonio-Kröger* theme, and a symbolic continuation of *Ewald Tragy*. The return of the Prodigal Son to the family is merely a renunciation of programmatic protest. He still refuses to be loved and to have ties to his family because that would rob him of his inner freedom. Only God could love him, through inspiration. "But He was still unwilling." Thus ends the diary of the frustrated, alienated poet.

In contrast to the fictional Malte, Rilke himself succeeded in the transformation of reality into a "second interpretation." In a great number of the poems from *Neue Gedichte* we find an abrupt reversal of meaning (Umschlag), which stresses the intention of transformation.[5] The poem "Der Schwan" represents this reversal in the form of a program in symbolic terms.

Diese Mühsal, durch noch Ungetanes
schwer und wie gebunden hinzugehn,
gleicht dem ungeschaffnen Gang des Schwanes.

Und das Sterben, dieses Nichtmehrfassen
jenes Grunds, auf dem wir täglich stehn,
seinem ängstlichen Sich-Niederlassen—:

in die Wasser, die ihn sanft empfangen
und die sich, wie glücklich und vergangen,
unter ihm zurückziehn, Flut um Flut;
während er unendlich still und sicher
immer mündiger und königlicher
und gelassener zu ziehn geruht.[6]

The Swan

This drudgery, to pass through undone things / clumsily and as if tied, / resembles the awkward [literally, uncreated] gait of the swan. / And dying, this inability to hold on / to the ground on which we stand, / day after day, resembles the timid lowering of the swan: / into the waters which receive him gently, / and which withdrawn from under him, / as if happy and past, flow by flow; / while it is pleasing to him to float, / with infinitely tranquil security, / gaining in royal sovereignty.

Let us first look at the form. In the *Neue Gedichte* the sonnet and variations on the sonnet appear numerous times.[7] In this instance there are two incomplete quartets, in each of which one line is missing, while the two tercets have been printed together in a six-line stanza. The turning point of this poem occurs before this stanza, at the "correct" position in a traditional sonnet. The two three-line stanzas in the beginning are bound together through the rhyme of "-gehn" and "stehn" in lines two and four. The poem, then, is divided into two parts. The first part consists of two statements, each a three-line stanza separated from the second part by a colon. The swan moves awkwardly on land and anxiously lowers itself into the water. These motions are compared with human activity, with moving in unfinished work, and with death. If one takes the sonnet form as point of departure, then the missing line in each of the two stanzas of the first part corresponds to the hesitation, the incompleteness, the alienation from his environment, which the swan on land represents. In the second part the swan is in its element; it swims majestically in the water. The way in which this conception is expressed in poetic language can be considered a high point in Rilke's works.

In the last two lines three comparatives occur: "mündiger," "königlicher" and "gelassener." The comparison is to the previous condition, which was not self-determined. The metaphor of a king describing the swan does not refer to power or action, but rather to the secure state of majesty, an almost timeless condition to which "wie glücklich und vergangen" alludes: metaphorical adjectives that refer to the carrying waves. In contrast to the incompleteness, the misery, and the anxious dying—the metaphors used for the motion of the swan on the shore—the swimming swan is the image of self-determined, timeless bliss, free of misery and removed from the present.

The regal image of the swan and what we know of Rilke's relation preclude a Christian interpretation of the poem. The Christian soul that goes to God after death or after the Resurrection of the Dead is not regal. The image of the swan represents rather a composed command over the language of the poem, a composure which Malte never achieves. The reversal (Umschlag) is one from the struggling poet to the finished work of art; the deliverance from the transitoriness of human, bourgeois life into the timeless bliss of the successful poem, of the perfected form, which admits no further change. The words of poetic speech are transformed; they are removed from their everyday context and, at the same time, are securely anchored in the poem's system of meaning. In this way they are freed from the day-to-day misery and, at the same time, are lifted above the transitory.

We can read even more closely and identify the first stanza with the poet who is working on a poem. That which is not yet accomplished (noch Ungetane) is a hindrance; it is heavy and inert. The word "ungeschaffen" suggests both "not (yet) created" and "awkward," forming a connection between the unfinished poem and the motion of the swan on land for which its feet are not suited. While the swan is still on the edge of its element, its "anxious lowering of itself" ("ängstliches Sich-

Niederlassen") reminds one of dying, but also, at the same time, of the "no-longer-understanding" ("Nichtmehrfassen") of the day-to-day bourgeois world from which the poet in the poem removes himself. His retreat is troubled alienation, but reverts to the beauty of the swimming swan. Rilke was occupied during his entire life with the relationship between the unredeemed poet, who is still only a striving bourgeois "who walks through the kitchen into the living room," as he wrote in the fourth elegy, and the redeemed poet, who found salvation in the poem and thus may show things to the angel. The idea of the transformation of the earthly into poetry in the *Duineser Elegien* and the idea of reversal in the *Neue Gedichte* are basically one and the same. There are stylistic differences; there are always contradictions in Rilke, but there is no programmatical change in principle between the Rilke of the *Neue Gedichte* and the Rilke of the *Elegien*. Rilke's idea of salvation through art remains constant.

The conclusion that the swan poem really does mean the transformation of the human poet into the perfected poem can be supported by the evidence of the surrounding poems. The poem that follows "Der Schwan" is "Kindheit." Here, as on other occasions in Rilke's works, childhood is evoked as a time in which normal measurable time is not valid, where fantasy still transforms everyday images, while adults attempt to tie the child to the only valid reality. The poem placed after "Kindheit" is called "Der Dichter" and is the reverse of "Der Schwan." Inspiration has abandoned the poet, has left him alone and useless. Thus he experiences the alienation of one who is not part of bourgeois life. The transformation of things through fantasy, their use as images in the poem and as symbols for the deliverance from reality, leaves the poet empty:

> Ich habe keine Geliebte, kein Haus
> keine Stelle auf der ich lebe.
> Alle Dinge, an die ich mich gebe,
> werden reich und geben mich aus.

> I do not have a beloved, no house,
> no place where to live.
> All the things to which I devote myself
> grow rich and spend me.

The words "keine Stelle auf der ich lebe" call to mind the passage quoted from *Ewald Tragy* concerning the empty center where the poet was supposed to be. The poem that appears before the swan poem is the sonnet "Römische Sarkophage." The quartets and the first tercet deal with the transitoriness of the human condition in the face of decay—a Baroque idea. The last tercet then deals with water, which in our days reflects (spiegelt) and glitters (glänzt) in the Roman sarcophagi serving as troughs. The mirror image is for Rilke a symbol for poetry. The mirror presents an inverted and alienated image.[8] The idea of the dissolution of individual substance in death leads to transfiguration in the mirrored image in this poem as well. The poem "Der Engel" precedes "Römische Sarkophage" in Rilke's order of the first part of *Neue Gedichte*. This angel "rejects whatever limits and obligates." It is obviously the angel on the roof of the cathedral of Chartres and, at the same time, like Jacob's angel, a symbol of inspiration, capable of breaking the poet out of his mold. All these poems take an element of experience from the world of the author and reader and transform it into a symbol of poetry. Religion, death, transformation through the imagination, and the human existence of the poet are topics that help to clarify the meaning of the central poem, "Der Schwan."

The poems "Der Schwan" and "Der Dichter" were written in the winter of 1905–1906, the poems "Römische Sarkophage" and "Der Engel," in May or June, 1906. "Kindheit" is dated by Ernst Zinn June 1, 1906. In the winter of 1905–1906 Rilke lived with Rodin in Meudon. From there he reported to Clara Rilke on the twentieth of September, 1905, that he usually sat in the evening with Rodin "an dem eingerahmten Bassin bei seinen drei jungen Schwänen" and held serious conversations.[9] We know that Rodin cherished *Fleurs du mal* highly. Rilke himself mentioned this in his Rodin book.[10] One can well imagine that Baudelaire's "Le Cygne" came up in these conversations about art held in front of the real swans or that Rilke then read the poem in *Fleurs de mal* in Rodin's home, especially since it is among the *Tableux parisiens*, a book of *Fleurs de mal* whose figures resemble the Malte side in Rilke.

Baudelaire's poem "Le Cygne," from the *Tableux parisiens* of *Fleurs du mal*, is a poem about alienation in the same sense that concerns Rilke and, above all, Rilke's Malte. Images of exile, of estrangement from one's homeland, from one's natural element, that is to say from authentic life, are brought together into a lament reflecting the poet who feels alienated in his bourgeois environment. The widow Andromache, carried off after the fall of Troy, sorrows over past greatness; a tubercular Negress in Paris remembers tropical Africa; the banished, the ship-wrecked, the imprisoned, the conquered, all have their parts. The image from which the poem gets its title is a swan escaped from a menagerie and met by the poet at a construction site. Its webbed feet rub against the pavement; it tries to bathe in the dust of a dry gutter. Baudelaire's swan wishes for a destructive tempest as it remembers the beautiful lake of its homeland. A convulsive motion of the neck upwards, where a blue sky seems to mock the wish for a cleansing thunderstorm, appears to be an accusing gesture against God. The construction site, which furnishes the background with its jumbled mess, represents the changed Paris. It is the bourgeois, progressive-capitalistic Paris of Napoleon III, which occasions the alienation and is then unconcerned about it. The poetic imagination holds the heterogeneous images of the poem together. Memory and interpretation form the poem.[11]

Edgar Lohner has considered "Le Cygne" in the context of its traditional background in his article "Das Bild des Schwanes in der modernen Lyrik."[12] As the bird of Apollo the swan has been the symbol for the poet. Since the time of Plato the swan that sings beautifully before its death has become a *topos*; the transformation of the poet into a swan is, since Horace, another traditional theme that was strengthened through the Zeus-Leda myth. Baudelaire perverts the motif by placing the swan on dry land and by having it wish for a storm upon the city with a wringing of his neck, a gesture of thirst and accusation. But Baudelaire used the tradition he perverted. The swan is the poet in his poem as in Rilke's. His suffering from modern ugliness is expressed and elevated to the heights of artistic form in the images of mythical and contemporary exiles.

The transformation of worldly imperfection into the beauty of poetry is the theme of Rilke's poem; he wanted to restore what Baudelaire had perverted. The painful pace of the swan on dry land may be seen as an allusion to the Baudelaire poem. Rilke did not wish to translate the pain of the alienated poet's existence into a lamentation; such a transformation had taken place in Baudelaire's poem. Rilke's swan, rather, is the image of this very transformation. By being transformed the swan returns to its element. Thus, Rilke's poem interprets the inner meaning of Baudelaire's poem. The swan on land in Rilke's poem is Baudelaire's swan. Rilke's swan in the water is the transformation that Baudelaire's poem had effected. Rilke's own experiences of creative euphoria enter into the image. Personal experience and literary allusion amalgamate.

Malte Laurids Brigge calls Baudelaire's poem "Une Charogne" incredible. He praises the transformation of a disgusting topic, a cadaver, into a poem with these words, "It was his [Baudelaire's] task to see the existing thing in this horrible sight which seemed to be merely disgusting. It retains its validity amidst all existence." Yet Rilke qualifies his statement: "Apart from the last stanza, he was right."[13] At the conclusion of the poem the speaker states that he has preserved the form and the divine essence from decay. With that Rilke could have agreed. What he has Malte protest against can only be the explicitness with which the poet expresses in discursive language what he had translated into imagery. A Symbolist theory is implied here and can be documented from the letters on Cézanne. In these letters to his wife Clara, Rilke, now in his own name, refers to the passage quoted from *Malte* and calls Baudelaire's cadaver poem the beginning of the development toward factual language, "Entwicklung zum sachlichen Sagen." Rilke writes: "The artist is neither permitted to select nor to turn away from anything existing. . . ."[14] This factuality (Sachlichkeit) is not the same as realism. A realistic author expresses himself in the language of the reader; he addresses the reader in his world. This is not how Rilke understands factual language (sachliches Sagen). He says of the apples in the pictures of Cézanne that "their edibility ceases; they become so concretely real, simply uneatable in their stubborn existence."[15] He attempts to exclude the human associations by transforming real things into "art-things" ("Kunstdinge"). If Rilke speaks of "dinghaft wirklich" he means that transformation of a real object into an "art-thing," a work of art, a painting or poem. The real thing, after being transformed into an aesthetic one, loses its reference to its former real environment, is isolated, exists for itself; it is no longer usable. In other words, we have before us not lyrical realism but rather symbolism, which has as its aim the presentation of a work of art, autonomous, consistent within itself and no longer subject to the laws of reality. Such a work of art is called "Ding" by Rilke and only in this sense can the *Neue Gedichte* be called "Dinggedichte."

Rilke developed his Symbolist aesthetics under the influence of Cézanne; nevertheless this aesthetics is really a poetics, it is derived more from Rilke's insights into his own creative process than from Cézanne.[16] The separation of the work of art from the author is a major theme of the aesthetics in Rilke's letters to Cézanne:

> After each experience the artist realizes more clearly how necessary it was to go even beyond love; as natural as it is for the artist to love every one of these things as he creates it: if he shows this love, he will make it less good; he is discussing it instead of stating it.[17]

That is exactly what Baudelaire had done in "Une Charogne." Rilke's own later works mix rhetorical discussion with the stating of images. Yet here his poetics aims at symbols free from discussion, or a total transformation of the intention into images. That is precisely what Rilke's swan poem expresses.

An often quoted passage from the Cézanne letters concerning colors can be read in the same sense, as consistent symbolic aesthetics.

> Still I wanted to say the following about Cézanne: that it has never before been shown how much painting depends on the relationship among colors, how one must leave them entirely alone so that they contend one against the other. The relations among them: that is what painting is. Whoever intrudes, whoever arranges, whoever allows his human opinion, his wit, his cause, his mental suppleness to take part in any way—he disturbs and tarnishes their action. The painter must not become conscious of his insights (like the artist in general): without taking a detour through his reflection, being enigmatic even to the artist himself, his development must enter so quickly into his work that he is not able to recognize it at the moment of entry.[18]

Rilke is not referring primarily to unconscious art, but rather to art which does not preach or does not contain its own interpretation. That the artist must not become conscious of his own insights, that he should not reflect, means—in the context of the aesthetics expressed in the Cézanne letters—that nothing should divert the artist from the task of creating an "art-thing" which exists in its own right. (In practice, Rilke knew exactly what he wanted to say. *Malte* and *Neue Gedichte*, among them, "Der Schwan," show that well enough.) We can disregard the romantic residual in the formulation; the important statement is that concerning colors: they are to exist in a system of correspondences without the painter's intrusion. When applied to poetry, it means that the poem should say what it says only in poetic, not in discursive, language—that is to say, not in such a way that the image can be translated directly into conceptual terms. That was the criticism Rilke directed against the last verse of "Une Charogne"; that is why he takes up Baudelaire's swan image and contrasts it with his own.

Rilke considered even using his aesthetic theory against his own inclinations. Again in the Cézanne letters he reports to Clara Rilke about his daily trip to the Salon d'Automne in Paris where the Cézanne paintings were on display. He passed through the Faubourg Saint Germain, past old aristocratic palaces whose unseen interior opened up to his imagination. "One senses, one believes there are royal interior rooms in these palaces; he has something in his blood which belongs there; and for a second the scale of all feelings lies there between the weight of bronze ancient Chinese porcelain pieces and the frivolous sound of a pendulum clock. . . ." Rilke's snobbism is surfacing here, the ostensible nobility with which he compensated for the feeling of classlessness which reigned in his family. He nevertheless wants to renounce his pet dream. In the gallery chamber, where the Cézanne paintings are, all this, he continued, has lost its validity, the affinity to noble mansions and "as a little blood feels which passes the heart from time to time, scenting like an aged essence." The formulation shows how strongly Rilke is still a prisoner of his snobbism even here where he rejects it. But he is determined:

> All this is to be abdicated, set aside, rejected. Even one who would speak of such mansions would have to view them in poverty and without presentiment, not as one who could be seduced by them. Certainly one must go so far with his neutrality that even vague remembrances of feelings, traditions of inherited predelictions and prejudices are not permitted to be interpreted. Instead, what emerges with these feelings, power, admiration and will, is to be applied pristinely and anonymously to one's own tasks. One must remain a pauper unto the tenth generation. Even for one's predecessors, one must be able to be poor, lest one only reaches back to their ascendancy, to their first glory. But one must feel beyond them to the roots and the earth itself. One must be able at every moment to lay one's hand on the earth like the first man.[19]

This avowal of primitivism is consistent with the style of his time. It is well known that Rilke would later proclaim the love of Earth solemnly in the *Duineser Elegien*. Because the passage in the Cézanne letters occurs in the context of an aesthetic theory, we should refrain from understanding Rilke's primitivism only philosophically but rather view it aesthetically as well. Primitivism for Rilke is a state of no presuppositions, that is, the separation of poetic language from the social context, including the social origins of Rilke himself. The poverty that Rilke is seeking is actually freedom from his origins, from all social ties, which include his pet aristocratic daydreams. The *Duineser Elegien* continue this idea; they deal with the justification of the asocial, totally nonbourgeois poet. Rilke's justification is the same as in the Cézanne letters: the poet transforms reality into art, real things into "art things." In poetry this transformation makes visible things invisible, it creates totally new associations that are available only in works of art and that suspend the transitoriness, sufferings, and joy found in real life.

Nevertheless, Rilke addresses his readers. Even though there are difficult passages in his poems, even if one must concede that the poems of his *Neue Gedichte* disclose their meaning only through painstaking interpretations, it is true that Rilke's poetry is more accessible to the reader than Mallarmé's hermetic symbolism. Mallarmé influences his elite readers through the enigmatic relationships that the images and half-images of his poems evoke. Rilke always presents recognizable images even as he distills from them his purely aesthetic, and not concrete, meaning. That must not necessarily mean that Rilke wants to make greater concessions to his readers than Mallarmé, or, as one might think at first, that Rilke is less modern or that he is more of a bourgeois realist.

Mallarmé also wrote a symbolist poem in which a swan appears. It is the sonnet which begins: "Le vierge, le vivance et le bel aujourd'hui. . . ."[20] It was published in 1885. Rilke might have been acquainted with it. The poem opens with the question whether the virginal, living, and beautiful new day will break the ice on the lake. But the question solidifies, as it were, in the image of a frozen lake. A fairy-tale swan is frozen fast in the ice. The poem does not, however, depend on this image. Rather the image is destroyed, taken back, and denied. The reader is not to identify the world of the poem and his own. The abstract is evocatively mixed with the concrete. The poem merely presents enigmatic associations that point to a basic structure in which freedom and constraint are opposed to each other.

The ambivalence of freedom and constraint describes, in Mallarmé's poem as in Rilke's, an aesthetic condition. The work of art is free from the social world but constrained by its nature because not one of its words can be exchanged for another. Its immutability hinders it from achieving true freedom.

Rilke, on the other hand, uses the swan symbol to offer freedom from the material world in the successful work of art. He does this without breaking his language up into enigmatic symbols. In "Der Schwan" the entire poem is the enigma that requires solution. While Baudelaire removed the swan from its element in order to suggest realistically a symbol for the alienation of the poet in the social world, and while Mallarmé freezes his symbol into an enigmatic system of allusions that point to unattainable beauty, Rilke returns his swan to its element as a symbol for the freedom of the poem from its real relationships.

A poetic program like the one behind the swan poem cannot be found in every poem of the *Neue Gedichte*. In some of them there is simply nothing more than the presentation of an "art-thing" that differs from the real thing, which had been its model, by way of a play with new, merely artistic nuances. This differentiation or transformation, whether it be more or less striking, is always the actual intention; it presupposes the reader's alienation from social reality; it is a Symbolist alienation from social reality; it is a Symbolist alienation effect.

Rilke's reader must share his principal unwillingness to accept the social order of the bourgeoisie (for which Rilke does not know a real alternative) as a valid order in the realm of art. His message is redemption and justification of human existence in the poem. This has political and therefore historical implications.

Egon Schwarz in his book *Das verschluckte Schluchzen* has shown that the poet preferred above all a conservative, anticapitalistic posture.[21] It was unique in that Rilke did not think nationalistically in terms of Germany or Austria. After initial amazement at the enthusiasm for the war in 1914 and temporary acclaim of this enthusiasm (not its cause) in the *Fünf Gesänge* (1914), Rilke became a determined pacifist. After the end of the war he returned again to prefascist sympathies, which went as far as approving, in a private letter, a speech made by Mussolini. Schwarz shows how Rilke's basic political position, especially the longing for the preindustrial age and for the social situation of the centuries preceding the French Revolution, corresponded with the political confusion that was common among the German middle class.

Rilke's prefascist tendencies grew out of the anticapitalism from the right. Fascism offered solutions to the alienation of the petit bourgeois in the industrial state who wanted to restore lost greatness. Mussolini did that by invoking antiquity. Alfred Schuler, a Bohemian student of ancient Rome who influenced Rilke as well as Hitler, preached a renewal of the blood by way of infusing the spirit of the primitive late-Roman subculture. Blood, for Schuler, was obviously a symbol. Rilke understood Schuler in his terms, Hitler in quite different ones. (We do not need to go into the Germanic folk-cults of the prefascists because Rilke was not interested in them.)

The solutions that Marxism offered for alienation were theoretical and unsymbolic. Rilke, like many others with the same level of education, saw modern technology, science, and socialism as threats to an organic world that still offered symbols by which one could live. The inclination toward fascism has, therefore, aesthetic reasons; it arises from the longing for a world ordered by symbols, which would end alienation. Redemption from the real, especially the technological, capitalist world by way of a symbolic *Weltanschauung* was widespread during Rilke's lifetime. The Expressionists hoped for the "new human," which was an essentially symbolic desire for change. Rilke had sympathies for some of them, even though most of the Expressionists identified with leftist political causes.[22] Rilke would identify with the call for newness as long as it was not couched in economic terms.

The emphasis on humanistic and aesthetic education in imperial pre-war Germany, together with the lack of practical political experience of the bourgeoisie under the Bismarck constitution, adds to the romantic German inclination to view politics not practically but from an aesthetic or philosophical point of view. The aversion to the orientation of the bourgeoisie within the bourgeoisie itself, the bourgeois alienation, is historically important by itself and should not exclusively be derived from its political consequence, fascism. The uneasiness within the aesthetically inclined intellectuals in the German bourgeoisie was by no means unequivocal. For example, one can show in the case of the two Mann brothers that their different political ways never relieved them of their need to defend aestheticism. The freedom of the artist from society remains the basis of their *Weltanschauung. Doktor Faustus*, to be sure, complains about aestheticism; but the novel presents this lament as an interpretation of German fate. The aestheticism of the upper class supposedly led to the fascist catastrophe. There may be some truth in that, but it is certainly not a sufficient theory of fascism. Nevertheless, it deserves to be noted that Adrian's flight into music, because of his need to rise above the banality of his fellow Germans, is similar to Rilke's flight into his theory of redemption through art.

The desire to transform the everyday world is basically the same as what we denote with the term "Verfremdung," or alienation effect, as used by Bertolt Brecht. The author has freed himself from the everyday world; he is alienated and shares this with the bourgeois theater audience, which he wants to lure out of its secure world. The alienation effect is to make the audience aware of the artificiality of the process. That is the intention of Brecht, who built the principle of the alienation effect into a program of basic realism in drama. He first addresses his audience in the context of its own world. Then he shatters that comfortable world so that the audience must change the world first in thought and then in deed. To what extent Brecht really relinquishes the autonomy of art with this program is a problem in itself. But it is clear that the alienation effect has at least an antirealistic component. Rilke's transformation has no realistic and no social goal at all. His political consciousness was faulty—like that of most of his readers. We can make such a sober statement and yet understand the internalized liberation of the aesthetically inclined bourgeois. This spirit of liberation often finds an excellent expression in Rilke's poems. His mature and regal swan is not only the image of a successful poem but also of a happy command of language. The calm joy about this mastery is evident in the form itself. This joy is the expression of happiness over the moment of self-determined freedom.

Rilke allows his reader to share in the enjoyment of this freedom. Already the *Stundenbuch* was concerned with the establishment of a developing artist-god of the future. It sought to destroy the traditional concepts of above and below. However, the romantic and cultic theme of the monk led to the reception of *Stundenbuch* as a substitute religion. In the *Neue Gedichte* and in *Malte* it becomes clear, however, that, in spite of all his misapprehension about his industrial environment, Rilke has no interest in the historical reality of his symbols. Older historical circumstances and religious myths interest him only insofar as they serve as sources for images or they support the belief that symbols were taken much more seriously in earlier times. But Rilke reinterpreted Biblical and historical themes without regard for their origin and meaning. Behind the appearance of humility and an affection for antiquity, the actual intention of Rilke's poems is to turn from the bourgeois-interpreted world to the openness of imagination where the poet rules as king. This Rilke meant by his concept of transformation into the invisible, which he employed in the *Duineser Elegien*. It is basically a nonconservative conception. Human existence is seen as tormenting in its homelessness and alienation; however, in the successful poem the lack of accord with a senseless world is reverted to a new majestic order which has aesthetic value.

Bourgeois freedom was historically the freedom from feudalism, which was based on land and on ancient heritage. When the propertied and the educated middle class surpassed the nobility economically, the middle class itself became conservative. The bourgeois tendency towards liberation turned into a socialistic cause for some discontent bourgeois outsiders, or else it became a tendency towards the relief from alienation and homelessness in aesthetic bohemianism. Bohemianism influenced Rilke's artistic education. The mature Rilke tried to bring his bohemian anarchism, his rebellion against his heritage and tradition, under the Symbolist's discipline of the autonomous work of art. The quality of Rilke's poems was based on the correspondence of the words with each other. But since such a poem depends on its autonomy, and since this autonomy is maintained in opposition to the established bourgeois world, one must consider anarchistic rebellion to be at the core of Rilke's poetry, externally balanced by Rilke's foible for old symbols and by his conservative attitudes.

NOTES

This essay was translated from the German manuscript by Alvin J. Mauler and the author.

1. See Egon Schwarz, *Das verschluckte Schluchzen: Poesie und Politik bei Rainer Maria Rilke* (Frankfurt am Main: Athenäum, 1972).
2. Rainer Maria Rilke, *Sämtliche Werke* (Frankfurt am Main: Insel, 1961), IV: 532. This edition (1955–1966 with several reprints) is hereafter quoted by volume and page only.
3. Ibid.
4. VI: 756.
5. See Judith Ryan, *Umschlag und Verwandlung: Poetische Struktur und Dichtungstheorie in R. M. Rilkes Lyrik der mittleren Periode (1907–1914)* (Munich: Winkler, 1972).
6. I: 510.
7. Cf. Judith Ryan, pp. 55–65.
8. Cf. Judith Ryan, p. 49.
9. Rainer Maria Rilke, *Briefe* (Wiesbaden: Insel, 1950), I: 116; September 20, 1905.
10. V: 152–53, 177.
11. *Les Fleurs du mal*, in Charles Baudelaire, *Oeuvres Complètes*, ed. Yves Florenne (Paris: Le club francais du livre, 1966), I: 952–53. Cf. also "L'Albatros" in *Les Fleurs du mal* (p. 923) where the poet is expressively compared with the bird who is alienated from his element. Both poems with English prose translation also in Baudelaire, *Selected Verse* (Baltimore: Penguin, 1961), pp. 8–9, 209–11.
12. In *Festschrift Für Bernhard Blume*, ed. E. Schwarz, H. G. Hannum, and E. Lohner (Göttingen: Vandenhock & Ruprecht, 1967), pp. 297–322.

13. VI: 775.
14. *Briefe*, I: 207; October 19, 1907.
15. *Briefe*, I: 187; October 8, 1907.
16. Cf. *Briefe,* I: 200 (comparison of the Cézanne-experience with *Neue Gedichte*), 205 (reference to the turning point in his work), 208 (reference to Malte Laurids Brigge on the basis of the Cézanne experience), cf. also 252 (letters of October 13, 1907; October 18, 1907; October 19, 1907; September 8, 1908).
17. *Briefe*, I: 199; October 13, 1907.
18. *Briefe*, I: 214; October 21, 1907.
19. *Briefe*, I: 211; October 20, 1907.
20. Stéphane Mallarmé, *Oeuvres Complètes* (Paris: Gallimard, 1945), pp. 67–68. Cf. Edgar Lohner's interpretation (see note 12 above), pp. 307–10.
21. (Frankfurt am Main: Athenäum, 1972).
22. For these connections cf. the documents cited by Joachim W. Storck in the catalogue of the 1975 Marbach exhibition *Rainer Maria Rilke*, especially pp. 190–241. The relations to Expressionist writers and leftist politicians were hidden from public view for a long time, since the publisher did not want to have them surface. Dr. Storck, who plans to publish a book on this aspect of Rilke's life, discussed these problems with me in 1975.

7

Rilke and Russia

LEV KOPELEV

"That Russia is my homeland is one of those great and mysterious certainties from which I live," Rilke wrote in 1903, three years after he had last been in Russia.[1] In the last year of his life he confessed in a letter to his old friend Leonid Pasternak that "everything which has to do with old Russia (the mysterious and unforgettable Skazka) . . . has remained near and dear and holy, forever fixed in the foundation of my life."[2]

Rilke's deep, many-leveled, and multifaceted relationship to Russia, to her literature, art, history, to her life with its religious festivals and day-to-day business, to her countryside and her people, all have been treated in numerous scholarly books and articles. But the complexity and significance of these relationships represent a challenge, for there are many problems that have not been considered, and many earlier observations require revision.

Rilke discovered Turgenev and Dostoevsky in 1897 as a young man of letters.[3] It is said that he read Tolstoy as a student even earlier, in 1893.[4] When, in 1907, he answered a questionnaire concerning the writers and books he considered important, he named the great Danish author Jacobsen, Turgenev, Dostoevsky, Ibsen, and the Bible. He wrote: "Dostoevsky . . . became . . . very important for me when, after I had been thoroughly prepared for him through his country and his language, I read and reread *Poor Folk* and finally translated a part of this naturally brilliant work" (*SW*, VI: 1021). When asked in 1924 by a literary scholar about the influences upon his life, Rilke named the Russians first, once again naming Turgenev among those who influenced his development in the "earliest stages" (and also included Jacobsen, Liliencron, Dehmel, George, Wassermann, Hofmannsthal, and Hauptmann). In that connection he wrote that "with the first trip to Russia (1899) and with the process of learning the Russian language . . . I then quickly and with hardly any difficulties experienced the enchantment of Pushkin and Lermontov, Nekrasov and Fet and so many others."[5]

At first he had read the works of Russian authors in German translations, and perhaps in French translations as well. But then he learned Russian very quickly. Rilke's early delightful excursion into the language and his especially keen musical-poetic feeling for the Russian word, for its powers of expression and richness in ideas, as well as for its inherent phonetic and rhythmical expressiveness, were also certainly advanced by his earliest relationship to his Czech homeland. Ever since his childhood he had been exposed to the Czech language, to Czech songs, fairy tales, and jokes; he had gotten to know many of his Czech fellow-countrymen and he had respected and loved them; he knew their traditional and often passionate dedication to their "great Slavic brothers in the East." One of Rilke's first literary teachers was Julius Zeyer (1841–1901), an epic poet, lyric poet, and dramatist, one of the leading figures of Czech Neoromanticism. Zeyer traveled to Russia several times in the 1870s and 1880s, and in 1882 he translated *The Campaign of Igor* into Czech. Rilke belonged to his circle of friends. Zeyer's favorite niece, Valerie von David-Rhonfeld, became Rilke's lover; it was to her that he dedicated his first volume of poetry, *Leben und Lieder*. He praised Zeyer in a sonnet that appeared in his next book of poetry, *Larenopfer*: "Du bist ein Meister . . ." ("You are a master . . .") (*SW*, I: 35–36).

Rilke's ties with his Czech homeland, with its people, traditions, culture, myths, and realities, were very fruitful for his creativity, in spite of many "inherited" prejudices and contradictions which were tied to his upbringing; they manifested themselves in his prose *Prager Geschichten* as well as in his poetry.[6]

The Czech sources of his youthful world of feeling and thought had prepared him for the reception of the Russian impressions. But Rilke's first direct contacts with Russia developed under the decisive influence of Lou Andreas-Salomé, whom the young poet met in May, 1897.

Lou, the daughter of a Russian general, was particularly perceptive to shades of thought and emotion in people and art. She was hardly twenty years old when in 1882 Nietzsche "fell madly in love with the bright, beautiful Russian girl."[7] But she refused his proposal of marriage. In 1894 she wrote one of the first significant works about him, *Friedrich Nietzsche in seinen Werken.*

Rilke was quite enthusiastic about her books on Nietzsche and Ibsen, as well as her critical theological essays. He even wrote anonymous letters of praise to her before he met her in Munich, in May, 1897. For the young twenty-two year old poet, still very excitable and tending frequently toward exalted expressions of feeling, the meeting with Lou was a decisive turning point in his life. The relationship with this attractive and intellectually superior woman fluctuated from the erotic to that of mystic exaltation. "I want to see the world through you; then I'll see not the world, but you, you, you!"[8] Lou's influence can be seen not only in his early poetry dating from his first Russian trip, but also later as he recounts, ". . . two years before I made my trip to Russia, I felt Russia's influence through a person who was close to me and who represented it in her nature. It prepared me to find what was my own" (*Br*, 880). For Rilke she was the personification of the Russian spirit and being.

II

During the first trip to Russia, April 27 to June 17, 1899, Rilke visited Moscow and St. Petersburg and added to his circle of Russian acquaintances. He visited Leo Tolstoy, Leonid Pasternak, Aleksandr Benois, and the sculptor Paolo Trubetzkoy. He corresponded with many, including Elena Voronina, art critic Pavel Èttinger, and Sofia Schill. After his return he was determined to link his future life with Russia. In a letter to his mother on August 12, 1899, he wrote ". . . the greatest part of my day belongs to my Russian studies." Again on August 28 he wrote ". . . I'm beginning to enjoy reading Turgenev and Lermontov in the original." On his twenty-fourth birthday: ". . . since I have finally chosen Russia, I must stand by it."[9] Though his plan to resettle in Russia never materialized, he recalled his earliest impressions of Russia in a letter to Lou from Rome.

> For me it was Easter just once; that was the time in that long extraordinary, uncommon, excited night when people were all milling about, and when Ivan Velikij struck, stroke after stroke. That was my Easter, and I believe it will suffice for a whole life; the message was given to me written strangely large in those Moscow nights, given into my blood and into my heart. I know it now. . . .[10]

In May, 1900, Rilke and Lou made a second trip to Russia, which lasted until August 22. They traveled from Moscow to Tula and Jasnaja Poljana. Here Rilke spent an afternoon with Leo Tolstoy and continued on to Kiev, to Kremenčug and Saratov, up the Volga to Samara, Kazan', Nižnij Novgorod, Yaroslavl', Tver', and finally to St. Petersburg. He spent several days in country houses, including that of the poet Spiridon Drožžin, and then visited the estate of Count Nikolaj Tolstoj. He visited the damp, dark underground catacombs in Kiev, saw the immense landscape of the steppes and breathed the breath of the gigantic land, which seemed so familiar and yet so darkly mysterious, so near yet unattainable.

In a letter to Ellen Key he described his first trip. "When I first arrived in Moscow everything there was known and long familiar; . . . it was the city of my oldest and deepest memories, it was a continual meeting again and greeting: it was home. . . ."[11] This corresponds also to the metaphorical expression, "the reappearance of all childhood." For Rilke the feelings of childhood are an essential source and milestone for his poetry, and one should not interpret the Russian experience as one German critic has: "[Rilke] gained essentially nothing, he found himself and his inner life reinforced in Russia. The Russian people became for him a symbol of certainties which had long sought expression in him."[12] Such an opinion is contradicted by virtually all of the documents from Rilke's first Russian experience, in his diaries, letters, and numerous later recollections. Furthermore, the otherwise sharpwitted researcher S. Brutzer is wrong when she maintains that Rilke recognized the Russian people "not as individual personalities" but "loved in them, the one, the Russian person. He was joyfully aware of a deep inner relationship with this patient, waiting nature . . . one which was slow to change."[13] Brutzer generalizes, in this instance rather narrowly, that Rilke's tendency toward abstractions (that is, "Ding," "Kunst-Ding") cannot be separated from the simultaneous concreteness ("Dinghaftigkeit") of his sense of reality.

Leonid Pasternak, who became Rilke's friend after their first meeting in May, 1899, admired the young, inquisitive poet, whose "soft, little beard and large, light blue eyes, with the questioning expression like those of a child, gave him the appearance of a Russian thinker." It impressed Pasternak that "Rilke had set himself the task of studying the religious and historic customs of the land and of becoming familiar with the unadorned, true life of the people."[14]

Rilke's command of the language was sufficient for him to compose his first letter in Russian on July 16 to Spiridon Drožžin.[15] He noted in his diary on November 29, "Today the first Russian poem came to me quite unexpectedly in the woods."[16] By December 7 he had composed six Russian poems, but these poetic excursions into the newly acquired language were not entirely "unexpected," in spite of his modest lines to S. Schill in February, 1900. "For me that would be the ultimate: to be able to compose Russian verses. Who could do it!" (*SW*, IV: 967–68). Then on August 17 he promised to send her "his first collection of Russian poetry."[17] Lou, to whom these poems and the diary were dedicated, mentioned them in her Rilke book and commented that they were "grammatically poor, yet somehow incomprehensibly poetic."[18] One can only agree with her. Rilke's Russian verses are filled with syntactical and lexical errors. Almost every line reveals a foreign melody in the phrase, the clumsy stammering of a foreigner. Yet one perceives in these poems a true poetry and the individual voice of the poet.

Rilke went to Paris where he found a new home and great teachers for his development as a poet. But Paris was for him "very large and full of sadness."[19] He wrote to Vogeler: "Paris? Paris is difficult. A galley. I cannot express how disagreeable everything is here, nor can I describe the rejection I feel as I walk here!" (*Br*, 44). This rejection, the fear and disgust he felt for Paris, was similar to the "frightened astonishment" he had had to overcome as a young cadet in military school. In the *Neue Gedichte* and in *Malte* he freed himself of these feelings in magnificently and powerfully worded language. He felt after the completion of the novel "like a survivor."[20] The experiences in his "adopted homes," France and Switzerland, and his trips to Italy, Spain, Germany, and Africa were all fruitful and an incentive for new creativity and forms. But none of these could diminish his Russian experience, particularly with respect to the intellectual and poetic activity and the lasting friendships that resulted. In his correspondence with Lou Andreas-Salomé, Rilke wrote on May 15, 1904: "I want . . . to continue to read Russian and from time to time to translate from Russian."[21]

Rilke and Lou had similar ideas, although they were not always of the same opinion. Certainly Lou's letter of July 9, 1917, expressed Rilke's own feelings about the Russian revolution:

> We both know that, what Russia is doing now, has little to do with what revolutions otherwise have done; all of Russia's denials are only a kind of rule by God. Even if it is destroyed by that, as a person is easily destroyed who understands too deeply the oneness of God and the earth (this is too

deep for politics!), there still remains the Russian land, which lives and "conquers" for all.[22]

For Rilke "oneness of God and earth" was the meaning of the world and human existence. This perspective of Russian life and the country that "borders on God" inspired his version of Lermontov's "I walk the way alone," which he sent to Lou in January, 1919.[23]

Lou's friendship was probably Rilke's most important connection with Russia, though other ties and friendships also remained strong during and after the war years. He renewed several old Russian acquaintances during his stay in Paris from January to August, 1925, among them Elena Voronina. He also became acquainted with Ivan Bunin and his works,[24] and he showed great enthusiasm for the Russian stage, represented in Paris by actor and director Georgij Pitoev, dancers Aleksandr and Chlothilde Sacharov, and the puppet theater of Julia Sazonova-Slonimski.[25] Rilke often reviewed their productions and met his Russian translator, M. Cetlin (Amari) there.[26] He also employed a Russian secretary, Ženja Černosvitova, who assisted him in reading Russian texts, and he even considered writing a book on Russia during this time.[27] His last stay in Paris was a return to the old Russia:

> . . . how strongly, with how much emotion, dear Leonid Osipovič Pasternak, I felt that last year in Paris: there I saw again old Russian friends and found new ones, and the young fame of your son Boris touched me in many ways . . . [I read] his poems, very beautiful ones (in a little anthology of Ilya Ehrenburg's, which . . . I . . . would have liked to reread). Now it moves me to think that not *he* alone, Boris, the already recognized poet of a new generation, knows about me and is familiar with my work. . . .[28]

When Boris Pasternak, whose own youthful development was strongly influenced by Rilke's works, learned of this letter, he wrote Rilke in a stormy surge of wonderment, love, and joy.[29] It was from Pasternak that Rilke received an introduction to the great Russian poetess Marina Čvetaeva, then living as an émigrée in France. Rilke wrote to her May 3, 1926:

> Dear Poetess, I have received at this hour a gripping letter from Boris Pasternak, filled to overflowing with joyous feeling. All the emotion and thankfulness his writing evokes in me, he asks me to transmit to you, and through you, to him! Both books (my last two publications), which will follow this letter, *are for you, are your property*. Two additional copies will follow when I have them: these should go to . . . if the censor allows it.

118

I'm so overcome by the fullness and strength of his devotion, that I can say no more today; but send my friend in Moscow the enclosed note! As a greeting.

Must I tell? You know that I have been able to count Leonid O. P. of Moscow as a true friend (for twenty-eight years!). After a long, long interruption, I received a letter this winter (at the beginning of the winter) from him, from Berlin, which I answered with all the joy that our finding one another again gave me. But I did not need the announcement from Leonid Ossipovič to know that his son has become a well-known, powerful poet: last year in Paris friends had already showed me his work, which moved me deeply. (I can still read Russian, though only after some searching and practice; letters are quite easy!) During my stay in Paris last year, almost *eight* months, I again had contact with Russian friends I hadn't seen for 25 years. But why, I must ask now, why haven't I been granted the favor of meeting *you*, Marina Ivanovna Tsvetayeva?!"

After Boris Pasternak's letter I have to believe that such a meeting would have meant the deepest inner joy for us both. Can it ever be retrieved?[30]

There are several additional letters to Marina Čvetaeva, whose texts are still unpublished. Although Rilke's friendship with her was short (he lived only a few more months), it was his source of inspiration for the elegy "O, die Verluste ins All . . ." and her New Year's requiem.

In the last year of his life, Rilke made plans to write a longer book on Russia that was to contain memories and essays on problems of Russian culture.[31] *The Family Chronicle* by Sergej Aksakov, an epic book about old eternal Russia, was kept on the nightstand by his deathbed.[32]

Rilke's relationship to Russian literature reaches from his first introduction to Russian books to this last selection. It spans the visits with the aged Leo Tolstoy and the naïve lyric poet Drožžin, and his friendship with Čvetaeva and Pasternak.

III

Russia permeated Rilke's life and creativity in many ways. He translated Russian epics, lyric poetry, and dramas. He composed poems in Russian and wrote essays on Russian art; he intended to organize exhibits of Russian painters in the West and even hoped to contribute to Russian journals. For a time he even made plans to immigrate to Russia. This emotion-filled, conscious searching for the "home of his soul" was strongest from 1897 to 1902, during Rilke's "Russian period."[33]

The works from this period showing the strongest Russian influence are *Das Stundenbuch* and *Geschichten vom Lieben Gott*. Even before his first Russian trip he began to translate Russian writers, and afterwards he translated not only for publication but for "his own use." He noted in his diary (December 2, 1899), concerning Dostoevsky's *Poor Folk*: ". . . I know of no book which can compare with it."[34] He had hoped to prepare a special edition and a German stage version of Tolstoy's *The Living Corpse*. However, he did not succeed in obtaining the manuscript from the author or his collaborators.[35] In a letter to Suvorin he indicates he translated Chekhov's *Seagull*,[36] though the manuscript has never been located.[37]

He did succeed in publishing a translation of a short story, *The Petition* (originally *Xodoki*), written by a young conservative journalist, V. Jančevetskij. It is a sweetly sentimental story of the selfless love of simple farmers for their czar.[38]

Rilke's most significant translation is *The Campaign of Igor*, an old Russian heroic song in free verse by an unknown author. He began the work in 1902 and finished it in Paris in March, 1904 (his adaptation was not published until 1930).[39] From 1899 to 1902 he translated poems by Lermontov, Fofanov, Hippius, and Drožžin; and in 1919, Lermontov's "Alone, I come on to the Road." The latter is one of the best translations of Russian poetry in world literature.

The lyric adaptations were an inevitable part of Rilke's poetic development. He only translated that which had direct poetic or spiritual appeal for him. This was particularly true of his first acquaintance with Lermontov's poetry.

He wrote Lou in September, 1899, "I long to read Russian," and asked her to send him "Lermontov, Volume 1, or something in prose."[40] Twenty years later, when he included a translation in a letter to Lou, he mentioned having written it down long ago in his notebook.[41]

Rilke read a great variety of books, essays, and poems, and carried on detailed correspondences about intellectual life in Russia, literature, theater, philosophy, and art with L. Pasternak, S. Schill, P. Ettinger, and A. Benois. In his letters to S. Schill in March and February, 1900, he emphasized the fruitful inner dialectic of Tolstoy's *The Resurrection*: ". . . a very significant book, full of artistic value. If one considers that it did not originate with the total application of his artistic talent, but in a constant battle against it, one understands the superhuman power of the artistic force which remains so wonderfully intense, despite the resistance of the aged Tolstoy."[42]

He expanded on his view of Chekhov in his correspondence with Èttinger, who had expressed a negative opinion of Chekhov's dramas and shown a preference for Maeterlink. Rilke, who had also been somewhat critical of Chekhov's dramas *Uncle Vanya, Three Sisters,* and *The Seagull,* clearly opposed Èttinger when he asserted that Chekhov, in comparison with Maeterlink, was more naïve and direct, more a realist, and more truly Russian in his attachment to the factual and concrete ("Dinglichem").[43]

His initial impression of Gorky's talent was also somewhat negative. He wrote Lou from Capri, December 13, 1906: ". . . Gorky lives here, part anarchist, part millionaire, with no regard for money or social threats, spoiled by fame, it would seem."[44] He did not favor Gorky because he felt his revolutionary ideas were "not only a contradiction to the artist, but also to the Russian" (*Br,* 251). But after meeting him, he wrote to K. Heydt that Gorky "possesses a great and touching goodness (that goodness which makes it possible for Russians to remain artists)."[45] Years later, after reading Gorky's memoirs of Tolstoy, he wrote to R. Zimmerman:

> Gorky has succeeded in offering a testament of love and admiration for the old Tolstoy, without presenting grounds for his powerful feelings; on the contrary, he does not spare himself the misery of detailing negative self-critcism and suspicions whenever such were inspired in him by that great phenomenon. That makes this little essay a very rare and penetrating document of veracity and one sees (and only a Russian could show this) that the will to truth does not harm love, if it has depth enough and is not afraid to suffer. Gorky's fragments impressed me all the more since I also had felt the same conflict at the time of my encounter with Leo Tolstoy, that powerful aging man. I was too young then to understand as fully as Gorky has succeeded in doing. [*Br,* 674–75]

In the letter to Drožžin (July 16, 1900), written in Russian, he said ". . . I found an enchanting book, *The Domestic Life of the Russian Czars of Sabelin,* in which the history of old Moscow is so brightly and sharply described as only in the pictures of Apollinarij Vasnetsov."[46] In a letter to Suvorin he mentioned the "Russian historical works by Pypin and Kostomarov."[47] From his diaries we know that between 1900 and 1904 Rilke read not only popular histories, Gogol, Gončarov, Chernyshevsky, and Garshin, but also old chronicles, heroic epics (*byliny*), texts from the sixteenth and seventeenth centuries (*Domostroj*), and memoirs of the fugitive czarist (*Djak*) Kotošixin and the revolutionary Prince P. Kropotkin.

121

Rilke's relationship to the visual arts is a chapter in itself. He wrote and published two larger essays on Russian painting, "Russian Art" (1901) and "Modern Trends in Russian Art" (1902).[48] Both indicate thorough, conscientious study and highly emotional interpretations of Russian artists and poets. The first is a survey of the sequential development of Russian art from the beginning and expresses a poetically elevated generalization about the "super-aesthetic" significance of Russian art.

> If one speaks of peoples as persons who are in the process of developing, then one can say: this person wants to be a soldier, another a merchant, a third a scholar. The Russian wants to be an artist . . . the two dangers, which threaten the Russian artist: first the contagious, shining influence of foreign beauty that alienates him from his people; second, if he belongs to the people, the ardent wish to further the art of the people. [*SW*, V: 495]

Only one particular painter is discussed in detail in this essay, Viktor Vasnetsov, whose work is "a shining example of the vivaciousness of the Russian god, and of the deep piety of the master toward life" (*SW*, V: 501–2).

On the other hand, the second essay is filled with names and facts. He begins, however, with the incorrect assumption that "great authors had virtually no connection with the visual arts" (*SW*, V: 613). It would appear that either Rilke did not know or perhaps did not remember Gogol's "Portrait," Turgenev's "Three Portraits," Tolstoy's use of art descriptions in *Anna Karenina*, Chekhov's *The House with the Mezzanine*, and many other stories about artists and art works. He continues with descriptions of several Russian painters, showing his preference for Aleksandr Ivanov, Ivan Kramskoj, and Viktor Vasnetsov.

He emphasizes these particular artists, but he also shows familiarity with other contemporary artists, Repin, Levitan, Serov, and Vasiljev. He had even hoped to organize a traveling exhibit of Russian artists in Germany, which was to include a young Maljavin, Korovin, and Somov. He attempted to interest German and Austrian publishers in the graphic artist Maliutin.[49] He had visited Repin in his studio and read his autobiographical and critical essays. He even suggested that Repin had helped him recognize "the metaphysical image of the eternal Russian."[50] For his theoretical observations, however, he departed from his own personal aesthetic of *l'art pour l'art* and poesie pure, exemplifying those artists whose work was clearly characterized by "super-aesthetic" ideas and ideals that transcended the realm and ends of art. He saw in A. Ivanov "the figure of the lonely fighter." He considered the long chain of such figures, ". . . kings, saints, prophets. . . . At the beginning of this chain is the pale visage of the Russian artist."[51] Of Kramskoj he writes, he is "the artist, the way to God . . . the Great Lover, who cannot be silent, whose riches spill from him in the form of art."[52]

Rilke was aware of the peculiar contradiction in his perception of the world. When he first began the two essays he only wished "to indicate his feeling toward the Russian people." It was not his intention to give a complete picture of Russian art, but more to show what "the experience . . . the Russian in his homeland" had meant to him (*SW*, VI: 1383).[53]

V

The first direct poetic expressions and transformations of Rilke's Russian experience were the *Geschichten vom lieben Gott* (1899–1900). This work contains recognizable Russian and Ukrainian background, sources, and material. They are in no way adaptations, retold tales, or versions of fables borrowed from folklore or literature, even though specific sources can sometimes be identified.[54]

The god in these stories is a unique combination of a Rilkean god and a Russian god. He is more a heathen god than the Biblical or Christian God. He combines humanity and nature, the universe and the minute, life and death, suffering and joy. He represents the unity of this indivisible diversity; he is fruitful, creatively productive, always present, and always becoming.

Years later (February 22, 1922) Rilke wrote to a young reader that

the contact and closeness with other human beings did not come about till late in my life and, without the times of my youth which I spent in Russia, the experiences would never have been so pure and complete . . . I began with things, which were my actual childhood companions . . . Then Russia opened to me and gave me the brotherhood and darkness of God where there was community. Even then I called him the God who overcame me, and I waited long on my knees in the anteroom of his name.[55]

He continues by describing his experience with God, which he uses in several places in *Das Stundenbuch*, as the "ascent of God from a sighing heart, covering the heavens, and his descent like falling rain . . . More and more we are obliged to set aside our Christian experience, the ancient God finally overshadows it."[56]

The ancient, ageless god that Rilke discovered in Russia and versified belongs to all religions, not to a dogmatic doctrine. It is the god of all believers, who has existed since the beginning of mankind and will exist as long as mankind is here. He is not a god for fanatics or hypocrites. Rilke's Russian God is poetic and artistic, omnipotent and personal, abstract and concrete, mystical and "neighborly."

The tale of God's hands introduces the collection of *Geschichten*. God's hands act independently "as long as he creates just 'things'. . . . He had created the things in his sleep, so to speak. . . ." Then as God's hands, independent of him, were shaping man, man prematurely escaped their grasp. "He was so impatient, man. He already wanted to live." So God became quite angry. In the next story, entitled "Der Fremde Mann," God had his disobedient hands cut off. He only permitted them to return when the concerned left hand pointed out that the hand which had become man was climbing Golgotha. "Hands" and "things"—words used literally or metaphorically in Rilke's poetic development of concepts—are particularly "favored" in his poetry and prose from this period. The first version of the end of *Malte* contained a description of a visit to Leo Tolstoy. The second writing of this ending was about seven pages long, two of which were devoted to a visual poetic description of a man's hands in a portrait that hung in Tolstoy's living room. The hands were a miracle. They showed the personality more clearly than all other parts of the picture and expressed the exciting experience of the painter, whose heart opened to the magnificence of the two hands (*SW*, VI: 974–75, and V: 275–78).

The philosophically potent words "hands" and "things" became necessary elements in the development of Rilke's perspective and mode of expression. A statistical example for this is the accompanying chart.

Work	Hands	Hand	Thing or Things
Leben und Bilder (1894)	8	16	....
Larenopfer (1895)	7	7	....
Traumgekrönt (1896)	8	4	1
Advent (1897)	15	3	....
Dir zur Feier (1897–1898)	19	1	3
Mir zur Feier (1898)	22	2	8
Studenbuch (1899–1903)	49	20	45

When one considers the quantitative evaluation and the structural significance of these word-picture concepts, their new value is considerably more striking, especially in the first part of *Stundenbuch*, which dates from around 1900. Rilke wrote in his diary at the beginning of his first Russian trip, "I feel in these days that Russian things will give me their names in exchange for the reverent piety of my being, which has from childhood longed to be a part of my art."[57]

Das Stundenbuch was completed in Paris and published at a time when Rilke saw in Paris his new, adopted home and in Rodin his teacher. Rodin "helped him overcome his lyric superficiality" and taught him "to work in front of nature, relentlessly conceiving and forming."[58] At this time he also wrote to Lou (August 15, 1903):

> . . . and the history of endless generations of things could be divined beneath human history, like a stratum of slower and more peaceful developments that come about more deeply, more intimately, and confusedly. Into this history, Lou, the Russian will perhaps fit sometime, who, as one becoming and enduring, is descended from things and related to them, the way Rodin is as a creator related by blood. The biding quality in the character of the Russian (which the German's self-important busyness with the unimportant calls indolence—) would thus receive a new and sure enlightenment: perhaps the Russian was made to let the history of mankind pass by in order to later chime into the harmony of things with his singing heart. He has only to endure, to hold out and like the violinist, to whom no signal has yet been given, to sit in the orchestra, carefully holding his instrument so that nothing may happen to it. . . . More and more, and filled with a deeper and deeper sympathy, I bear within me my affection for this wide, holy land; as a new ground for solitude, and as a high hindrance against others.[59]

Das Stundenbuch "contains my love for Russia," he wrote in a letter to L. Pasternak (July 11, 1906). Much later he explained, ". . . Russia [you see this in books such as *Das Stundenbuch*] became the foundation of my experience and receptivity."[60] Literary critics, such as Sophie Brutzer, see this experience as building blocks in this foundation. "Without Kiev *Das Stundenbuch* is unthinkable." A. Rogalskij agrees with her,[61] as does Batterby, who is convinced that *"Das Stundenbuch* would not have been written but for the impact of Russia."[62]

This book—his first poetically mature work—has its roots in the dark rooms of the catacombs of Kiev. The sources of the poetic atmosphere and thoughts in the melodic verses of "Vom mönchischen Leben" and "Von der Pilgerschaft" are the Russian earth itself, the Dnieper, and the Volga. But as in *Die Geschichten vom lieben Gott* the direct sources have undergone a uniquely Rilkean transformation. The following poem may serve to illustrate this significant process:

> Du bist der raunende Verrußte,
> auf allen Öfen schlaefst du breit.
> Das Wissen ist nur in der Zeit.
> Du bist der dunkle Unbewußte
> von Ewigkeit zu Ewigkeit.
>
> Du bist der Bittende und Bange,
> der aller Dinge Sinn beschwert.
> Du bist die Silbe im Gesange,
> die immer zitternder im Zwange
> der starken Stimmen wiederkehrt.
>
> Du hast dich anders nie gelehrt:
> Denn du bist nicht der Schönumscharte,
> um welchen sich der Reichtum reiht.
> Du bist der schlichte, welcher sparte,
> Du bist der Bauer mit dem Barte
> von Ewigkeit zu Ewigkeit. [*SW*, I: 276–77]

> You're that smoked whisperer, extended
> on every stove in drowsiness.
> Time bounds our comprehendingness.
> You are the dark uncomprehended
> throughout all everlastingness.
>
> You are the trembler and entreater
> who makes all meanings hard to tell.
> You're that recurring syllable,
> forever tremulously sweeter
> in strong-voiced hymning audible.
> Never else apprehensible.
>
> For you're not one whom rich and clever
> surround, but one whose simpleness
> makes putting-by his chief endeavour:
> the peasant with the beard, from ever-
> lasting to everlastingness.[63]

The gentle, fearful Russian God, waiting by the fire, who "aller Dinge Sinn beschwert," became part of Rilke, after he saw the Russian churches, the Kremlin at Easter, after his discussions of faith and superstition with Leo Tolstoy, and after extensive readings of classical and contemporary literature in 1900.

"Because he was homesick for Russia and Paris seemed so hard and cold to him then, the third part of *Das Stundenbuch* was written, possibly due to the influence of Tolstoy, whose works Rilke particularly studied during this time."[64] This view of Alfred Rammelmeyer is well supported by many characteristics of the last part. However, it seems necessary to explain that in this case Paris represents any metropolis in western civilization. His longing for Russia, which was particularly strong in the first years of the century, determined his melancholy disgust for this civilization, and an inseparable fear accompanied it: the deep fear of the large city.

VI

Rilke "struggled with form" and with many means of expressing his Russian experience without actually giving it up. This effort went far beyond *Das Stundenbuch*. As he studied Nietzsche's *Geburt der Tragödie* in 1900 he recorded his thoughts "with reference to Russian things" as follows: "Isn't the Dionysian element still the moving force in Khorovod of the Russians? . . . And is the Russian mythos of the masses the only one close enough to be used as a comparison for the free life of sound?" (*SW*, VI: 1175). It is difficult to point to an aspect of Rilke's thought or works where his relationship to Russia does not play a significant role. Certainly the poetry of his *Buch der Bilder* and *Neue Gedichte* reflects it. But since a comprehensive treatment of this topic is not possible in the scope of an essay, we must limit our discussion to certain highlights.

On March 17, 1904, he wrote Lou, "I began a larger work in February, a sort of 'Lieben Gott' book, Part II. I'm now right in the middle of it and don't know if it will continue, when or how. . . ."[65] That was the beginning of *Die Aufzeichnungen des Malte Laurids Brigge*. He spent six years working on it, writing wherever he was, Paris, Prague, Germany, Sweden, Belgium, or Italy. He finally finished the manuscript in Leipzig (February, 1910).[66] He initially intended to close the work with the essay to Leo Tolstoy. Why he didn't, we can only guess, since we do not have his own comments on it.

The theme of death, of "one's own death" and death in general, woven into much of the plot of *Malte* is stubbornly reminiscent of the motifs in Tolstoy's works. Rilke elaborated in his diaries on Tolstoy's presentation of dying, "Having to become one, so that one ceases to exist. . . . sometimes it develops in only a few hours and with great force in a dying person. . . ."[67] Rilke also wanted to create similar death scenes in *Malte*. Several years later he wrote in a letter about the main problem in *Malte*. He knew of few writers other than Tolstoy who had ever "reflected more clearly, calmly and grandly about death." Particularly in the story "The Death of Ivan Ilich" and the two volumes *Steps of Life*, Rilke is extraordinarily impressed by Tolstoy's use of the death motif: ". . . his enormous experience of Nature (I hardly know anyone who so passionately devoted himself to studying Nature) made him astonishingly able to think from a sense of the whole and to write out a feeling for life which was so permeated with the finest particles of death, that death seemed to be contained everywhere in it as an odd spice in the strong flavor of life" (*Br*, 510-15).

In Malte's childhood memories one can recognize in the matriarchial family of Graf Šulin distinct characteristics of Turgenev, and especially Goncharov, whose ability "to rest in heaviness . . . and to reflect back to the very beginnings" Rilke so admired.[68] Malte's neighbor from St. Petersburg, the good natured, schizophrenic Nikolaj Kusmič, who feels the "passage of time" and the movement of the earth so keenly and painfully that he attempts to spite these forces by simply lying in bed, who recites poems by Pushkin and Nekrasov, who marvels exceedingly at all "who walk around and endure the movement," is closely akin to Gončarov's idle character, Oblomov. Kusmič's extreme peculiarness, like the entire atmosphere in which Malte's two neighbors from St. Petersburg live, is clearly reminiscent of Dostoevsky's novels and stories.

The fate of Griša Otrepjev, the "false Dimitri," is a strong counterpart for Malte. His need "to no longer be anyone's son" is a prophecy for the closing essay. The Biblical story of the Prodigal Son is also uniquely and poetically transformed. Rilke's prodigal son pleads for "no one to love him," leaving Malte in perplexingly stoic loneliness. Rilke uses his material in much the same way Pushkin uses Russian history in *Boris Godunov*.

S. Brutzer believes that Rilke's comments on the artist figure Alexander Ivanov express theoretically the same ideas about reality and the personal inner world of the sensitive, artistically inclined personality and reality that were then artistically realized in *Malte*.[69] She also points out marked similarities in the dark atmosphere of the Parisian hospitals and their surroundings, and the letters of the painter Feodor Vasiljev, who had died as a young man in a Crimean spa in 1872.[70]

Rilke elaborated on many aspects of his work in the correspondence with Witold Hulewicz, his Polish translator. He wrote that Malte demands life, ". . . which is continually withdrawing into the invisible, intelligible to himself through evocations and images; these he finds now in his own childhood memories, now in his Paris surroundings, now in the reminiscences of his wide reading. And all that, *wherever* it may be experienced, has the same valency for him, the same duration and presentness."[71] The original Russian elements of the phenomena and images in *Malte* are mainly literary reminiscences from Rilke's childhood, like Graf Šulin, Griša Otrepjev, and the neighbors from St. Petersburg. In other episodes that picture the human relationships and inner stance of the narrator, one can readily identify the objective and yet warmly subjective narrative style of Turgenev, Tolstoy, Gončarov, and Garshin, and the traditional style of the Russian epic.

Professor Vladimir Admoni sees in Rilke's prose and poetry "the seemingly incomprehensible movement of the soul" comprehended and "a profound analysis of the problem of inner life joined with magical lyricism," and in this aspect of his writings, Rilke's strongest and most intimate ties to Russian literature.[72]

One could certainly find many more examples of how Rilke's romantic, pantheistic, enthusiastic mythical image of Russia, though still uniquely Rilkean, relates to the *mythos* present in certain streams of contemporary Russian literature. The sources of this mythical imagery are his love for Lou, travel impressions, Russian friendships and literature, the vastness of the Volga, the churches and cloisters, and other objective realities to which he gave poetic potency. To a certain extent, his view of Russian art and Russian literature was also mythical.

Rilke wrote Lou triumphantly on February 11, 1922, the day he finished the last Duino elegy: "Think! I have been allowed to survive up to this. Through everything. Miracle. Grace.—All in a few days. It was a hurricane."[73] Rilke was referring to Sonnet XX of Part I:

Dir, aber, Herr, o was weih ich dir, sag,
der das Ohr den Geschöpfen gelehrt?—
Mein Erinnern an einen Frühlingstag,
seinen Abend, in Rußland—, ein Pferd . . .

Herüber vom Dorf kam der Schimmel allein,
an der vorderen Fessel den Pflock,
um die Nacht auf den Wiesen allein zu sein;
wie schlug seiner Mähne Gelock

an den Hals im Takte des Übermuts,
bei dem grob gehemmten Galopp.
Wie sprangen die Quellen des Rossebluts!

Der fühlte die Weiten, und ob!
Der sang und der hörte—, dein Sagenkreis
War in ihm geschlossen.
                    Sein Bild: ich weih's. [*SW*, I: 743–44]

But what shall I dedicate to you, master, say,
who taught the creature their ear?—
My memory of a day in Spring,
its evening, in Russia—, a horse . . .
Across from the village came the white horse alone,
on one fore fetlock the hobble,
to be alone for the night on the meadows;
how his shock of mane beat
on his neck in time with his high-mettled spirit,
in that rudely obstructed gallop.
How the springs of his steed's blood leapt!
That horse felt the distances, and how
he sang and heard!—your cycle of myths
was closed in him.
                    His image: I dedicate.[74]

The following year he wrote to Clara Rilke, "Isn't it beautiful that the white horse [the "Ex-Voto," Part I, sonnet 20, p. 26] which I 'experienced' with Lou on a meadow in Russia, in 1899 or 1900, leapt through my heart again?! How nothing is ever lost!" (*Br*, 835).

From the time of his youth in Bohemia and Prague, and as a result of his extensive travel, Rilke understood well the insatiable suffering of an ailing national consciousness, and the vulnerable, heated passion to which national feeling can degenerate. But in Russia he saw "the first step of a developing Russian art, which is uninhibited by growing feelings of nationalism, and which will perhaps be able to express supreme and universal humanity when it has forgotten everything foreign and conspicuous, everything not Russian" (*SW*, V: 504–5). This agrees with similar opinions expressed by V. Solovjév, A. Blok, and Dostoevsky (the speech on Pushkin).

These ideas and feelings of Rilke's have never been refuted. Even the stormy events that have changed the historical existence and consciousness of millions of Russian people require no significant revision of the Rilkean perspectives on cultural and aesthetic development. Although his entire mythological picture of Russia was virtually destroyed and lost in history, some aspects do remain intact.

Rilke never relinquished his Russian dream, even at the end. In a letter to Leonid Pasternak in March, 1926, he wrote:

> Yes, we have had to let much change pass over us, your country above all: but, even if *we* are no more to experience it in its resurrection, the deep, the real, the ever surviving Russia has only fallen back into its secret root-layer, as once formerly under the Tartars, who may doubt that it is *there* and, in its darkness, invisible to its own children, slowly, with its sacred slowness, is gathering itself together for a perhaps still distant future? Your own exile, the exile of so many most loyal to it, is nourishing this in a sense subterranean preparation: for as the real Russia has hidden itself away under the earth, in the earth, so all of you have only gone away in order to remain true to its momentary hiddenness. . . ."[75]

If one reads what Rilke wrote between 1900 and 1926 and realizes that nowadays in Moscow and Leningrad young people are discussing Dostoevsky, Solovjëv, Berdjaev, Baxtin, Solzhenitsyn, Sakharov, and others, and are talking about theological and esthetic problems that appeared solved to earlier generations, one must grant the dreamy poet, the "summer tourist in rosy dreams," the creator of myth, Rilke, the stature of prophet.

According to Ivan Rožanskij, Moscow philosopher and Rilke scholar, "unity . . . unified wholeness" was what the young Rilke sought and believed to have found in Russia. He identifies in *Das Stundenbuch* a strange Rilkean "trinity," an inseparable unity that holds together, indissolubly, the concepts: the Russian, the Creator, and the God.

The awareness of this unity became Rilke's means of creating the union or wholeness he desired. The basis for this development was his "Russian experience."[76]

Unity of art and life, of literature and the world of thought, means unity of the irrational, barely conscious, spontaneous feelings that press for self-expression with the conscious will to form or shape the material in the practical manner of a craftsman. Indispensable is the unity of personality or individuality with society, and the unity of solitude or even the divine solitariness of poetic creativity with the deep-rooted attachment to the language and life of the people as well as to national history and religiosity. One of the most significant elements of this multifaceted Rilkean work is his contradictory concept (mythical and real) of Russia. It is his own, as is his search for unity between visible things or art things ("Kunst-Dingen") and their invisible counterparts, between life and death, between "the infinite longings and finite deeds" of permanent art, created by mortal artists.

These longings, desires, and deeds expressed in the eternal Rilkean world are particularly meaningful now, when uncertain crises threaten the fate of nations and act to stifle art and literature. From the *Sonette an Orpheus*:

> Wandelt sich rasch auch die Welt
> wie Wolkengestalten,
> alles Vollendete fällt
> heim zum Uralten. [*SW*, I: 743]

> Even though the world keeps changing
> quickly as cloud shapes,
> all things perfected fall
> home to the age-old.

> Wir sind die Treibenden.
> Aber den Schritt der Zeit,
> nehmt ihn als Kleinigkeit
> im immer Bleibenden. [*SW*, I: 745]

> We are the driving ones.
> O but the stride of time,
> take it as trifle
> in the ever remaining.[77]

Rilke is one of the few well-known poets of the West whose life and work have been so thoroughly shaped by his Russian experience and whose works have found acceptance in the Soviet Union.[78] Discussions and research about the importance of Russia for Rilke can serve to improve the intellectual climate and to promote favorable relations and mutual understanding among peoples.

NOTES

The author wishes to dedicate his essay to the memory of Marina Baranovič. The translation of the original German manuscript was prepared by Jennifer Liebnitz.

1. *Rainer Maria Rilke—Lou Andreas-Salomé, Briefwechsel*, ed. E. Pfeiffer (Zürich: Niehans, 1952), pp. 109–110. In the preparation of this essay the author is indebted to the pioneering works of Asadovskij, Čertkov, Rudnicki, and Frank.
2. Rainer Maria Rilke, *Briefe aus Muzot, 1921–1926* (Leipzig: Insel, 1935), p. 363.

3. Rainer Maria Rilke, *Sämtliche Werke* (Frankfurt am Main: Insel, 1966), VI: 1021; henceforth abbreviated *SW* and inserted in the text.

4. C. Sieber, *René Rilke: Die Jugend R. M. Rilkes* (Leipzig: Insel, 1932), p. 108.

5. Rainer Maria Rilke, *Briefe* (Wiesbaden: Insel, 1950), p. 859; henceforth abbreviated *Br* and inserted in the text.

6. Peter Demetz, *René Rilkes Prager Jahre* (Düsseldorf: Diederichs, 1953).

7. Albert Soergel and Curt Hohoff, *Dichtung und Dichter der Zeit* (Düsseldorf: A. Bagel, 1964), I: 319.

8. Hans Egon Holthusen, *Rainer Maria Rilke in Selbstzeugnissen und Bilddokumenten* (Hamburg: Rowohlt, 1973), p. 34.

9. All of Rilke's letters to his mother are located in the Rilke Archives, and they are quoted here from Sophie Brutzer, *Rilkes russische Reisen* (Königsberg, 1934; reprinted by the Wissenschaftliche Buchgesellschaft, Darmstadt, 1969), pp. 4–5.

10. *Briefwechsel mit Lou*, p. 135.

11. Ellen Key, *Seelen und Werke, Essays* (Berlin: S. Fischer, 1911), p. 159.

12. Lilly Zarnke, "Rilke und Dostojewski," *Theologische Blätter* 11 (1922): 135.

13. Brutzer, p. 12.

14. Leonid Pasternak, "Vstreči s R. M. Rilke," in *Rainer Maria Rilke*, ed. I. Rožanskij (Moscow: Iskusstvo, 1971), pp. 422–23. Henry Glade has described this book in the following way: "Unquestionably a major event of the literary year was the publication of the selected works of Rainer Maria Rilke (Iskusstvo, 50,000 copies). One Russian critic observed that this book is fated to be less read than treasured. Read or not, it is obviously treasured, since it already achieved rare book status by the day of publication, which is very unusual even in Moscow. The editor of the collection, I. Rožanskij, is a former physicist, a Germanist and a respected authority on Rilke. In his introduction Rožanskij says that his criterion for the selection of the material was 'the theme of art in the works of Rilke.' The book includes, among other items: 'Worpswede' (Rilke's views on painting and painters such as Vogeler and Runge); an essay on Auguste Rodin; *Brief an einen jungen Dichter;* about fifty letters; selections from his poetry including *Das Stundenbuch, Neue Gedichte, Duineser Elegien,* and *Die Sonette an Orpheus;* his article on basic tendencies in contemporary Russian art; his poems in Russian; selections from *Geschichten vom lieben Gott;* and L. O. Pasternak's article 'Encounters with R. M. Rilke.' Rožanskij's forty-page introduction gives an excellent over-view of Rilke's life and works; and the final article by V. Mikuševič, one of the two poetry translators, on language, style, and thematics in Rilke's verse shows expert knowledge of the subject.

"A good one-fourth of the material is concerned with Rilke in Russia. There is a fascinating account ('Rilke's Russian Encounters') in which two young Leningrad scholars, K. Asadovskij and L. Čertkov, summarize previous findings and draw on additional archival sources. Such an emphasis is, of course, justified in view of the tremendous impact Russia had on Rilke's spiritual and artistic development. None of his contemporaries was more closely linked to Russia than Rilke. Twenty years after his first trip to Russia the author summarized his feelings in a letter: 'Russia made me what I am, from there my inner life proceeded, the home of my instincts, all my deepest origins are there.'

"V. Levik's lengthy review of the Rilke book [*Inostrannaia literatura (Foreign Literature)*, No. 11] is, to my mind, fair and thorough. Although he praises individual elements of the collection (the translations, for example) he decides that it has several glaring faults. First the reviewer does not agree with the editor's selection of genre. The Russian reader who cannot read German is not well acquainted with Rilke's poetry; therefore more poetry should have been included. Since there is such heavy emphasis on art, the editor might have offered some pointers on such obscure figures as Vogeler and Runge. Rožanskij in his introduction points up the basic trends in Rilke's life and works, but Levik is critical of the book's failure to chart the development of Rilke's views on fine arts and discuss these in the general frame of Rilke's esthetics. Finally, Levik laments that there are no reproductions of the works about which Rilke wrote—strange indeed in a book of this sort published by Iskusstvo (Art)." Henry Glade, " 'Germanistics' in the Soviet Union during 1971," *Russian Literature Triquarterly* (1972), p. 459.

15. Rilke had written him a postcard even earlier, announcing his and Lou's arrival. Lou must have helped him write it, although it contains a few errors. But the letter from Petersburg was written by Rilke alone, as was the second long letter to Drožžin from Worpswede on December 29. *Central-nyj gosudarstvennyj arxiv literatury* (henceforth *ZGALI*), Moscow. Fond 176, EX 1035–6, and Fond 176, EX 1035/1.

16. Brutzer, p. 15.

17. Brutzer, p. 15.

18. *Briefwechsel mit Lou*, p. 90.

19. Holthusen, p. 74.

20. *Briefwechsel mit Lou*, p. 53.

21. Ibid., p. 166.

22. Ibid., p. 393.

23. Ibid., pp. 405–6.

24. M. Betz, *Rilke vivant* (Paris: Emile-Paul, 1936), p. 152; K. Asadovskij, "L. Čertkov. Russkije vstreči Rilke," in I. Rožanskij, p. 110.

25. Ibid., p. 229, *SW*, VI: 1238; K. W. Jonas, "Rilke und Kl. Sacharoff," *Monatshefte* 68 (1966): 6.

26. Betz, p. 229.

27. Ibid., p. 148.

28. *Briefe aus Muzot*, p. 364. (Translator's note: in this case and in a number of others the Greene-Norton translation of Rilke's letters was consulted.)

29. Boris Pasternak, "Ljudi i položenija," *Novyj mir* I (1967).

30. On the basis of the manuscript, written by M. Čvetaeva, now in Moscow.

31. Betz, p. 148.

32. J. R. von Salis, *Rainer Maria Rilkes Schweizer Jahre* (Frauenfeld: Huber, 1952), p. 252; Lou Andreas-Salomé, *R. M. Rilke* (Leipzig: Insel, 1928), p. 112.

33. Asadovskij, p. 380.

34. Brutzer, p. 46.

35. Letter to V. G. Čertkov. *ZGALI*, Fond 552, EX 2408; Asadovskij, p. 365.
36. *ZGALI*, Fond 459, WX 3598, op. 1/II.
37. Brutzer, p. 68; Asadovskij, pp. 365–66.
38. *Literarische Beilage zu Bohemia*, January 5, 1902. The author became a successful Soviet writer of historical novels in the 1930s and 1940s, and he was the recipient of a Stalin Prize.
39. *Briefwechsel mit Lou*, p. 166.
40. Ibid., p. 36.
41. Ibid., p. 405.
42. Brutzer, p. 51.
43. Rainer Maria Rilke, *Briefe und Tagebücher* (Leipzig: Insel, 1931), pp. 383–85; Brutzer, p. 65.
44. *Briefwechsel mit Lou*, p. 228.
45. Brutzer, p. 52.
46. *ZGALI*, Fond 176, EX 1035.
47. *ZGALI*, Fond 459, EX 3598.
48. *Die Zeit* (Vienna), vol. 29, no. 368, October 19, 1901; *SW*, V: 493–504; *Die Zeit*, vol. 33, no. 424, November 15, 1902; *SW*, V: 613–22, and VI: 495.
49. Brutzer, p. 29; Asadovskij, pp. 367 and 373–76.
50. Brutzer, p. 26.
51. Rilke's letter to P. Èttinger. Brutzer, p. 35.
52. Ibid., p. 38.
53. The opposite view is expressed in *Briefwechsel mit Lou*, pp. 84–90.
54. See the convincing report of the Kiev literary historian Dmytro Nalyvajko, "Ukrajinski motywy w poesiji Rilke," *Showten* (1971), p. 135ff.
55. *Briefe aus Muzot*, pp. 184–85.
56. Ibid., pp. 185–86.
57. *Briefe und Tagebücher*, pp. 15–16.
58. *Briefwechsel mit Lou*, pp. 84–85.
59. Ibid., pp. 104–5.
60. *Briefe aus Muzot*, p. 370.
61. Brutzer, p. 5; "Rilke i Rossija," in *Zycie i mysl* (1959), nos. 11–12, p. 38.
62. K. A. J. Batterby, "Russia or France," *Rilke and France* (Oxford, 1966), p. 30.
63. Trans. J. B. Leishman.
64. A. Rammelmeyer, "Russische Literatur in Deutschland," in *Deutsche Philologie im Aufriß* (Berlin: Erich Schmidt), p. 385.
65. *Briefwechsel mit Lou*, p. 136.
66. *Briefe*, pp. 256, 258, 261, and 264.
67. Brutzer, pp. 51–52.
68. Brutzer, pp. 53–54.
69. Ibid., pp. 34–35.
70. Ibid., p. 40.
71. *Briefe aus Muzot*, p. 319.
72. Cf. I. Rožanskij.
73. *Briefwechsel mit Lou*, pp. 464–65.

74. Trans. M. D. Herter Norton.
75. *Briefe aus Muzot*, pp. 363–64.
76. I. Rožanskij, p. 28.
77. Translation of the sonnets by M. D. Herter Norton.
78. The reception of Rilke in Russia will constitute a large and problematic chapter yet to be written. Not even the published works and the letters from Marina Čvetaeva and Boris Pasternak have yet been considered thoroughly. There is still considerable material to be examined in the archives of both of these famous poets; and the field of Russian Rilkeana, including countless critical works, adaptations, and translations, has hardly been touched. Contributions to the study of Rilke in Russia have been increasing steadily since the early 1960s and include works by such noted writers as Konstantin Bogatyrev, Sergej Petrov, Vladimir Mikuševič, and Éugenij Vitkovskij in Russia; Grigorij Kočur and Mikola Lukaš in the Ukraine; Vaxtang Kotetišvili in Georgia; and Maris Čaklais in Latvia.

In this essay the method of transliterating names has been the one employed in scholarly journals of Soviet studies, but in the case of certain well-known names (e.g., Dostoevsky, Tolstoy, Gorky, etc.) we have adhered to the generally accepted spelling.

8

Rilke's Poetic Cycle "Die Zaren"

DARIA ROTHE

R. M. Rilke's cycle of poems entitled "Die Zaren" is contained in the second edition of *Das Buch der Bilder*, which appeared in 1906. The cycle consists of six poems, and all but one were first written in Meiningen in the late summer and early fall of 1899. They were later reworked in Paris in 1906. Only poem three has no version other than the one of 1906.

On May 27, 1899, Rilke, whose first Russian journey was coming to an end, writes from St. Petersburg to Frieda v. Bülow, a mutual friend of his and Lou Andreas-Salomé's:

> My Russian journey is now practically over. Next week we will travel to Schmargendorf. . . . I intend to join you in Meiningen during the last days of July—certainly by the first of August. In the meantime, I will prepare myself to provide peace and resonance for those upcoming summer days. There will be much work for us to do together, not the least of which will be such work as was inspired by Russia.[1]

With the first impression of Russia vividly in his mind, Rilke set out to deepen his knowledge by gathering the historical and literary background he needed to make it more than a fleeting experience.[2] Thus, during the six-week stay with Frieda v. Bülow, he and Lou Andreas-Salomé embarked on a feverish period of study concerning anything Russian. This was done with such intensity that the hostess felt rather neglected. After the departure of her guests, she writes in a letter dated September 20, 1899:

> I have seen very little of Lou and Rainer during this six week stay together. After their long Russian journey which they [including Lou's husband]

made this spring, they have given themselves body and soul to the study of things Russian. All day long, with phenomenal industry, they studied the language, literature, art, world history and cultural history of Russia as if they had to prepare themselves for a horrendous examination.[3]

The first fruits of Rilke's Russian harvest was the "Zaren" cycle, which then consisted of five poems. It was followed by *Das Buch vom mönschischen Leben* in September, and the *Geschichten vom lieben Gott* in November of 1899. By March, 1900, Rilke had translated Chekhov's *Seagull* and continued to prepare himself for the second trip, which began in May and ended in August of that year. The poetic yield of the second journey did not come so quickly. Rilke expresses his disappointment about this in two entries in his diary, one dated September 1, the other September 27. The second one reads: "The Russian journey with its daily losses is an infinitely alarming proof of my immature eyes, which do not know how to be receptive, how to hold on and how to let go. Burdened by tortured images, they go by beauties on to disappointments. . . ."[4] But in the winter of 1900 a second harvest begins. In December he writes the eight poems in Russian. They are followed by "Das Buch der Pilgerschaft" in 1901, as well as articles on Russian art and translations. In Westerwede, Viareggio, Paris, and Rome, Rilke continues to hear the Russian hours. *Das Stundenbuch* is finished in 1903 in Paris, the translation of *Slovo o polķu Igoreve, Das Igorlied*, is completed in 1904 in Rome. By 1906 most of his works that were inspired by his Russian experience were behind him. But when the second edition of *Das Buch der Bilder* was prepared for publication, Rilke returned to "Die Zaren," which had been left untouched since the summer of 1899. In a letter to Clara Rilke, dated February 1, 1906, he writes that he is working on these poems, but wishes that he had more time to devote to them. In the next letter to Clara, dated February 5, 1906, he writes: "The czars. I have been much occupied with them these last few days. There have been some changes made and things have opened up a little; with unparalleled joy I am helping my old things to come to the surface. The czars will be a new treasure in the middle of the book (as I plan to insert them), right after Charles XII. . . ."[5]

The poems were included in the 1906 edition of *Das Buch der Bilder*. Throughout the "Zaren" cycle run threads of Russian literary and historic tradition from pre-recorded times to the reign of Fëdor Ivanovich, the last descendant of the Rurik dynasty. In fact the cycle can be looked upon as a poetic account of the origins and end of the house of Rurik.

Although only poems three through six directly deal with the czars, namely Ivan IV and his son Fëdor, the founding of the dynasty dates back to the Nordic invasions in the ninth century. This coincides with the time frame of the tale of Ilya of Murom, on which the first two poems are based. The dynasty is thus an important cohesive element in the cycle.

Underlying the whole mood of the cycle is Rilke's belief that Russia was to be the land of the future. It was not a concept that originated with Rilke. He took it over from Russian history, which he reportedly studied with great diligence after his return from the first Russian trip in 1899.

At the center of the cycle stands Fëdor Ivanovich, son of Ivan the Terrible. Three of the six poems deal with him. It was during the reign of Fëdor that the belief that Moscow was to be the Third Rome became particularly popular. It is obvious that Rilke was fascinated by the figure of this pale, gentle, other-worldly king, who seemed to be so ill-suited for the throne that he occupied. I will discuss two of the Fëdor poems, numbers four and five, for they illustrate Rilke's belief that Moscow was to be the Third Rome, a belief which he superimposed upon other material of Russian origin, thus creating his own myths. For example: the Ilya of Murom whom we encounter in the first poem and the nightingale we meet in the second poem are quite different from their counterparts in the Russian *bylina* (*byliny* are ancient tales in the oral tradition). The one of Ilya of Murom tells us of a time dating back to the early Middle Ages. One of the main figures of the tale is Vladimir, prince of Kiev, who ruled from 978–1015.

Ilya is a lame peasant boy who is miraculously cured of his infirmity and becomes a great knight, the central figure of the heroic tale that bears his name. One of his deeds is the defeat of "solovej rasbojnik," a notorious outlaw whose ability to make magical sounds makes him invincible to all but Ilya. "Solovej" translated into German is "Nachtigall," the enigmatic creature which appears in the second poem of the cycle.

In the first poem Rilke chooses to treat Ilya's transformation from cripple to knight as an awakening to the call of destiny. The process of awakening becomes a recurring motif in the poem, so that Ilya, the awakening giant, becomes a symbol for the country to whose literary tradition he belongs.

From the initial awakening of the country in the first poem we come to the building of a civilization in poem two. The primeval destructive force, which the cry of the nightingale evokes, is overcome by patient endurance on the part of "die Überstarken, die Alten." They are able to guide others to safety. "Die Alten" is a translation of the Russian "startsi," meaning church elders and founders, that is, the builders of the Kievan Rus.

The third poem deals with a much later period. We find ourselves in sixteenth-century Moscow at the court of Ivan IV, Ivan the Terrible. We witness the old czar's growing isolation and ever-increasing fear, as his mind spirals out of control and ends in a state that no longer differentiates between the self and the outer world.

The remaining three poems concern themselves with the successor of Ivan IV, Fëdor Ivanovich.

Poem four begins with a two line stanza telling us of an occasion on which the empire admires its own many-faceted splendor:

Es ist die Stunde, da das Reich sich eitel
in seines Glanzes vielen Spiegeln sieht.

It is the hour when the vain realm assembles
to gaze upon its mirrored majesty.

The second stanza introduces the emperor in whose honor the festivities take place, and one becomes immediately aware of the great contrast between empire and emperor—a break underscored by the shortness of the first stanza.

Der blasse Zar, des Stammes letztes Glied,
träumt auf dem Thron, davor das Fest geschieht.

The pale Czar, last of all his family,
dreams on his throne before the pageantry.

He is not part of the celebration but a passive figure whose dreaming removes him from his surroundings. It soon becomes apparent how far removed in mood and character the emperor is from his empire:

und leise zittert sein beschämter Scheitel
und seine Hand, die vor den Purpurlehnen
mit einem unbestimmten Sehnen
ins wirre Ungewisse flieht.

and just perceptibly his shamed head trembles,
as do his hands, that flee, as from the spurning
of those impurpled armrests, with vague yearning
into confused uncertainty.

The adjective describing the top of his head is "beschämt." The noun it modifies, "Scheitel," rhymes with "eitel" of the first stanza and again draws our attention to the contrast between emperor and empire. His trembling hand flees the royal armrest "mit einem unbestimmten Sehnen ins wirre Ungewisse." The flight into this vague world, which is symbolically expressed by his hand, is mirrored in the composition of the last three lines of the stanza. With one enjambment after the other, they inevitably glide "ins wirre Ungewisse."

The next stanza focuses on the boyars, the nobles, who pay homage to the czar. The boyars, after all, represent the empire.

> Und um sein Schweigen neigen sich Bojaren
> in blanken Panzern und in Pantherfellen,
> wie viele fremde fürstliche Gefahren,
> die ihn mit stummer Ungeduld umstellen.

> And all around his silentness extending,
> bright-mailed and panther-skinned, from many nations,
> boyars like strange royal perils are low-bending,
> perils encircling him with dumb impatience.

The description of the dress of the nobles of the realm not only emphasizes that they are *like* the foreign dangers that threatened the Russian throne at the time, but also makes one wonder which dangers are the most imminent. Shining armor is usually associated with battle, and the fur of a panther brings to mind a highly dangerous, predatory animal.

Historically, there has been a constant struggle for power between the boyars and the czars. It was particularly violent and bloody during the reign of Ivan IV, Fëdor's father. The association of "Bojaren" and "Gefahren" becomes even closer because the two words rhyme. They are a potential danger waiting to be realized, as the "stumme Ungeduld" of line four points out. That danger is effectively enclosed between the first and the last lines of the stanza. The stanza begins and, quite properly, ends with the ceremony of giving obeisance to the new emperor: "Tief in den Saal schlägt ihre Ehrfurcht Wellen" ("Far through the hall their awe excites vibrations").

In stanza four, the boyars quite naturally think of the predecessor of the new czar:

> Und sie gedenken eines andern Zaren,
> der oft mit Worten, die aus Wahnsinn waren,
> ihnen die Stirnen an die Steine stieß.

And to another Czar their thoughts are tending,
one who, with words insanity was sending,
would often thrust their brows against the stone.

The "andere" is clearly Ivan IV, as "Worten, die aus Wahnsinn waren" of the second line confirms. He controlled the boyars by terror and violence, but as their thoughts about him continue, it becomes evident that in their minds the tyrant was in some ways better suited to occupy the throne than his pale son:

Und denken also weiter: *jener* ließ
nicht so viel Raum, wenn er zu Throne saß,
auf dem verwelkten Samt des Kissens leer.

And when that Czar was seated on the throne
he did not leave, as further they recall,
so much room on the faded silk below.

When he sat on the throne, one did not take notice of the pillow. From the italicized "jener" in line four, Fëdor's shortcomings become all too apparent, and he does not fare well in the comparison with his father. The boyars realize that they had not remembered that the seat of the throne was red in color. Although the old czar was "der Dinge dunkles Maß," as the many deeds of Ivan IV show, he majestically filled the throne, and his robe lay heavy upon it:

Er war der Dinge dunkles Maß,
und die Bojaren wußten lang nicht mehr,
daß rot der Sitz des Sessels sei, so schwer
lag sein Gewand und wurde golden breit.

He was the obscure scale of all,
and the boyars had long since ceased to know
that the throne's seat was red, his robes lay so
ponderously there in outspread goldenness.

The wide, golden royal robe of Ivan IV is compared to the royal robe of the present czar. Like its wearer who dreams on the throne, the royal robe is in a state of slumber. The new czar is seen as a boy for whom the throne is too large:

Und weiter denken sie: das Kaiserkleid
schläft auf den Schultern dieses Knaben ein.
Obgleich im ganzen Saal die Fackeln flacken,
sind bleich die Perlen, die in sieben Reihn,
wie weiße Kinder, knien um seinen Nacken,

und die Rubine an den Ärmelzacken,
die einst Pokale waren, klar von Wein,
sind schwarz wie Schlacken—

And go on thinking: the imperial dress
slumbers upon those shoulders infantine.
Although throughout the hall the torches flare,
pale are the pearls that in seven rows incline,
like pallid children, round his neck, and where
the sleeve-enclasping rubies used to glare
like crystal goblets filled with wine,
they're now as black as cinders there—

The royal robe does not look very imposing on Fëdor, the rubies in the sleeves look dull, the pearls no longer shine. There is no vitality in the worldly splendor of that garment. The czar is "blaß" (line one, stanza two), the pearls are "bleich." Clearly, their pale boy emperor is not meant to wear the robe. The stanza breaks off with a dash, and it is followed by a staccato one-line stanza: "Und ihr Denken schwillt" ("And their thinking swells"). There is not much doubt as to what they are thinking. It is their opportunity to seize power:

Es drängt sich heftig an den blassen Kaiser,
auf dessen Haupt die Krone immer leiser
und dem der Wille immer fremder wird;
er lächelt.

And presses on that pallid monarch tighter,
for whom the crown he carries even lighter,
and willing ever more remote will seem;
he smiles.

They crowd to take a closer look at the obstacle in their way. The potential danger of stanza three is about to become realized—yet the only response of the czar is a smile. The imperial crown on his head commands no authority, the imperial will "wird immer fremder." It becomes obvious that, in the struggle for power, the czar has missed his cue. Encouraged by this, the boyars test him further. Reminiscent of the way a predatory animal sizes up his prey before moving in for the kill, they come closer. They are still bowing, but the "Ehrfurcht" of stanza three is supplanted by "schmeicheln," which becomes more obvious, more desperate:

Lauter prüfen ihn die Preiser,
ihr Neigen nähert sich, sie schmeicheln heiser,—

The appraisers' cautiousness grows slighter,
their bows draw near, their flattery rings unrighter,—

Their flattery is unmasked by losing all subtlety and becoming hoarse. After the dash in line five it becomes a naked display of force. The poem ends with the following line: "und eine Klinge hat im Traum geklirrt" ("and now a sword has rattled in his dream"). There is the jarring sound of a sword being drawn in a dream. But whose dream is it? The line is ambiguous. It only tells us that the sound is being perceived. Its vagueness, however, causes us to associate it with the czar. He is so far removed from the situation that he is unaware of both the potential and the real danger that surrounds him. Just as he does not respond in an expected manner to the crowding of the boyars around his throne (in the beginning of the last stanza), he does not respond to the sound of the sword being drawn any more than if it were a sound in a vague dream.

The first line of poem five assures us that the czar will not die by the sword:

Der blasse Zar wird nicht am Schwerte sterben,
die fremde Sehnsucht macht ihn sakrosankt;
er wird die feierlichen Reiche erben,
an denen seine sanfte Seele krankt.

Made sacrosanct, though, by his strange obsessions,
the pale Czar will not perish by the sword,
but will inherit all those wide possessions
with which his gentle soul is so abroad.

While he is ill-suited to be heir to a realm in which the sword is the ultimate authority, Fëdor, by the same token, has nothing to fear from the sword. Here it becomes important to know something of Russian history of the time. N. Zernov, in *The Russians and Their Church*, writes:

Theodor [or Fëdor], the last representative of the House of Rurik, displayed a complete detachment from all earthly concerns. . . . He grew up into a man of childlike simplicity and candor, of pure heart and mind, whose sole interest was centered in divine worship. His life was the very denial of worldliness and he remained quite unmoved by the passion for earthly possessions which played such a prominent part in the life of this father and forefathers . . . he was one of the "fools in Christ" ["iurodivy"], whom the Russians believe to be under God's special protection. . . . The presence of such a "fool" on the throne of Russia brought comfort and consolation to the nation deeply stricken by the terror of Ivan's reign. The Russians knew that their Tsar was not able to rule over them properly, but they were sure that he could pray and that his prayers, his childlike simplicity and faith, his very helplessness and profound humility were their shield and protection and a source of sanctification for the whole nation.[6]

During Fëdor's reign "the greatest ambition of the Russians was at last fulfilled—the Metropolitan of Moscow was elevated to the status of Patriarch."[7]

Thus, "die feierlichen Reiche" of line three (stanza one) alludes to the realm in which the sword wields no power, the spiritual realm to which Russia saw herself heir. Particularly after the fall of Constantinople in 1453, the belief that Moscow was to be the Third Rome was widespread. It was formulated quite concisely by the monk Philotheus (about 1510–1514) in the following words: "All Christian realms will come to an end and will unite into one single realm of our sovereign, that is, into the Russian realm, according to the prophetic books. Both Romes fell, the third endures, and a fourth there will never be."[8] This defined Moscow as the sole defender of the true Faith, and the late fifteenth-century *Tale of the White Cowl* played a significant role in the development of this belief.

However, the strange yearning that protects Fëdor from violence and makes him "sakrosankt" has an ailing quality about it. His soul is overcome to the point of suffering from the "feierlichen Reiche" of line three.

In the second stanza he stands at a window of the Kremlin and has a vision of a new Moscow:

> Schon jetzt, hintretend an ein Kremlfenster,
> sieht er ein Moskau, weißer, unbegrenzter,
> in seine endlich fertige Nacht gewebt;
>
> Already, from a Kremlin window gazing,
> he sees a Moscow whiter, more amazing,
> wrapt in its night so long a-fashioning;

It makes one think of St. John's vision of the new Jerusalem, particularly as one reads about the night that has been finally fashioned to receive the new city: "And the city had no need of the sun, neither of the moon, to shine in it: for the glory of God did lighten it, and the Lamb *is* the light thereof" (Revelation 21:23). The Moscow Fëdor sees has a freshness of a spring morning about it:

> so wie es ist im ersten Frühlingswirken,
> wenn in den Gassen der Geruch aus Birken
> von lauter Morgenglocken bebt.

> such as it is in wakening Spring's first lurches,
> when in the streets the fragrance of the birches
> with many bells is quivering.

The bells are the voices of its churches, and the Moscow that vibrates with the sound of bells made a profound impact on Rilke. In a letter to Sofia Nikolajewna Schill written by Rilke during his second stay in Moscow in 1900, he mentions those great deep bells.[9] He again speaks of them in an often-quoted letter to Lou Andreas-Salomé written in Rome at Easter of 1904. It begins with the traditional Easter greeting, "Christ is risen," and contrasts Easter at Rome with that of Moscow. He writes: "Alas, but Rome is no Easter city and no place which knows how to lie under the great bells. . . . I experienced Easter one single time. . . ."[10]

The third stanza begins with the great bells:

> Die großen Glocken, die so herrisch lauten,
> sind seine Väter, jene ersten Zaren,
> die sich noch vor den Tagen der Tataren
> aus Sagen, Abenteuern und Gefahren,
> aus Zorn und Demut zögernd auferbauten.

> The mighty bells, that sound so dominating,
> are those primeval Czars, his ancestry,
> who, even before the Tartar cavalry,
> through sagas, perils, rage, humility
> have hesitantly been inculminating.

Each line of the above stanza is in iambic pentameter and ends in a feminine rhyme that echoes the ringing of the bells. The great concentration of the vowels "o, au, a" in disyllabic words in the stanza reinforces the audial sensation of bells ringing at various pitches.

The historic Fëdor was particularly fond of bell ringing, and he was quite skilled at the art. "The inhabitants of Moscow would be often awakened in the early hours of the morning by the deep sound of the great Kremlin bells, and they knew that their Tsar was personally calling his people to prayer," writes Zernov.[11]

Fëdor looks at the great bells as his ancestors, the illustrious members of the house of Rurik, who built the empire. Those who came before the Tartar invasion were the princes of Kiev. They built the Kievan state by force and ambition; but they were also responsible for bringing Christianity to their country, thus the tension of opposing forces in "Zorn and Demut" in the last line of the stanza.

Stanza four reads:

Und er begreift auf einmal, wer sie waren,
und daß sie oft um ihres Dunkels Sinn
in seine eignen Tiefen niedertauchten
und ihn, den Leisesten von den Erlauchten,
in ihren Taten groß und fromm verbrauchten
schon lang vor seinem Anbeginn.

And who they were, he fathoms suddenly,
and that, to find their own dark meaning, they
had often dived into those depths of his,
and him, the mildest of the majesties,
had used in great and pious purposes
long before he himself saw day.

While his ancestors were often not sure about their purpose, as "zögernd"
in the last line of stanza three and "um ihres Dunkels Sinn" in line two
of stanza four indicate, Fëdor sees his purpose clearly: "er begreift auf
einmal." Because of the darkness of their perception, they drew upon the
energies which were meant for him, which came from his depths, "seine
eigenen Tiefen." Thus, he seems to be a victim of the ambitions of his
ancestors. But instead of feeling resentful for having his energies used up
long before he was born, he is overcome with gratitude for their having
been spent so lavishly:

Und eine Dankbarkeit kommt über ihn,
daß sie ihn so verschwenderisch vergeben
an aller Dinge Durst und Drang.

And a great gratitude comes over him
and they were so extravagantly giving
him to all being's thirst and stress.

His ancestors' lavishness as well as the overflowing quality of his gratitude is expressed in the words themselves: "verschwenderisch vergeben."
Suddenly, this pale czar, who seems to be wanting in so many positive
qualities, sees himself quite differently:

Er war die Kraft zu ihrem Überschwang,
der goldne Grund, vor dem ihr breites Leben
geheimnisvoll zu dunkeln schien.

He was the strength for their unboundedness,
the golden ground before which their large living
mysteriously seemed to dim.

He realizes that he has been a vital element in the accomplishments of his ancestors. Stanza five builds to a crescendo, which is reached in the last stanza of the poem:

> In allen ihren Werken schaut er *sich*,
> wie eingelegtes Silber in Zieraten,
> und es giebt keine Tat in ihren Taten,
> die nicht auch *war* in seinen stillen Staaten,
> in denen alles Handelns Rot verblich.

> He sees himself in all they could avail,
> like silver in fine jewelry intertwisted;
> there's not one deed of which their doing consisted
> that has not once in his quiet states existed
> wherein all action's redness has grown pale.[12]

Fëdor sees himself in all the works of his ancestors, but it is obvious that we are only dealing with the great, noble deeds. He sees himself as inlaid silver in the great ornamentations that represent their deeds.

His realm is not one of action, yet it incorporates all the deeds of his ancestors, since they were inspired and made possible by drawing upon the energies of the spiritual realm. The robust quality of action, represented by the color red, fades "in seinen stillen Staaten." The verb "verbleichen" draws our attention to the silver to which Fëdor likens himself and recalls the adjective "blaß," which is used to describe the czar. "Die stillen Staaten" of the last stanza echoes "die feierlichen Reiche" of the first stanza and shows us that the czar, who seems not to belong to this earth at all, has very much been part of his country's history. The spiritual and religious aspects that "die feierlichen Reiche" represents are an integral part of the design of Russian history. During Fëdor's reign a high point was reached in the spiritual realm with the installation of the first patriarch of all Russia. In the document marking this event (1589) there appears a sentence which repeats almost verbatim the prophetic statement of Philotheus (previously quoted). The sentence ends with these words: "thy great kingdom, O pious Tsar, is the third Rome." The document continues: "It surpasses in devotion every other and all Christian kingdoms are now merged in thy realm. . . ."[13] None of the deeds of Fëdor's vigorous predecessors could compare with this accomplishment.

The cycle ends with Fëdor standing in prayer before the great Icon of the Annunciation. The czar addresses the icon with words that are full of impatience and reproach, for the promise of the Anunciation has not been fulfilled. His people and he are still waiting for the Son who is yet to come. Trembling, the czar stands in his imperial robe, which appears to be superimposed upon him, as the glowing overleaf of the icon is superimposed upon the painted image. His face is deep set in the collar of the golden robe, like the face of the Virgin in her golden frame. Finally, the czar and the icon look as if they were mirror images of each other.

It is not coincidental that Rilke ended the cycle with this poem. The time of fulfillment for both the icon and the czar lies in the future, and the whole "Zaren" cycle is based on Rilke's belief that Russia was to be the land of the future. The concept of the Third Rome, which underlies the Fëdor poems, was available in Russian history. But when Rilke finds no support for his belief in Russian history or legend, he turns to legends of his own making. This is a very important aspect in Rilke's stance in respect to Russia or things Russian, not only in this cycle, but also in his other works.

In "Die Zaren" Rilke takes the *bylina* of Ilya of Murom and changes it so that a new myth emerges, in which Ilya becomes the awakening giant, a symbol for his country which is yet to awaken. The "solovej," or nightingale, is transformed into a creature whose song arouses primeval forces of sexuality that bring about destruction. Thus mythopoesis and history combine to form Rilke's "Zaren" as well as Rilke's concept of Russia.

A letter written by Rilke in 1921 to a former teacher at St. Pölten, a Major General Sedlakowitz, reveals the psychological need for that land. The very long and sometimes cumbersome letter reads in part:

> The Russian individual has demonstrated to me in so very many instances that affliction and servitude, even in an extreme form . . . do not necessarily have to bring about the destruction of the soul. There is a degree of submission . . . which is so complete that it deserves to be called perfect. . . . It creates a secret playing-ground for the soul, a fourth dimension . . . in which . . . a new boundless and true freedom begins.[14]

Rilke, who saw his own being threatened by what he called "the block of impervious misery," which was rolled upon him during his early years, needed to believe in the possibility of his salvation. Russia, the land of the future, and the Russian individual who, in spite of his misery, was capable of saving himself from destruction, provided Rilke with that possibility. The Russia Rilke chose to know became the secret playing-ground of his soul, the fourth-dimensional country in which his spiritual freedom began.

NOTES

I would like to thank Professor Ingo Siedler for his critical comments on this essay.

1. Rainer Maria Rilke, *Briefe und Tagebücher aus der Frühzeit, 1899–1902* (Leipzig: Insel, 1931), p. 17.
2. Ibid., p. 22. In a letter to Leonid Pasternak, Rilke writes: ". . . nun muß ich Ihnen zunächst erzählen, dass Rußland mir, wie ich es Ihnen auch vorausgesagt habe, mehr als flüchtiges Ereignis war,—dass ich seit August vorigen Jahres fast ausschließlich damit beschäftigt . bin, russische Geschichte, Kunst, Kultur und nicht zu vergessen: Ihre schöne unvergleichliche Sprache zu studieren. . . ."
3. Hans Egon Holthusen, *Rainer Maria Rilke* (Hamburg: Rowohlt, 1958), p. 39.
4. Rilke, *Briefe und Tagebücher*, p. 342.
5. Rainer Maria Rilke, *Briefe* (Leipzig: Insel, 1930), II: 297.
6. Nicolas Zernov, *The Russians and Their Church* (London, 1964), pp. 67–68.
7. Ibid., p. 69.
8. Serge A. Zenkovsky (ed.), *Medieval Russia's Epics, Chronicles and Tales* (New York, 1963), p. 265.
9. Rilke, *Briefe und Tagebücher*, p. 36.
10. Rilke, *Briefe*, II: 144.
11. Zernov, p. 69.
12. Rainer Maria Rilke, *Selected Works*, trans. J. B. Leishman (London, 1960), II: 125–26.
13. Zernov, p. 71.
14. Rilke, *Briefe* (Leipzig: Insel, 1937), V: 354–55.

9

Rilke's "Das Bett"

ANDRZEJ WARMINSKI

Aside from cursory treatment in general works on *Neue Gedichte*, "Das Bett" has received little attention.[1] Yet J. B. Leishman, in his introduction to *New Poems*, singles out the poem to attack it:

> There is only one poem in *New Poems* which I find almost totally incomprehensible, and that is *The Bed*, a poem in which there is an unhappy combination, and even confusion, of allegory, symbolism, and personification, and where Rilke seems to be trying (perhaps not hard enough) to say something about the act of love. It is the only one of *New Poems* where what is said, or shown, seems to have no independently significant meaning, and to "stand *for*" something else, some idea, which, if one has the patience, one is being invited to worry out. It is the only poem which definitely requires some sort of key to unlock it, which there would be any sense in trying to interpret equationally (A=X, B=Y, etc.), and which, if not profitably, at least not wholly nonsensically, might be endlessly "explicated" and argued about in theses or in letters to the *Times Literary Supplement*. It is not only perhaps the most un-Rilkean poem that Rilke ever wrote; it is also the only really bad poem in *New Poems*, and I mention it in order to indicate what all the other poems in this collection are essentially *not*.[2]

Although Leishman's recognition of the poem's difficulty, even obscurity, is valuable, his reasoning can be questioned. "Das Bett" is difficult precisely because it is one of the most Rilkean poems that Rilke ever wrote, and, as such, it refuses any attempt to unlock it by means of "equational" interpretation. Even a mechanical listing of some of the poem's nouns betrays its typically Rilkean character: in addition to the title, "Theater," "Chor," "Lied," "Stunde," "Hintergrund," "Geliebte," and "Tier" are all elements of recurring, if not obsessive, configurations of

Rilke's *oeuvre*. But this recognizable typicality also facilitates a particular, two-sided kind of reductive interpretation. It is no answer to treat these typically Rilkean words (equationally) as code-words with equivalences in "real life" or "experience" (the poet's or our own), or to use the "word field" method and thereby bury the specificity of *these* words in the context of *this* poem under the weight of numerous examples of these words in *other* contexts, because these latter contexts, whether they be called "life" or "poem," are themselves texts with a specificity that in each case has to be interpreted before it can be advanced as "evidence" to clear up the difficulties of another text. But since any interpretation necessarily entails speaking about *one* language in *another* language it is inevitably reductive. The real problem is not whether an interpretation is or is not reductive but whether it is self-conscious enough to resist self-satisfaction and to allow the text to put in question the assumptions that lie at the base of any act of reading and interpretation. The following reading questions the poem less in the expectation of finding answers than in the hope of discovering more questions.

> Laß sie meinen, daß sich in privater
> Wehmut löst, was einer dort bestritt.
> Nirgend sonst als da ist ein Theater;
> reiß den hohen Vorhang fort—: da tritt
>
> vor den Chor der Nächte, der begann
> ein unendlich breites Lied zu sagen,
> jene Stunde auf, bei der sie lagen,
> und zerreißt ihr Kleid und klagt sich an,
>
> um der andern, um der Stunde willen,
> die sich wehrt und wälzt im Hintergrunde;
> denn sie konnte sie mit sich nicht stillen.
> Aber da sie zu der fremden Stunde
>
> sich gebeugt; da war auf ihr,
> was sie am Geliebten einst gefunden,
> nur so drohend und so groß verbunden
> und entzogen wie in einem Tier. [I: 626][3]

"Das Bett" is an unveiling: a curtain is ripped aside to reveal action and actors. But what is unveiled, where is this theater? What? "was." Where? "dort." The clause "was einer dort bestritt" ("What one fought there") contains only one word ("bestritt") that points to some decipherable—that is, paraphrasable—sense. Although indicating specific directions, the others ("was," "einer," "dort") point as if in a vacuum—where is "there" when "here" is unknown —an area where pronouns have no antecedents. Even "bestritt" depends upon the other elements of the clause for its meaning, for, in itself, "bestreiten" has a wide range: it can mean "to deny," "to fight against," "to pay for." The unveiled drama will have to unveil "was," "einer," and "dort." It seems to do so in that the progress of the scene leads to another revelation and another relative clause: "was sie am Geliebten einst gefunden" ("what she had once found on the beloved"). Here interpretation appears to be on surer footing: a subject pronoun which presumably has an antecedent in the preceding drama, an identified "dort" ("am Geliebten"), and a form of "finden," a verb that does not have the wide horizon of meaning of "bestreiten." But in order to determine which "hour" (if either one) is the antecedent of "sie," it is necessary to make arbitrary choices based on an understanding of the drama. In addition, a new disruptive element appears in the second "was" clause. The arena of ambiguity has shifted from indefinite subject ("einer") and mysterious *place* ("dort") of action to indeterminate *time* ("einst") of action. In the transaction between "was einer dort bestritt" and "was sie am Geliebten einst gefunden," the definiteness of "sie" and "am Geliebten" has been obtained at the expense of the temporal definiteness of "bestritt," which has been replaced by the vaguer "gefunden"— past participle with an implied but absent auxiliary verb. But since the "was" retains its position in the second clause, little has been gained. The poem can be seen as a drama unveiling a twofold "was": it is a box within a box. "Was" is both the question and the response.

This movement toward simultaneous revelation—in terms of spatial definition—and concealment—in terms of temporal definition—is characteristic of the poem, and it takes place on all levels. Coupled with the "was" clauses at the beginning and the end of the poem is an analogously duplicitous structure involving another "invisible" word[4]—"da," before and after a colon—and which is schematized as a chiasmic reversal in the accompanying diagram.

da *ist* ein Theater——————— : ———————da *tritt* . . . *auf*
da sie zu der fremden——————— : ———————da *war* auf ihr
Stunde *sich gebeugt*

The parallel terms are the paired occurrences of "da" organized around colons, and the crossed terms are the verbs: that is, linking verbs ("ist," "war") designating situation (where?) and constitution (what?) in *space* versus verbs ("tritt . . . auf," "sich gebeugt") designating action in *time* (when?). In other words, the parallel occurrences of "was" and

153

"da" create a neatly symmetrical frame for the drama between the colons; but, schematized as a chiasmic reversal, this arrangement at the same time reveals a tension between time and place at the center of the poem. While holding the poem together, "da" also threatens to tear it apart, for the word carries both a spatial ("there," "in that place") and a temporal ("then," "just then") meaning. Although the first two occurrences of "da" would suggest a relatively clear distinction between "there" and "then," the last two uses of "da" are uncompromisingly ambiguous, and the phrase "zu der fremden Stunde" contributes to this ambiguity. In terms of the drama staged by the poem, one personified hour is bending down *to* another strange hour, but in most other contexts the phrase "zu der fremden Stunde" would mean "*at* this strange hour." Like this phrase, the final "da" of the poem, while seeming to signify a stable "there," "in that place," also means "just then," "at that moment."

These ambiguities involving temporal definition would require a discussion of verb tenses in the poem, but the usefulness of such an undertaking is severely limited because it is handicapped by the same concealments and ambiguities. In the first stanza, for example, a clear temporal difference is posited between the present tense verb "löst" ("dissolves") and the past tense verb "bestritt" ("fought"), but the temporal relation *between* these two actions is far from clear, for it is impossible to tell whether (and which) one of the actions follows the other or whether they are simultaneous. This impossibility is due to the fact that the relations among the three "places" named in the first stanza —"in privater Wehmut," "dort," "da"—cannot be determined with certainty: are they different places or do they coincide? The second and third stanzas are characterized by the same interplay between the present and the past tense—the interweaving of actions performed by one subject in the present with those performed by another subject in the past tense— and the same impossibility of determining precise temporal definition. The problem is caused in part by the nature of the actors in the drama: "hours," personified units of time definable only as hours *during which something occurred.* One is an hour from the past ("bei der sie lagen") taking action *now* ("tritt . . . auf")—that is, in some way making the past present—and the other is an hour which protect*s* itself and writhe*s* in the background. These contrasted hours and their actions are the only "fixed" points in the poem and are therefore in need of unveiling and interpretation. Although the moment of revelation and resolution does take place in the last stanza—something that was once "found" ("gefunden") on the lover is unveiled "on her" ("auf ihr")—this moment also contains all the unknowns and ambiguities running through the first three stanzas. It is not only that the "was" still needs to be identified on the basis of the preceding drama, but also that the problematic distinction between present and past tense is given up altogether at the moment of revelation. Turned into participles, verbs abdicate their specific roles as indicators of time in order to assume the temporal innocence of adjectives: "drohend" ("threatening"), "verbunden" ("bound up"), "entzogen" ("withdrawn"). The sequence can be understood as a moment of simultaneous presence and withdrawal, but, in terms of semantic progression, it is best understood as successive moments of approach ("drohend"), arrival ("verbunden"), and departure ("entzogen"). Either reading is possible, for the invisible word "und" can express both simultaneity and succession. On account of these strategically invisible and ambiguous words ("was," "da," "und") the precise relation—complicity or tension—between spatial definition and temporal indefiniteness, presence and absence, in the poem cannot be determined before an interpretation of the poem's many-sided "was": what is the theater? What is the moment dramatized? What is the moment of revelation? And, ultimately, what is "what"? But while attempting to answer these questions and identify these "what's," the interpretation cannot leave sight of the fact that it is the possibility of precisely this activity—knowing as *knowing something: what*—that the poem problematizes and puts in question.

The hour—"jene Stunde . . . bei der sie lagen"—is the hour of sexual encounter. This hour steps out from the continuity of past and future time and tears her clothing and accuses herself because she could not console the other hour "with herself." The other hour is protecting herself and writhing in the background. Perhaps she is in the background, in infinity, because her time has not yet arrived, but such a distinction is useless here, for both hours are "present," singled out, on a stage that contains all hours. If "jene Stunde" is the hour of sexual encounter, then the other hour is the hour of labor-pains and childbirth: not only the labor-pains and childbirth of the woman who conceived during the hour "bei der sie lagen," but the birth of the hour itself. This hour, "die sich wehrt und wälzt," is the child of the other hour: that is, the hour of sexual union conceives the hour of childbirth. When the first hour "takes place"—that is, when she steps out from infinity—she makes the second hour inevitable. The hour of childbirth is protecting herself against the inevitability of time, the necessity of becoming herself (the hour of childbirth), the necessity of being born. The hour of sexual union could not *still* the other hour in three ways: the verb "stillen" can mean "to still," "to calm or allay pain," or "to nurse a child." To begin with the last meaning, although the hour of lovemaking is the "mother" of the hour of childbirth, she cannot nurse her: she is separated from her by a temporal gap. She also cannot allay the pain of the other hour, just as the memory of the hour of love cannot ease the pain of the hour of childbirth. Last, she cannot "still" the other hour, she cannot stop her from occurring by rendering her motionless, because it is precisely she that has made her inevitable. In short, the drama of the second and third stanzas is that of one moment giving birth to another. But the moment giving birth is separated from the moment born by the temporal gap between them: although the hour of love is present on the stage, she must witness the birth of her child at a distance. This is a motherless birth, for the real mother is time. Time, the temporal difference between the hours, is simultaneously that which makes the two moments possible and that which makes it impossible for them to be anything *but* moments. The poem establishes a distance between the hour of love and the hour of childbirth, but in spatializing the relation between them by placing both on the stage "at the same time," it introduces the possibility of a reconciliation.

On a first reading of the poem, the evidence for this moment of childbirth may appear slim. There is, of course, the verb "stillen" which can mean "to nurse or suckle," and the verb "sich wälzen" which can mean "to writhe" or "to be convulsed," but both of these verbs can have other meanings. Yet an ear familiar with Rilke's language cannot help but recognize the hour of childbirth, for it is suggested as early as the opening lines of the poem. If "sie" and "einer" are understood as an opposition of "her" and "him," then the lines can be paraphrased as follows: let *her* think that what he bore there, during the moment of lovemaking, dissolves ("löst") itself in private sorrow ("Wehmut"). Although the meaning of "Wehmut" may appear unproblematic, it is a compound word: are there "Wehen" ("labor-pains") in "Wehmut"? Rilkean language is definitely aware of this compound word's suggestive power: for example, Malte uses it in a short description of pregnant women—"And what a sorrowful beauty ["wehmütige Schönheit"] it gave to women when they were pregnant . . ." (VI: 721)—where clearly a "Wehen-mütige" as well as a "wehmütige Schönheit" is meant. "Weh" as a suggestion of "Wehen" may also be combined with other words; the opening word of Rilke's attempt at a poem about childbirth is "Wehtag." It is worthwhile to quote this fragment—"Schwangere" (1909)—because it is also a useful example of the way a Rilkean childbirth *sounds*:

> Wehtag, da sie heulend in dem Hause
> heiß sich an die Säulen drängt
> aufgerissen und die Augenpause
> maskenfaltig und verhängt
> von dem Haar an dem sie raufend reißt. [II: 371]

> Day of woe, when howling in the house / she presses herself against the bedposts / ripped open and the forehead / mask-wrinkled and covered / by the hair on which she pulls and tears.

Forms of the verb "reißen"—"aufgerissen" and "reißt"—appear twice in these five lines, and "heiß" in line two provides a similar kind of sound. No doubt "reißen" is used because it evokes the violence of labor (in the Rilkean universe) while at the same time suggesting (in its present tense form) the sound of the verb that means "to be in labor": "kreißen." It is no accident, then, that "Das Bett" uses the same kind of violence—"*reiß den hohen Vorhang fort . . . und zerreißt ihr Kleid und klagt sich an*" —to evoke a moment of childbirth. To return to the opening lines of "Das Bett," the interpretation of "in privater Wehmut" as a scene of childbirth suggests an additional meaning for the verb "löst" in line two: "lösen" can mean "to loosen, free, or dissolve," but it can also mean "to untie, unbind, or detach." A new paraphrase could read: let her think that what he fought, denied, during the lovemaking dissolves itself, detaches itself like the child from the mother, in the private sorrow of labor-pains.

At this point it may be in order to introduce one of Rilke's most complete and explicit statements—from his *Briefe an eine junge Frau* (January 19, 1920)—about the nature of the "Liebesaugenblick," since this statement is directly relevant to the problems of "Das Bett." In the course of replying to the bitter question of an abandoned young wife who asks "whether all the labor of loving and all the pain of unrequited love was merely for the purpose of giving life to a child" Rilke writes:[5] "It is a terrifying thought that the moment of love ["der Liebesaugenblick"] which we regard as something so completely and deeply personal and our own ["als einen uns so völlig und tief eigenen und eigentümlichen empfinden"] could yet be so entirely determined on the one hand by the future (the future child) and on the other by the past. . . ."[6] The moment we consider special and our own is really determined by past and future. Clearly, these are the two views of the situation articulated in the first stanza of "Das Bett": she (or perhaps "they," people in general) thinks that the "Liebesaugenblick" is dissolved in her private sorrow, but it is precisely *here*—in the moment of sexual union, in the moment of childbirth—that a theater exists. It is a theater of time where past, present, and future take on roles: each determined by the others, each containing the others. This determining and determined character of the "Liebesaugenblick" is what makes it almost impossible to define the temporal relation of one moment to another in the first two lines of the poem. Since these lines are still about *people* and not yet about *hours*, they contain both "Liebesaugenblick" and labor-pains. It is only in the theater of hours that each moment's enslavement by time is revealed, where it is shown that *no* moment belongs to us but that *all* moments belong to time. This temporal quandary of the poem is exacerbated and resolved by the "presence"—does this word still have any meaning in reference to "Das Bett"?—of a *third* moment which can be introduced by continuing the quotation of the letter to the young wife:

> but still *then*: there would still remain in the experience its indescribable depth as an escape into the personal, our own ["als Ausflucht ins Eigene"]. . . . This would agree with the experience, how much every one of our deepest raptures makes itself independent of duration and passage ["von Dauer und Verlauf sich unabhängig macht"], indeed, they stand vertically upon the courses of life, just as death, too, stands vertically upon them; they have more in common with death than with all the goals and strivings of our vitality. Only from the side of death (when death is not accepted as an extinction, but imagined as an altogether surpassing intensity), only from the side of death, I believe, is it possible to do justice to love.

The indescribable depth of our moments of rapture creates a way for an "Ausflucht ins Eigene" and makes these moments our own. They stand vertically on the horizontal directions of life and somehow are independent of "Dauer und Verlauf" since they have more in common with death than with any goals of our vitality: "nur vom Tode her . . . läßt sich der Liebe gerecht werden." Present in "Das Bett" along with the hour of love and the hour of childbirth is a third one: "Sterbestunde."

It is virtually a banality to say that in Rilke's work the moment of death is bound up with the moment of childbirth. Sexual union, childbirth, and death form a unit, and it is almost impossible for Rilke to mention one moment without naming at least one of the others. A good example is the previously mentioned passage in *Malte* about pregnant women: "And what a sorrowful beauty it gave to women when they were pregnant and stood there, and in their big bellies, upon which their slender hands involuntarily rested, were *two* fruits: a child and a death. Did not the tight, almost nourishing smile on their completely blank faces come from their sometimes thinking that both were growing?" (VI: 721). The death growing inside the pregnant woman may be her own death or it may be her child: that is, in giving birth to a child, the woman gives birth to a death since (sooner or later) the child will die. This theme of giving birth to a death is a commonplace in Rilke's work —it is evident as early as *Das Buch von der Armut und vom Tode* (1903) —and there is no need to multiply examples in order to demonstrate the likelihood of "Sterbestunde" in "Das Bett."[7] Supporting evidence for the constellation death/theater may be found in the poem "Todes-Erfahrung" (*Neue Gedichte*), in which death is a dramatic character "den ein Maskenmund tragischer Klage wunderlich entstellt" ("whom a mask-mouth of tragical lament strangely disfigures") (I: 518), and in a passage where a full comparison between "Bett" (and particularly "Sterbe-bett") and "Bühne" ("stage") is made by Malte.[8] If the hour that "protects herself and writhes in the background" is the hour of death as well as the hour of childbirth, then her convulsed resistance becomes even more understandable: she does not want to be born because her birth also means her death, just as the woman's giving birth to a child means death in Rilkean language.[9] Such an understanding of the second hour as "Sterbestunde" also completes the significance of the hour "during which they were lying" and her actions: she laments not only the inevitable moment of childbirth but also the death for which she is responsible. On the stage, such violent complaints (like tearing her clothing) would be very appropriate as expressions of grief and remorse on account of a death. But all these distinctions (as tenuous as they are) among moments, hours, and times break down completely in the final stanza as one hour bends down to another hour (at this strange hour) and obliterates all lines of definition. This is the timeless moment—independent of "duration and passage," as the letter to the young wife formulates it—the moment of synchrony and synchronization when the minute-hand makes its "final" round and inevitably coincides with the hour-hand at midnight —"die fremde Stunde"—no matter how that hour-hand may resist this configuration. It is indeed a strange hour. What does it mean?

Once again it is necessary to withdraw from "Das Bett" in order to approach it and to read the riddle contained in the "was" of the last stanza. The fascination with looking and *the* look is probably the greatest commonplace of Rilke's work: "schauen, sehen, der Blick," and "das Gesicht" play fundamental roles in both poetry and prose. One of the strains of this fascination is a concern with the different "looks" of animals and men. From "Der Panther" to "Eine Begegnung" to *Malte* there is a veritable obsession with the "Blick" and "Gesicht" of animals, and whenever an animal appears in Rilke's work, its look is sure to be an important part of the discussion. The most extensive unfolding of this problem is the eighth Duino elegy (1922), in which the look of animals and men is contrasted: while animals see the open ("das Offene"), we see death. We "turn around" the eyes of children when they are still young so that they too no longer see the open—"was draußen *ist*" (I: 714)—but only death. Yet under certain conditions even men can approach this look—"free of death"—of animals, and, paradoxically, the moment near death is one of these conditions: "Denn nah am Tod sieht man den Tod nicht mehr / und starrt *hinaus*, vielleicht mit großem Tierblick" ("For close to death one no longer sees death / and stares *out*, perhaps with the vast look of an animal") (I: 714). Lovers also approach this kind of look: "Liebende, wäre nicht der andre, der / die Sicht verstellt, sind nah daran und staunen" ("Lovers, if it were not for the other who / displaces the view, are near to it and wonder?") (I: 714). Rilke's explanation of "the open" in general, and its meaning for lovers in particular, can help towards an interpretation not only of the eighth elegy but of the last stanza of "Das Bett" as well:

> You must understand the concept of the "Open," which I have tried to propose in the elegy, in *such* a way that the animal's degree of consciousness sets it into the world without the animal's placing the world over against itself at every moment (as we do); the animal is *in* the world; we stand *before it* by virtue of that peculiar turn and intensification which our consciousness has taken . . . By the "Open," therefore, I do not mean sky, air, and space; *they*, too, are "object" ["Gegenstand"] and thus "opaque" and closed to the man who observes and judges. The animal, the flower, presumably *is* all that, without accounting to itself, and therefore has before itself and above itself that indescribably open freedom which perhaps has·its (extremely fleeting) equivalents among us only in those first moments of love when one human being sees his own vastness in another, his beloved [nur in den ersten Liebesaugenblicken, wo ein Mensch im anderen, im Geliebten, seine eigene Weite sieht], and in man's elevation toward God.[10]

All of this letter's and the elegy's concerns—"der Tierblick," "das Offene," "der Tod," and "der Geliebte"—are found in the last stanza of "Das Bett." When one hour bends down and coincides with the other hour, the poem returns to the categories of its first two lines. It is difficult to determine *which* hour bends down, for the action of bending down unites them and makes them indistinguishable, and the only way these two hours can be fused together is in a human being: that is, in the woman who *experienced* the hour of lovemaking, the hour of childbirth, and, now, the hour of death. But because of the essentially equivalent nature of these experiences there is no use in saying that the moment of sexual union occurred *then* and the moment of childbirth occurs *now*. For all intents and purposes—for Rilke—the woman experiences all these moments *now*, at the same time. So that "da war auf ihr" ("there was on her") does not refer to *one* of the hours but to the woman, to *both* of the hours. The bending down marks the passage to the third hour; the fusion is the moment of death. "What" is revealed on the woman is the look ("Blick") that she had once found on her lover during the "Liebesaugenblick." Although it is stated in the eighth elegy that the presence of the other ruins "den großen Tierblick" of lovers, according to the explanatory letter that look is at least a momentary possibility "in der ersten Liebesaugenblicken, wo ein Mensch im anderen, im Geliebten, seine eigene Weite sieht." What the woman had once seen on the lover ("am Geliebten") was her own vastness: a lover herself, she looked at him "mit großem Tierblick" and saw her own look mirrored in his. This is the look discovered *on her* in the last stanza: the look that sees the open, the look "wie in einem Tier" because it *is* "der Tierblick" and also because the open is *in* this look. (In lines eight and nine of the elegy the open is described as being *in* the look and face of the animal: "das Offene, das im Tiergesicht so tief ist.") Although the look on and in the woman *now* is the one she had found on the lover, the look that sees "das Offene," it is not precisely the same look, for this final moment surpasses the "Liebesaugenblick" and gives it a meaning: shortly before death is the only other time men approximate the look of animals.

A brief interpretation of the "open" is in order before a consideration of this "Sterbeblick"—"drohend," "so groß verbunden," and "entzogen." According to the eighth elegy, the look of the animal that sees the open is "frei von Tod": the animal "has its decease perpetually behind it" and "so goes in eternity." In contrast, men see only death, always "the world" and not the open; their fate is "to be up against ["gegenüber sein"] and nothing else and always up against." According to the letter to the Russian reader, men, unlike animals, are not "in the world" but "before the world" ("vor der Welt"). To contrast the temporal awareness of men and animals is one way of reducing these differences to a constitutive opposition: the animal does not see death and goes in eternity because it has *no* temporal awareness; constantly seeing the world as "Gegenstand" —as *objects* to be used in time—men are aware of time and therefore see the death waiting in front of them. The human "Sterbeblick," a "Tierblick," then, can be threatening just as the look of an animal can be threatening. Or, seen and described from outside by a time-bound observer, a look that sees or is about to see the open is threatening to detach itself from time and to enter the eternity "known" by animals: it is the threat of imminent loss. Such a look is also as threatening as death itself: although the dying person no longer sees death, her look betrays its coming: If "drohend" is the imminence of "Sterbestunde," the phrase "so groß verbunden" signifies the very moment itself. The look of the dying woman is "verbunden" because it sees the open, it is no longer "vor der Welt" but "in der Welt," bound up, at one with "Himmel, Luft und Raum." The senses in which the look is withdrawn ("entzogen") parallel the senses in which it was threatening. On a first level, it is withdrawn because the look of animals refuses more than a momentary eye-to-eye confrontation,[11] but also because such moments of "Verbundenheit" can *only* be moments precisely on account of their status as perpendicular to the horizontal directions of time-bound life. In other words, what is most "their own" (and therefore most *our* own insofar as we are time-bound creatures) about these moments is their very status *as* moments: as always already *withdrawn*. Several eloquent examples could be adduced for this characteristic Rilkean position,[12] but the following lines from one of the *Sonette an Orpheus* serve the purposes of this interpretation best in that they make a direct comparison between the fleeting nature of time and the fleeting look of an animal:

Rufe mich zu jener deiner Stunden,
die dir unaufhörlich widersteht:
flehend nah wie das Gesicht von Hunden,
aber immer wieder weggedreht,

wenn du meinst, sie endlich zu erfassen,
So Entzognes ist am meisten dein. [I: 766]

Summon me to the one among your hours / that unceasingly resists you: / imploringly near as a dog's face, / but ever and again turning away / when you think at last you're grasping it. / What is thus withdrawn is most yours.[13]

Addressed (by Rilke in a footnote) to the reader, this sonnet may appear to mean something quite different from "Sterbestunde." But as Rilke wrote in the letter to the young wife, it is precisely death that has the indescribable depth which makes it "Ausflucht ins Eigene": like "so Entzognes," it is simultaneously "most" and "for the most part" our own. The look is withdrawn because the person has died. This hour of death, then, gives the other two moments their depth, and it is only from the viewpoint of death that they can be understood as our own (in being withdrawn). In death the woman (re-)experiences the moments of conception and childbirth. On her is the look: threatening, united, and withdrawn, like the male in sexual union, like the child in childbirth, and, overshadowing these, like death. The poem answers the question "What is a bed?" "Liebesbett," "Wochenbett," and "Sterbebett" have become "das Bett."

"Seeing" a bed in terms of the way it is experienced—as bed of love-making, childbirth, and death—would be to a certain extent in agreement with the phenomenologist's view "that in experience (consciousness) the thing and the appearance of the thing cannot be distinguished, that the description of the experience of the thing is identical to the description of the thing itself."[14] Implicit or explicit, this position is at the basis of most interpretations of Rilke's so-called "Dinggedichte," but it cannot account for the necessary contradictions of "Das Bett." Namely, such a view sees experience as unproblematically given, present-to-itself, while "Das Bett" puts in question the very possibility of such unmediated, taken-for-granted experience. The moments we think of as most present, personal, and our own are precisely those which are least present; they are our own only insofar as they are metaphors for the ultimate negation of presence: death. Death is most our own in being withdrawn because it is simultaneously proper to all human beings *and* the negation of all human beings. But perhaps poetry can *re*present these moments of total presence/absence in such a way as to transcend the negativity of their momentariness and to enable us "to read the word 'death' without negation."[15] How would "Das Bett" answer the question posed by Paul de Man in reference to Rilke's work in general? "It is a matter of establishing if Rilke's writing reflects on itself to the point of putting in question the authority of its own affirmations, above all when these affirmations refer to the kinds of writing it extols."[16]

As early as the prose text "Zur Melodie der Dinge" (1898), Rilke expresses the task of the artist in terms of theater, stage, and drama. A "melody of life" ("Lebensmelodie"), a "background" ("Hintergrund"), is postulated behind all human activity, and this melody of the background is what enables human beings to come together in a "common hour" ("gemeinsame Stunde") (V: 417). The melody forms an altar between two lovers: their communion is so profound, they hardly need to speak. When such people are put on the stage, however, the melody of the background is lacking, and it is impossible to convey why these lovers are happy. The background chorus has to be transferred onto the stage:

> It is a question of expressing on the stage the common hour, that in which the characters speak. This song, which in life is left to the thousand voices of the day or the night, to the rustling of the forest or to the ticking of the clock and its hesitating striking of the hour, this vast chorus of the background ["dieser breite Chor des Hintergrundes"], which determines the beat and tone of our words, cannot be made comprehensible, above all on the stage, by the same means. [V: 420]

The background chorus cannot be reproduced on the stage by "mood" or "atmosphere" ("Stimmung") or by artificially produced sounds, for such methods emphasize only *one* voice when it is a matter of a *thousand* voices. According to this text, the only way to bridge the gap between the thousand voices of the chorus and the individual voices of the action ("Handlung") on stage is "Stilisierung": that is, the creation of a balance, a harmony, between them—when the dramatist "tunes the vast and wordless down to words" ("das Große und Wortlose zu den Worten herunterstimmt") (V: 421)—and it is this harmony of the background chorus and the action that in turn creates "the common hour" on stage. From the brewing of this hour rises a "voice" ("die Stimme . . . breit und unpersönlich")—the voice of the chorus on stage, which is "the basis from which that quieter song (the action) frees itself and into whose womb it, more beautiful, finally falls back" ("die Basis ist, aus der jenes leisere Lied ["die Handlung"] sich auslöst und in deren Schooß es endlich schöner zurückfällt") (V: 423). There is hardly any need to make more explicit the parallel between this configuration of "Chor," "Hintergrund," "Stunde," and the configuration in "Das Bett." The poem not only creates a drama according to the specifications of "Zur Melodie der Dinge," it dramatizes *how that drama comes into existence*: that is, how "the vast and wordless" is turned into words, how a poem comes to be.

The "action" of a drama, the "quieter song" given birth by the voice of the background chorus, is a poem, and its birth is the action of "Das Bett": one hour steps out and begins her own song in front of the song of infinity sung by the chorus. In terms of "Zur Melodie der Dinge," the tension and division on the stage of "Das Bett"—"jene Stunde . . . zer-reißt ihr Kleid und klagt *sich* an . . . sie konnte sie mit *sich* nicht stillen"—would be due to the hour's seeking the "common hour" in her-self: "All division and error is due to the fact that men seek the common *in* themselves instead of seeking it in the things *behind* themselves, in the light, in the landscape, in the beginning and in death" (V: 424). But by the end of "Das Bett" this hour too seeks "das Gemeinsame" in the "beginning and in death" and returns, more beautiful, to the womb of the common hour. She is a poem: "Das Bett" dramatizes the birth of a poem as well as the births of an hour and a child.[17]

Malte's description of how a poem comes into existence reads like a rearrangement and a transformation of "Das Bett" into prose. His view is expressed in organic terms: verse must not be written too early, for it has to "ripen." "For verse is not, as people think, feelings (those one has early enough),—it is experiences" (VI: 724). Then Malte provides a list of at least twenty kinds of experiences one must have and be able to think back upon in order to write verse, but even this is not enough:

> One must have memories of many nights of love, none of which was like the others, of the screams of women in labor, and of light, white, sleeping women in childbed, closing again. But one must also have been beside the dying, must have sat beside the dead in the room with the open window and fitful noises.

Yet even having these memories does not suffice:

> And still it is not yet enough to have memories. One must be able to forget them when they are many and one must have the great patience to wait until they come again. For it is not yet the memories themselves. Not till they have turned to blood within us, to glance and gesture, nameless and no longer to be distinguished from ourselves—not till then can it happen that in a most rare hour the first word of a verse arises in their midst and goes forth from them ["daß in einer sehr seltenen Stunde das erste Wort eines Verses aufsteht in ihrer Mitte und aus ihnen ausgeht"].[18]

The first word of a poem *steps out* (like the hour in "Das Bett"), and it is also *born* (like the "quieter song" in "Zur Melodie der Dinge") in that a childbirth is suggested here by a language of impregnation: the memories have to become "blood, look, and gesture" ("Blut, Blick und

Gebärde") in us and indistinguishable from us. In addition, the *kinds* of memories one must have in order to write poetry are the very experiences dramatized in "Das Bett"—"nights of love ["Liebesnächte"] . . . screams of women in labor ["Schreie von Kreißenden"] . . . the dying ["Sterbenden"]"—and their rapid enumeration once again stresses their analogous nature. "Das Bett" describes the feelings, experiences, and memories necessary for the writing of poetry *and* their transformation into poetry.

In being a poem "about" the sexual act, childbirth, and death, "Das Bett" is also a poem "about" the origins of poetry. This is not to say that the poem is "really" about poetry, for what it questions is precisely this notion of "really." Whether "poetry" is really a metaphor for the sexual act, childbirth, and death or whether these moments are really metaphors for poetry cannot be said, for both readings are true: in Rilke's language the origins of poetry and these "original" moments have the same structure of simultaneous presence *and* withdrawal. As "Zur Melodie der Dinge" and the passage from *Malte* demonstrate, a poem's origins and meaning lie not in any prior, isolable experience, memory, or reality, but in a process of harmonization and mediation between what are ordinarily called "life" and "poetry." In "Zur Melodie der Dinge," "life" with its background chorus and its action is already structured like poetry (a tragedy); in *Malte*, it is neither feelings nor experiences, nor memories, nor forgotten memories that are the origin of poetry but the entire process of temporal differentiation from one to the other. In using a language of impregnation and childbirth to describe the origins of poetry, both texts suggest a genetic pattern, but in both cases the immediate "mother" of poetry disappears either in a complicated system of mediations or in a long stretch of narrative. As in "Das Bett," these births are motherless births, for the real mother is time. For Rilke, poetry cannot be the transformation of a self-present, self-sufficient "thing" or "experience" into a self-present, self-sufficient language because both the former and the latter originate in a constitutive absence, a difference from themselves. Neither experience nor poem is present to itself, to its own meaning; both are separated from their meaning by a temporal difference which is both the condition and the negation of meaning. It is only by means of forgetting its temporal origins—like the forgetting (in "Zur Melodie der Dinge") of the thousand voices of the background, which takes place when the chorus is transferred onto the stage by means of "Stilisierung," or like the forgetting of memories in *Malte*—that poetry is able to grant itself a moment of existence. The poem asks *Was?* in order not to ask *Wann?*

Rilke's later poetry asks *Wann?* with such an insistence that sometimes it seems to ask nothing but *Wann?*[19] The temptation to set up a genetic pattern and thereby explain (away) Rilke's work as a progression *from* an origin of self-deception and blindness *to* an end of self-awareness and insight is strong,[20] but to succumb to it would be overly hasty in light of as self-conscious an early text as "Zur Melodie der Dinge." Rilke's work (from the 1890s to 1926) is an acutely self-conscious language, and it would be a precarious task to impose some kind of periodization on its insights. If nothing else, a reading of "Das Bett" should be a caution to any attempt at an unproblematic genetic totalization of origin and end, no matter what relation such an attempt may choose to oversimplify: the relation between "reality" and the poem, between the poet's life and the poem, between another poem and the poem, etc. Yet such caution is, in a sense, impossible in practice insofar as reading means to follow, interpret, and understand a text which—as the many births in "Das Bett," "Zur Melodie der Dinge," and *Malte* make abundantly clear—is *nothing but* the positing of an (imaginary) origin and the elaboration of a genetic pattern. Fortunately (or unfortunately), however, Rilke's language is always already more self-conscious than any critical language could be, and it is hardly necessary to stray from its logic to arrive—but what (or when) is "arrival" when origin and end do not coincide, when "origin" is its own forgetting and "end" is remembering the impossibility of any other origin?—at its simultaneously founding and subverting insights. Quotation and paraphrase would remain the languages closest to and farthest from claiming Rilke for their own: "So Entzognes ist am meisten dein."

NOTES

1. The only full-scale interpretation of the poem is K. Deleu, "R. M. Rilke, Das Bett," *Tijdschrift voor Levende Talen* 18 (1952/53): 202–13. Its methods and findings differ considerably from those of the present essay.
2. Rainer Maria Rilke, *New Poems*, trans. J. B. Leishman (New York: New Directions, 1964), p. 21.
3. All page references unless otherwise identified are to Rainer Maria Rilke,

Sämtliche Werke (Frankfurt am Main: Insel, 1966), and are given by volume and page number. A literal paraphrase of the poem: Let them (or her) think that what one fought there dissolves in private sorrow. Nowhere else but there is a theater; rip the high curtain away: there steps out in front of the chorus of nights, which began to say an infinitely wide song, that hour during which they were lying, and rends her garments and accuses herself, on account of the other hour, which defends herself and writhes in the background; for she could not still her with herself. But when she bent down to the strange hour: there was on her what she had once found on the beloved, only so threatening and so greatly bound up and withdrawn as in an animal.

4. Cf. *Die frühen Gedichte*: "Die armen Worte, die im Alltag darben, / die unscheinbaren Worte, lieb ich so" ("The poor words that starve in the every-day, / the invisible words, I love them so") (I: 148).

5. See appendix two in Rainer Maria Rilke, *Duino Elegies*, trans. J. B. Leishman and Stephen Spender (New York: Norton, 1963), p. 112.

6. Rainer Maria Rilke, *Briefe an eine junge Frau* (Leipzig: Insel, 1934), p. 21. Translation in *Duino Elegies*, trans. Leishman and Spender, p. 122.

7. In the *Buch von der Armut und vom Tode* the poem "Herr: Wir sind ärmer denn die armen Tiere" complains that we do not die *our* deaths and contains the lines:

> Sind wir nur Geschlecht
> und Schooß von Frauen, welche viel gewähren?—
> Wir haben mit der Ewigkeit gehurt,
> und wenn das Kreißbett da ist, so gebären
> wir unsres Todes Fehlgeburt. [I: 348]

> Are we merely the sex / and womb of women who allow too much?— / We have whored with eternity, / and when it is time for child-bed, we bear / our death's dead abortion.

The "Requiem" of 1908 would be another example:

> So starbst du, wie die Frauen früher starben,
> altmodisch starbst du in dem warmen Hause
> den Tod der Wöchnerinnen, welche wieder
> sich schließen wollen und es nicht mehr können,
> weil jenes Dunkel, das sie mitgebaren,
> noch einmal wiederkommt und drängt und eintritt. [I: 653]

> So you died, as women of old died, / you died in an old-fashioned way in the warm house / the death of those women in child-bed who / want to close themselves again and cannot, / because that darkness which they bore along with the child, / returns again and presses and enters.

8. Malte's comparison reads: "those women who grew very old and small and then on a huge bed, as on a stage ["wie auf einer Schaubühne"], before the whole family, the household and the dogs, passed away in discreet and seigniorial

168

dignity." Rainer Maria Rilke, *The Notebooks of Malte Laurids Brigge*, trans. M. D. Herter Norton (New York: Norton, 1964), p. 23.

9. The specific use of the verb "wehren" as defense against death occurs in *Malte*. The "Sterbende" encountered in the cafe is described as one who has stopped defending himself: "So he sat there and waited for it to happen. And no longer defended himself ["und wehrte sich nicht mehr"]." In order to contrast his own desire to live, Malte continues: "And I still defend myself. I defend myself ["Und ich wehre mich noch. Ich wehre mich"]" (VI: 755).

10. As quoted in Martin Heidegger, *Poetry, Language, Thought*, trans. Albert Hofstadter (New York: Harper and Row, 1971), p. 108. Originally quoted in Maurice Betz, *Rilke in Frankreich* (Vienna: Herbert Reichner, 1938), p. 291.

11. Such a withdrawal, a letting go, is expressed in the "Requiem" of 1908:

    Dann aber will ich, wenn ich vieles weiß,
    einfach die Tiere anschaun . . .
    will ein kurzes Dasein
    in ihren Augen haben, die mich halten
    und langsam lassen, ruhig, ohne Urteil. [I: 649]

    Then I would like, when I know a great deal, / simply to look at the animals . . . / would like to have a short existence / in their eyes, which hold me / and slowly let go, quietly, without judgment.

12. For example, the famous lines from the *Sonette an Orpheus*: "Wolle die Wandlung" (I: 758); or the last line of the eighth elegy: "so leben wir und nehmen immer Abschied ["so we live and are constantly taking leave"]" (I: 716).

13. Rainer Maria Rilke, *Sonnets to Orpheus*, trans. M. D. Herter Norton (New York: Norton, 1962), p. 115.

14. Käte Hamburger, "Die phänomenologische Struktur der Dichtung Rilkes," *Rilke in neuer Sicht*, ed. Käte Hamburger (Stuttgart: Kohlhammer, 1971), p. 92.

15. Rainer Maria Rilke, *Die Briefe an die Gräfin Sizzo, 1921–1926* (Wiesbaden: Insel, 1950), p. 37.

16. See the introduction to Rainer Maria Rilke, *Oeuvres*, ed. Paul de Man (Paris: Éditions du Seuil, 1972), II: 14.

17. A discussion of the relation between "Zur Melodie der Dinge" and Nietzsche's *Geburt der Tragödie* would discover much material to work with, especially since Rilke's "Marginalien zu Nietzsche, 'Die Geburt der Tragödie'" (1900) has been published (VI: 1163–1177).

18. *The Notebooks of Malte Laurids Brigge*, trans. M. D. Herter Norton, pp. 26–27.

19. For example: "Wann wird, wann wird, wann wird es genügen das Klagen und Sagen?" (II: 134); or the lines from the *Sonette an Orpheus*:

    Gesang ist Dasein. Für den Gott ein Leichtes.
    Wann aber *sind* wir? Und wann wendet *er*
    an unser Sein die Erde und die Sterne? [I: 732]

20. Even Peter Szondi—at the end of his sensitive reading of the ninth Duino elegy—is in danger of succumbing to this temptation as he maps out three periods (very traditional ones in Rilke criticism) in Rilke's career, which imply a movement from blindness to insight: "the first, whose medium is pure feeling, the experience. . . . The second period . . . begins with the first turn due to Rodin's example, with the turn to precise, relentlessly comprehending and reproducing observation, to work of the sight. . . . But the second turn, in which the Duino Elegies are grounded, is from the work of sight to heart-work: this heart-work is defined by the ninth elegy as the saying of things [das Sagen der Dinge]: man—according to the elegy—has the task of saying the things. . . ." Peter Szondi, *Das lyrische Drama des Fin de siècle* (Frankfurt am Main: Suhrkamp, 1975), p. 481.

10

The Devolution of the Self in
The Notebooks of Malte Laurids Brigge

WALTER H. SOKEL

A duality seems to run through *The Notebooks* that is most clearly apparent in the contrast between the two families whose union produced Malte—the paternal Brigges and the maternal Brahes. The two grandfathers, Brigge at Ulsgaard and Brahe at Urnekloster, stand at opposite poles in their attitude toward or experience of death, and offer themselves as apt points of departure for examining this duality and its significance.

Malte recalls that old Chamberlain Brigge died his own death. The powerful individuality and authenticity of his whole existence seemed to be manifested in his long-drawn-out dying. But not only he, most members of the Brigges, including even their children, had had their own deaths. Death was for them fruition and fulfillment, and each death confirmed, as it sealed, the unique character of the life it ended.

In contrast to this existentially authentic dying of the Brigges stand not only the anonymous assembly-line deaths in the Parisian hospitals, but also the Brahes' refusal to recognize death at all. At Ulsgaard, the home of the Brigges, everything proclaims the powerful impact of individual personality and the distinctive phases of the individual's life. At Urnekloster, ancestral home of the Brahes, the opposite prevails. Here, one is oblivious of the time of day. Death is not recognized because linear time, dividing existence into the three dimensions of past, present, and future, plays no role. The long-deceased might be expected as dinner guests. And why shouldn't they, if there is no distinction between past and present? The dead meet what is expected of them by putting in appearances. In the Brahes, we encounter an ideal concept of time which, as Beda Allemann has shown, is characteristic of the mature Rilke.[1] It is the idea of *Weltinnenraum*, of the world's inner space in which the distinctions within linear or directed time disappear in favor of the experience of the unity and consequently the simultaneity of all being. The Brahes are closely connected to Rilke's mystic inspiration, which served him as the point of departure for the first two Duino elegies in 1912, and which he described in the following year in the strange prose piece "Erlebnis" ("Inner Experience").[2] But this experience goes back to an even earlier illumination that had seized Rilke in Capri in 1907, that is, in the midst of his work on his Parisian novel.

The contradiction between the linear time dimension, implied in Brigge's dying, and the simultaneity of all being, which underlies the Brahe complex of the novel, has escaped attention, despite its importance and the obvious problems it raises. In terms of intellectual history, the Brigges may boast of a truly Nordic genealogy. They derive from the aestheticism of Jens Jacobsen, author of *Niels Lyne*, through whom the influence of Kierkegaard, a fellow-Dane now more famous than Jacobsen, might have first reached Rilke.[3] This Danish lineage is wedded in Rilke to reminiscences of Nietzsche, mediated to him by their common lady friend, the fascinating Lou Salomé. The Brahe sphere, on the other hand, while pointing ahead to the mysticism of the Duino "experience," is also rooted in the pantheistic penchant present in Rilke's work from its beginnings. The duality expressed by the two families is an instance of "the law of complementaries," which Ulrich Fülleborn has shown to be a basic structural principle of the novel.[4] The Brigges embody the law inherent in the *Gestalt* that grows toward its point of pre-ordained development and constitutes a unique and definite individuality, or in Malte's term "das Eigene," that which is peculiar to the individual. The Brahes, on the other hand, embody the principles of exchangeability of identities, of the commingling of all the forms of the universe, and consequently of the unreality of separateness and distinction. The Brahes experience the melting together of all contours, which is grotesquely displayed by Mathilde Brahe's overweight body, her somehow overflowing, shapeless flesh. Another example of the same element is the dimness of the hall at Urnekloster, which seems to enlarge the room on all sides so that its walls can no longer be seen. The indefiniteness of Old Brahe's features and personality, to which no name or label seems to adhere, belongs to the same context. These vague negativities produce the ghostlike atmosphere of the Brahe residence, later repeated at the Schuhlins. The masklike smile, which Malte notes as characteristic of his maternal grandfather, is part of the eeriness of Urnekloster, as is the whole spectrum of Malte's mask and mirror experiences, which all occur there. The mask, in *The Notebooks*, is a sign of the loss of identity and betokens a transcendence of the ego. The fact that "das Eigene," one's own distinct individuality, is part of the male line of Malte's descent, while the blurring and mingling of all boundaries mark the female line, would appear as not without significance to anyone familiar with the assumptions on which Rilke's view of the sexes, as expressed—for instance, in his doctrine of love— rests. To develop this aspect of Rilke's thought would lead us too far afield here. Our task is to pursue further the theme of the contrast that the two lines of descent exemplify.

The contrast reappears as an open contradiction in Malte's conflicting views of God. Early in *The Notebooks*, in its nineteenth section, appears a series of questions, each initiated by the words: "Is it possible?"

> Is it possible that there are people who say "God" and mean that this is something they have in common?—Just take a couple of schoolboys: one buys a pocket knife and his companion buys another exactly like it on the same day. And after a week they compare knives and it turns out that there is now only a very distant resemblance between the two—so differently have they developed in different hands. [*TR*, 29–30][5]

The passage strikingly resembles a very similar one in Montaigne, in which Renaissance individualism seems to reach its apogee.[6] At the same time, the influence of Jacobsen, and through him of Kierkegaard, cannot be overlooked here. For Malte, God is the opposite of the universal. He is the absolute individual in whom and through whom each individual experiences and reveals his subjectivity as true being; and Malte's rhetorical question: "Is it possible?" expresses his horror at mankind's failure to grasp that ultimate reality is, and must be, utterly individual, unrepeatable, and unique.

However, a remark of Malte's near the end of his notebooks stands in sharp contrast to what has just been established. There Malte says: "Let us be honest about it, then; we have no theatre, any more than we have a God: for this, community is needed" (*TR*, 196). Here the individual is negated as absolute reality, and God, in conformity with the Dionysian principle, to which the theater seems to point, appears as based upon the collective. We find in this contradiction another version of the contrast between the Brigges and the Brahes.

Yet, we shall see that this duality is only apparent. Its two poles not only complement each other; they unite to form a third force in which we shall come to discern, as the unifying theme of *The Notebooks*, the process of the overcoming of the self, the letting go of the ego.

Our concern here will be to examine how the process of the breaking of the self described by Malte reveals the duality of Brigges and Brahes as a unity, consisting of the tension between two poles.

Let us begin with the castaways, those figures of the lowest depths far beneath society, who seem to emerge from the underground into the streets of Paris to haunt Malte and beckon him to follow them into an inconceivable abyss. They function like messengers from future horrors that leave the imagination of the present utterly behind. This future seems to be taking aim at him through them. These homeless beggars and grotesques seem to be grinning at him, winking at him everywhere. Even the Bibliothèque Nationale fails to protect him from them. They draw him to them with bonds of dread. Disguised as mesmerizing anxiety, an overpowering temptation issues forth from the castaways. With constantly diminishing strength, Malte struggles against their lure. "Who are these people? They are refuse, husks of human beings, whom destiny has spewed up" (VI: 743).[7]

The wording of this first characterization of the castaways, given by Malte, already hints at what it is they seem to urge upon him. It is the purging of the ego from his being. He calls them "husks" of human beings, "Schalen," which could also mean "peels" or "shells." This metaphor then conjures a fruit which has lost its inner core and flesh, and has been reduced to the worthless frame of its former being. The metaphor establishes the castaways as the counterpart and opposite of Old Chamberlain Brigge, Malte's powerful paternal grandfather. For the full, ripe, or maturing fruit is the image of his existence, which was full-bodied, unique, and mighty in his death as well as in his life. The image of the ripening fruit reaches back to the third book of the *Stundenbuch* of 1903, the year in which *Malte* was first conceived.

> Denn wir sind nur die Schale und das Blatt.
> Der grosse Tod, den jeder in sich hat,
> das ist die Frucht, um die sich alles dreht.[8]

Brigge contained this fruit, his own personal and unique death, within himself from the beginning. His existence had a destiny. The castaways are at the opposite pole. They are deprived of that interiority and substance that "everyone" carries within himself. Nothing can make them be compared to an organic being. They are without that which ripens toward fruition and fulfillment of its inner law. The word "refuse" ("Abfälle"), with which they are described, refers in its root meaning to something that has fallen off or been removed and thrown away from something greater to which it originally belonged but now no longer belongs. They are the peels without the fruit they once contained; they are the exteriors without the corresponding interior; they are enclosures without anything to enclose. They exist at the most extreme remove from the world of the Brigges in which life enjoyed the favor of fortune and possessed the time to mature into the fruit of its own death. But the castaways have been robbed of their organic being. They are no longer persons.

In his long letter to Lou Andreas-Salomé of July 18, 1903, Rilke still invests the castaways with a fate. Here he writes of them: "And they were passersby among passersby, left alone and undisturbed in their fate."[9] In the novel, however, they are already "spewed up by fate (or destiny)"; it is destiny which has thrown them away and made them into "refuse." This is a consistent elaboration of the meaning of "being left alone," which Rilke already expressed in his letter. If we look into the further use of the term "Schicksal" (fate or destiny) in *Malte*, we find that it is called the "inventor" of "patterns and figures," and that it is put in contrast to "life." Whereas the "difficulty" of "destiny" lies in its "complexity," we read that "life is heavy from simplicity" (VI: 898–99). The castaways share their lack of destiny with the saints and the female lovers who are not loved in return. They have become shapelessly simple like "eternal ones." Like the saints and the women, whose love goes un-requited, their lives have ceased to change. "But they maintain them-selves almost like eternal ones. They stand at their street corners each day, even in November, and they do not scream because of the winter. Fog comes and makes them indistinct and uncertain: yet they are. I had been away; I had been sick; for me many things had passed; but they have not passed away" (VI: 904). The castaways exist in a state in which the un-stable self that is subject to linear time, occupied with projects, ambitions, cares, chores, and affairs, no longer is. In this respect, the castaways are like the women lovers who have given up all hope for love requited. These women are likewise "deprived of destiny" and stand as though eternal "next to the beloved man who is subject to metamorphoses" (VI: 899). The difference between the castaways and the women lovers lies in the passivity of the former. The castaways endure only passively like "puppets with whom life has played," what the women have "resolutely" chosen for themselves. Like the saints, the women have deliberately refused destiny, whereas the castaways merely happened to lose it. Circumstances have robbed them of it and made them slowly and gradually "slide down" (VI: 904) into the fateless abyss of misery. However, despite the superiority of the unloved lovers *vis-à-vis* the castaways, the result common to both must not be ignored.[10] It is the absence of self that raises both beyond time. Both, after all, are compared to "eternal ones."

Like the unloved lovers, the castaways have, together with the self, thrown off caprice, deception, and shame. When Malte sees the beggar woman daily offering the stump of her arm to the view of the people at sidewalk cafés, he admits to himself his own inability to attain such an utter disregard to self-consciousness and shame. He would lack the strength and indifference for it, ". . . but I would make a vain boast if I claimed to be like them. I am not. I would have neither their strength nor their measure" (VI: 904). Having shed the constantly striving and worrying ego, they have allowed being to appear in them. "Yet they *are*," says Malte of them. But through himself, time still passes, many things have happened to him; and with his ego involved, he has been and still is the victim of time which robs and changes all. They, on the other hand, have already traveled so far away from destiny that time no longer occurs in them. From dupes and victims of time, they have become its equals. Now they themselves are time. The blind newspaper vendor at the fence of the Jardin du Luxembourg no longer faces time the way the self, constantly dwindling in time, but desperately clinging to its illusory gifts, has to face time, the great and invincible enemy of selfhood. The blind newspaper vendor is one with time. He is the measure who measures all that changes, but who himself does not change.[11] Malte comments: "And the world is so arranged that there are people who pass their entire lives in that pause when he, more silent than anything that moves, inches forward like the hand of a clock, like the shadow of such a hand, like time" (VI: 900).

We have run ahead from the first appearance of the castaways to the meaning that they will assume for Malte near the end of *The Notebooks*. Between these points lie phenomenological descriptions of the process of losing selfhood. They follow immediately upon the first emergence of the castaways. In a series of infernal scenes, Malte depicts the eruptions and visitations that first threaten and then smash the self. They serve as prefigurations and allusions to his own calling and destiny. The scenes begin with the stranger whose dying Malte witnesses in the dairy café, the creamery, and culminate in the eruption of the St. Vitus's Dance on the Pont du St.-Michel. The horrors of Malte's childhood, his encounter with the hand under the table, and his near-suffocation under the mask form remembered parallels from Malte's past to the scenes of horror witnessed in his Parisian present. I call these descriptions or evocations phenomenological because they represent the phenomena described not from the perspective of a mimetic convention—that is, as fictional fact—but openly as elements of the consciousness that describes them.[12]

The dying man in the creamery, who throws Malte into such shock that he runs away from the scene in panic and races through the streets, is described in this passage:

> The connection between us was established, and I knew that he was stiff with terror. I knew that terror had paralyzed him, terror at something that was happening inside him. Perhaps one of his blood-vessels had burst; perhaps, just at this moment, some poison that he had long dreaded was penetrating the ventricle of his heart; like a rising sun that was changing the world for him. With an indescribable effort I compelled myself to look in his direction, for I still hoped it was all imagination. But then I sprang up and rushed out; for I had made no mistake. [VI: 749–55, *TR*, 50–51]

This death in the creamery is a synthesis between the two kinds of death encountered by the reader so far. It combines the anonymous assembly-line dying in the hospitals with the "personal death" of Chamberlain Brigge. Like the death of the chamberlain, the dying in the creamery erupts from within. It explodes, as it were, from the interior space of the individual. It removes its victim from all accustomed things and makes him a stranger to the world. In that sense, his death is like the death of Chamberlain Brigge. On the other hand, this dying is certainly not seen in terms of the ripening of a fruit. It is not at all conceived of in terms of an organic development fulfilling an inner law. Rather, it is experienced as a sudden breakthrough inside. It is not the highest point of growth, but a catastrophe. In the context of a history of sensibility, the distance traversed between the remembered death of Old Brigge and the dying observed in the creamery would serve to illustrate the development from the age of Goethe, Romanticism, and neo-Romanticism to the Expressionist and post-Expressionist way of perceiving the

177

world. For all its terror and alienation, the dying of Old Brigge still encompassed a long-drawn-out, gradual evolution, the leisurely ripening of a pre-ordained organic development. What confronts us in the dairy café is a sudden volcanic metamorphosis, which points ahead in essential respects to the "metamorphosis" of Gregor Samsa only a few years later, or to Georg Heym's poem "Der Krieg," in which war suddenly emerges from its subterranean concealment and engulfs the modern metropolis. It is the visualization of apocalypse that links this aspect of *Malte* to Expressionism and to the existentialism of the subsequent decades. The emphasis no longer rests, as it still does in Old Brigge's case, on the organic development of the individual personality, even into his death, which is uniquely his own. This dying in the creamery belongs to the anonymity of the modern megalopolis from which the nameless man emerged and to whose infernal world he belongs. The radical aloneness of this dying, in the midst of the metropolitan bustle rushing past it, without awareness, is an extreme case of the shabby anonymity of those thousands of deaths occurring in the city hospitals every day. It occurs to Malte that, at Duval's, the elegant café, they would not even have admitted this moribund patron of the creamery; the fashionable bourgeois world has banished dying out of sight. In the hospitals, meanwhile, the dying exist as mere statistical numbers and cases, deprived of everything they might call theirs. However, it is precisely in this anonymous isolation that the existential horror of death hits Malte with full force. Here there is no longer the solace of authenticity, of one's own personal death. For the aestheticizing world view, individuality is the supreme value. However, individuality falls away with the illusion of special privilege contained in the idea of dying one's own personal death. The absolute isolation that the dying in the creamery establishes opens up the abyss of the no-longer-conceivable, which dying is, and flings it into Malte's and the reader's consciousness.

In contrast to the imperious death of Old Chamberlain Brigge at Ulsgaard, the silent dying in the creamery is an example of both loss and transcendence of self. In the dying in the creamery the emphasis lies not on the quality and individuality of a personal death, but on dying as a process and on its consequences. The individual and historical aspects of existence, which still found such powerful expression in Old Brigge's dying, lose all significance here. It is the pure happening without a past—the metamorphosis taking place in the present moment—which is described or rather conjured here. The word "perhaps" repeated three times and initiating each of the questions shows that Malte is only able to circumlocute here, and that what is actually occurring must remain conjecture. The three catastrophes evoked—the bursting of a blood vessel, the entrance of poison into the heart, the eruption of a brain tumor—these three catastrophes are speculations surrounding the inconceivable reality. In contrast to the powerful roar of Brigge's dying which dominates the environment and makes this dying unquestionably an event imprinting itself, as did his whole life, upon the world, the dying in the creamery proceeds in a sinister soundlessness. The dying man surrenders defenselessly to what is happening in and to him. "So he sat there and waited until it should have happened. And defended himself no longer" (*TR*, 51). Here occurs the birth of that equanimity which later, in the blind newspaper vendor, shall become exemplary.

A comparison of the time structure in the death scenes reflected upon and witnessed by Malte is illuminating. In the death of the chamberlain the emphasis is on the linear development which leads from the lived past into the dying present. Living and dying are situated on the same single line. The mass dying in the hospitals is empty present, unconnected with anything preceding or following. But in the anonymous dying of the stranger in the creamery, the present is being swept into a future as yet inconceivable. The tumor bursting in the man is compared to a sunrise "that transformed the world for him." It thus heralds the dawning of a new day, a newborn world. Spine-chilling though it is, this dying is pregnant with a future. We can discern this from the effect this death has upon Malte and the significance it assumes for him. It becomes a call for his rebirth, a milestone on the road to his Damascus. Malte knows that he must obey the call that this death expresses. It is a sign, a signal, which he grasps not conceptually as yet but, as it were, intestinally. The death in the creamery signifies for Malte the need "to change [his] life." It has the effect that the work of art has upon the beholder, as expressed in the last line of the "Archaïscher Torso Apollos."

> . . . denn da ist keine Stelle,
> die dich nicht sieht. Du mußt dein Leben ändern. [I: 557]

> . . . for there is no spot
> that does not see you. You must change your life.

For Malte, this implies the severing of all remaining bonds to his vanished and relatively sheltered past, the kind of weaning of existence from the maternal ground of being which we find more explicitly expressed

179

in the third Duino elegy. It also means renunciation of yearning for the sheltered existence lived by the celebrated poet—who has been identified as Francis Jammes[13]—whom Malte reads in the Bibliothèque Nationale, hoping in vain to escape through him from the threatening ambush of the castaways. This poet is still housed in a world that he can call his own. But Malte, like the dying man in the creamery, has to "remove himself and take leave of everything."[14]

The dying in the creamery, in a sense, becomes a transition from the world of the Brigges to the world of the Brahes. Malte thinks that the dying man might no longer be able to distinguish objects; and it is precisely this inability that makes his dying so horrifying, and yet, from a hidden perspective that only gradually becomes explicit, so exemplary, for Malte.

> Yes, he knew that he was now withdrawing from everything: not only from human beings. A moment more, and everything will have lost its meaning, and that table, and the cup, and the chair to which he clings, all the near and the commonplace will have become unintelligible, strange and heavy. So he sat there and waited until it should have happened. And defended himself no longer. [I: 755; *TR*, 51]

What the Brahes have proudly attained—namely, the transcendence of distinctions between the discreteness of objects—is here still experienced as a loss, as terrifying impotence and negativity. "There was nothing." But even here, Malte realizes that it is the perspective of his own anxiety that posits this experience as a loss, a horror, and an emptiness. He senses and indeed knows that, in place of seeing nothing, a wholly new way of seeing would emerge, a readiness "to see everything differently."

The learning "to see differently" is of course the theme of the book. But it can only come about by a surrender of the ego. It is a selfless seeing. For Malte it will mean a kind of writing radically different from the one he has practiced so far. His pen will no longer obey the dictation of his conscious will. "But here there will come a day when my hand will be far from me, and when I bid it write, it will write words I do not mean . . . this time I shall be written" (VI: 756; *TR*, 52). For Malte, the poet, that yielding of self, which he has described among the castaways and the women whose love went unrequited, will manifest itself as a profoundly changed form of creativeness. His writing will cease to be "Erlebnisdichtung," which is the expression of the ego and its experience. Malte knows that the time must come when he will have to give up all claim to personal distinction and ambition for his authorship and all self-willed individuality in his style. He will have to renounce the self-pleasing image of creator and lower himself to be mere medium, poor husk, pure vessel of something other and greater than himself.[15]

But Malte's prophecy "but this time I shall be written" poses the question of the identity of that greater author whose medium or whose subject—the distinction is not made—Malte will become. Who is the author who shall write *Malte* or write by means of Malte? The section dealing with the victim of the St. Vitus's Dance on the Boulevard St.-Michel will lead us further in this quest.

The description of the dancer on the Boulevard St.-Michel shows, in anticipation of the fifth elegy, that the self is a will, a concentrated effort at control. The will seeks to maintain an appearance. The victim of the nervous disorder, in whom Malte comprehends himself, is intent on preserving the appearance of a normal existence. The man strains to protect himself against the eruption of an uncontrollable urge to twitch and toss about his limbs. He clings to a cane, which serves him as an instrument of self-control, but also represents the symbol of bourgeois respectability in pre–World War I Europe. He is in Malte's words, "still defending himself," even as Malte himself is desperately resisting the suction issuing from the castaways. "And I am still defending myself," he tells himself, putting a distance between himself and the dying wretch in the creamery. Yet he knows that his defense is as doomed as the spastic's efforts to hide his seizures.

This resistance is identical with the ego, the individual will, the organizing consciousness, seeking to assert its control over the body and over the environment. It is the upkeep of an image of respectability aimed at the others; it is the ambition to avoid becoming an object of derision, contempt, and pity. The self is here identical with appearance and repute. In anticipation of Sartre's concept of "bad faith," the self is a role tailored to the expectations and opinions of others. "This posture [of putting his cane against his back] was not striking; at most it was a little cocky; the unexpected day of spring might excuse that. No one thought of turning round to look; and now all went well. It went wonderfully well" (VI: 772; *TR*, 64–65). The self corresponds to what Heidegger calls "das Man." It is the crowd turned inward. Anxious regard for people's opinions becomes the yardstick for self-judgment. This self can be equated with the loved ones in Malte's (and Rilke's) doctrine of love, who are dependent on their lovers, try to live up to the role expected of them, and allow their lovers to determine them. Insofar as the lovers tolerate and foster this self-enslavement of the beloved, they themselves are not genuine lovers. Only by transcending the beloved and no longer hoping for love returned can they fulfill the force and freedom that true love is. Short of that, neither partner in a love affair lives authentically, in the freedom and pure activity of emotion that true love is. In the false lovers' case, the self takes its measure from the partner; in the spastic's and in Malte's case, from the others, the impersonal crowd, the faceless "Man" or "people."[16] Insofar as the self depends on the recognition and regard accorded to it by someone else, it is a façade and not a truth, and the defeat of its wish to appear to others in a certain light is, in a sense, a liberation of its truth. This is what the scene with the victim of the St. Vitus's Dance shows.

As we have seen, his self consists of his maneuvers to conceal the terrible force that lies waiting inside him. The inward truth in his case is his sickness coiled inside him to be released. The victim's desperate attempt to hide what victimizes him is a form of vanity or shame, a pretense at being what he is not, or what Kierkegaard called the first stage of "the sickness unto death." Malte identifies completely with the victim of the nervous disease. He follows him, anxious and fascinated, down the whole length of the Boulevard St.-Michel, and would like to help him with a portion of his own strength. The thoughts that he projects into the sick man are, of course, all Malte's own thoughts. The sick man is Malte's *alter ego*, literally a projection of his own self and situation. Like the sick man, Malte is anxiously concerned about his external appearance. The same anxiety dominates him as the sick man—the fear of letting it be seen that he is about to lose his footing and slide down into an inconceivably shameful condition. He too makes strenuous efforts not to forfeit the semblance of normality and bourgeois respectability, even though these have long ceased to correspond to his real state of affairs.

> True, my collar is clean, my shirt and underwear too, and I could, even as I am, enter any pastryshop I pleased, preferably on the Grands Boulevards, and could calmly reach into the cake plate and take some: No one would find that surprising, and no one would scold me and show me the door, for mine is still a hand that belongs to respectable circles; a hand that is washed four or five times a day. Indeed there is nothing under the nails, the index finger is without ink-stains, and the wrists particularly are irreproachable. Poor people don't wash so far up; that is a known fact. [VI: 742; *TR*, 41]

It is Malte's own self which, in this passage, is unmasked as a façade.

Malte's "eigenes Leben" is precisely that part of him that he tries to hide from people. It lies in his anguish, his exposure, his wretchedness. His negativity is what is positive and promising about him. In this context, the afflicted creature on the Boulevard St.-Michel becomes a symbol and prefiguration of Malte's own existence. The wretch's pathetic clinging to his respectability, embodied in his cane, cannot resist the gigantic force welling up in him and waiting to break out from under his pitiful pride. And as he gives in and his will collapses, something incomparably greater, mightier, and truer leaps forth from him. ". . . and then he gave in. His cane was gone, he spread out his arms as if about to take off and fly, and there burst out of him something like a natural force and bent him forward and pulled him back and made him nod and bow, flinging the power of the dance out of him into the crowd. For many people had already gathered around him and I saw him no more" (VI: 774; *TR*, 66).

This is a scene of horror, which leaves Malte utterly empty and exhausted. A human being, with whom the narrator identifies, loses his dignity, in fact his human status. Will and consciousness prove impotent. Man is helplessly handed over to his dreadful disease and to the pitiless derision of the world. A self goes under, literally, when we think of the concluding words of the scene: "For many people had already gathered around him and I saw him no more." The reader is depressed and crushed by this total defeat of human self-control, this total loss of the autonomy of the human will. We share Malte's dreadful melancholy in witnessing the event.

But Rilke gave the advice to read his *Malte* "contre son courant."[17] In light of this advice, we must raise the question whether a purely negative evaluation of this scene is justified, no matter how strong the first impression would speak for it. For the depressing content is contradicted by a linguistic structure that clothes and surrounds this destruction of the self with a triumphant exultation. Choice of vocabulary and syntactical structure show the defeat and dissolution of the will as the liberation of an enormous power. The expansive gesture, the spreading out of his arms, with which the dancer lets go of his cane, indicates relief and liberation. How paltry and false his previous clinging to the cane now appears from the vantage point of this gigantic expansion of arms to wings! The image makes the positive aspect of the ego's destruction appear more significant than the negative meaning suggested by the narrator's perspective and the reader's preconceptions of what man should be. Seen as pure description, the gesture presents a liberation, a broadening and freeing of the figure. In the context, it is a liberation from the constant burden of having to suppress what is strongest within oneself. We have seen how this self had previously been intent on holding back, on keeping down, on covering up, on oppression, pretense, and façade. The main function of the conscious self seemed to be not to allow what was most important inside to become visible—the compulsion to dance that was vibrating in his muscles and nerves.

The simile "as if about to take off and fly" raises the horizontally expansive gesture of the spreading of arms to the vertical dimension of wings going into action. The simile "like a natural force" counteracts all associations of degeneration and negativity implied by the idea of the nervous disorder, and elevates that which the conscious will sought to repress to the rank of a force that not only overwhelms man, but is also in accord with, and part of, nature.

The following phrases, connected by the paratactic conjunctions "and"—"and bent him forward and pulled him back and made him nod and bow"—must of course appear to Malte and to the reader as describing utter horror. For these phrases show man degraded to a puppet and, in the cruellest way, mock our sense of human dignity. However, as Jacob Steiner shows in his discussion of the symbol of the puppet in Rilke's fourth elegy, the puppet embodies for Rilke the highest degree of authenticity. The fact that in the puppet "there is no background (no reaching into interiority and memory) guarantees that appearance and depth are not separated . . . into pretense and actuality, as they are in the human dancer."[18] In *Malte*, too, the puppet or puppetlike condition can be interpreted affirmatively, if the text is read "against the current." The description of the afflicted man's fit, which reduces him to the state of a puppet, is framed, on the one end, by the majestic similes that compare his attack to "a natural force" and, on the other, by the exhilarating metaphor that shows the victim as flinging "the power of the dance" to the crowd. Word order and syntactical structure thus show the following: Negativity—that is, the grotesque reduction and destruction of the human person—is bedded into a highly positive, uplifting, and expansive phrasing. The paratactic arrangement of the sentence most intimately conjoins positive and negative evaluation and, in fact, equates them. The destruction of the individual thus appears as the reverse side of a tremendous expansion and elevation. Destruction becomes, as it were, the necessary precondition for the release of elemental power. The grammatical structure—"something" being the subject, bursting out of the person, and the person being the helpless object in its grip—precisely embodies the existential situation shown. Impersonal force completely dominates the individual. This sentence structure thus represents the total reversal of the accustomed subject-object relationship. Man, who normally conceives himself and is conceived as the subject and ruler of the world of objects, here appears as the defenseless object of the impersonal "something." This "something" attains the rank of "a force of nature." At the same time, it is the donor of the joyous power of the dance. What it takes from the individual, it squanders on the crowd. It transforms man's loss into the enrichment of mankind.

The "something" that bursts forth and submerges the individual is akin to Nietzsche's concept of the Dionysian. Not only words like "force of nature," "power of the dance," and "crowd" point to this connection— the entire structure of the vividly dramatic scene establishes such a link. As already mentioned, the individual literally disappears in the multitude, is swallowed up by it. The structure of this event corresponds exactly to the principle of Greek tragedy as interpreted by Nietzsche.[19] The tragic hero, by virtue of being the most powerful and extreme individual character, embodies in his person the principle of individuation. By his fall, he affirms the triumph of cosmic unity as embodied in the chorus. In the victim of the St. Vitus's Dance on the Pont du St.-Michel, the attempt of man to assert himself as an individual comes to naught as drastically as in the hero of Greek tragedy. Despite the obvious vast differences, this fundamental structural analogy establishes a profound identity between the royal and mythic protagonists of Attic drama as seen by Nietzsche, and the pathetic representative of the anonymous horrors of Parisian street life, as observed by Malte.

Our reading of the scene on the Pont du St.-Michel shows linguistic formulation in contradiction to the writer's conscious perspective, which, however, filters the scene to the reader. What is actually described stands in contrast to the way it is experienced. It is a striking confirmation of the need to heed Rilke's advice and read his novel *contre le courant*. Throughout the novel, the scenic presentation runs ahead of the conceptually formulated insights. The dance shows in purely scenic terms, without conceptual grasp and comment, something that Malte will later, in the second part of *The Notebooks*, be able to formulate explicitly. In the second part of *The Notebooks* Malte distinguishes between a "bad" fear and a "genuine" (or authentic) fear, a distinction in which Bollnow sees the heart of the book.[20] This genuine fear increases with "the force which produces it. We have no conception of that force except in our fear" (VI: 862). This fear is the token of a power within us that is accessible to our consciousness only negatively, namely as fear. Thus fear is the yardstick for our strength. For this strength "is so utterly inconceivable, so totally opposed to us, that our brain disintegrates at the point where we strain to think it. And yet, for some time now, I have believed that [this fear] is *our own* power, all our power, which is as yet too great for us. . . . we do not know it, but is it not that which is most our own of which we know the least?" (VI: 862; *TR*, 145).

The scene of the dance expresses this insight by its linguistic and visual terms. That which Malte describes there is the eruption of an enormous power that threatens and crushes the self, and makes it disappear. Yet, this power has welled forth from the depths and innermost recesses of the same self that it destroys. It is the self's own power that transcends the empirical ego so far that it can and must be experienced, at least at first, as menacing and destructive strangeness. Even after the encounter in the creamery, Malte had had an inkling of this: "Only one step," he tells himself, "and my profound wretchedness would be bliss" (VI: 756). The structure of *The Notebooks* is such that that "bliss" shows itself first as its reverse. In the novel itself, Malte never attains this bliss. It remains mere wish and projection. The last sentence of *The Notebooks* contains the words "not yet." But throughout the metropolitan inferno that Malte has to go through, that possibility of an unknown "bliss" is somehow present, the way, in the "negative theology" of Karl Barth, God speaks to us in and through His absence.

The structure of the dance closely corresponds to the poetics contained in *Malte*. We have already, in connection with the dying in the creamery, referred to the passivity and lack of resisting will, which point to an entirely new way of writing. "There will come a day when my hand will be far from me, and I shall bid it to write, and it will write words I shall not mean." Passivity appears as the poet's openness to his inspiration, which the mind's deliberate intentions would only block. The grievous process of self-abandonment will be the precondition for inspiration. The hand that writes will no longer obey the conscious mind, and it will write down words not intended by the self. And yet, the image of the hand far removed from the self shows that the dissolution of the ego is at the same time a tremendous expansion of the self. For this hand that will refuse to write down the words commanded by the ego will yet be Malte's own hand. It will still belong to him and begin to write at his bidding. Thus the self will not have vanished. It will be removed from the control of that narrow and superficial segment which is conscious intention. It will no longer be subject to what the ego "means." But in exchange, the space between Malte and his hand, which is the self in a larger and greater sense, will be enormous and extend into cosmic reaches.

This future type of writing—what Malte calls "the other interpretation"—can be compared to the wild dance dictated by a deeper force within the victim. As the ego-destroyer *par excellence*, this force is surely "against us." Yet it is "our strength," it is that "which is most our own." The efforts marshaled to repress this power constitute a kind of self-alienation, since they aim at preserving a pretended self, an appearance of "normal" respectability, in place of the real and total self which includes the dance. The pedestrian clinging to his cane and desperately courting the effect he intends to achieve, symbolizes, like Malte himself, that which Heidegger was to call "das Verfallen des Daseins" ("the fallenness of *Dasein*").[21] This façade, this pretense of health, is not the dancer's "own life," but only an effort to live up to the expectations of others. It is a deception which reality unmasks. His "Eigenstes," his "ownmost" is not the impression he tries to make, but the gigantic power which he seeks to conceal and which is called disease.

When this "ownmost" achieves its eruption, it establishes the possibility of a much more real relationship between the self and the others than the image of "normality" he tried to cultivate. That image amounted to an apparent and negative tie to others. It aimed at a negation, at not arousing attention and derision. Now, however, the barrier of negativity has fallen, and there is an acknowledged link between the dancer and his public. Instead of guarding against being noticed, he flings "the power of the dance" "among the crowd." He infects and moves them, and the crowd literally receives him. We are told that he disappears in it. For Malte's eyes, he has become one with the multitude, and no distinction is left between the self and mankind.

Thus we have arrived at the synthesis of the two apparently antithetical principles embodied in Malte's blood—the Brigge principle of individuation and the Brahe principle of the simultaneity and unity of all states of being. That which is most profoundly our own, the principle of the Brigges, is at the same time that which overwhelms and dissolves us as separate, individual entities. The old chamberlain's "own death" is, on the one hand, the crowning of unique authentic existence. On the other hand, this authenticity is by no means the same as the empirical self or ego, but on the contrary is hostile to it. Growing within him, as the fetus in the womb, his death metamorphoses the personality of old Brigge and makes it strange to all who had known him. His maturing death usurps the self's place. It is no longer Brigge who rules at Ulsgaard, but his death, and that is something very different, as Malte explicitly informs us. His death is the force that originates within the self, yet transcends and annihilates it. Thus the culmination of what is most "our own" is at the same time a falling asunder of ourselves. Fulfillment is transformation and transcendence of that which is fulfilled. That which is most our own is always that which completely transcends our empirical self. It is precisely the Brigges' insistence on the authenticity of "their own" that, if carried out with sufficient thoroughness and consistency, permits the advance toward the realm of the Brahes, where what is our own is no longer felt as distinct from all being.[22] This expansion of the self to a cosmic dimension can only proceed by the devolution of the empirical personality or ego. For, as our analysis of the St. Vitus's Dance scene has shown, the ego is the elaborate concealment of the self's true reality.

NOTES

This essay is a revised, translated version of the article, Walter Sokel, "Zwischen Existenz und Weltinnenraum: Zum Prozeß der Ent-Ichung im *Malte Laurids Brigge*," in *Probleme des Erzählens in der Weltliteratur,* ed. Fritz Martini (Stuttgart: Klett, 1971), pp. 212–33. Reprinted by permission of the publisher.

1. Beda Allemann, *Zeit und Figur beim späten Rilke* (Pfullingen: Neske, 1961).
2. *Sämtliche Werke* (Frankfurt am Main: Insel, 1966), VI: 1036–1042. Cf. also Allemann, pp. 20–25.
3. Cf. Else Buddeberg, *Rainer Maria Rilke* (Stuttgart: Metzler, 1954), pp. 129, 139, 141, 150–51.
4. "Form und Sinn der Aufzeichnungen des Malte Laurids Brigge," in *Deutsche Romantheorien*, ed. Reinhold Grimm (Frankfurt am Main: Athenäum, 1968), p. 260.
5. Rainer Maria Rilke, *The Notebooks of Malte Laurids Brigge*, trans. M. D. Herter Norton (New York: Horton, 1949; reprinted New York: Capricorn Books, G. P. Putnam's Sons, 1958). All quotations from this translation are

indicated in the text with the designation *TR* followed by the appropriate pagination.

6. Cf. Montaigne's essay "On Experience," book 3, ch. 13, para. 1. There Montaigne asserts that the most universal categories are individuality and differentiation.

7. Wherever I believed that Norton's translation does not reproduce the meaning of the original adequately, I use my own translations. They are based on the following edition of Rilke's text: Rainer Maria Rilke, *Sämtliche Werke*, ed. Rilke-Archiv, Ernst Zinn, and Ruth Sieber-Rilke, vol. VI (Frankfurt am Main: Insel, 1966). All quotations followed in the text parenthetically by the Roman numeral VI and the appropriate page number refer to my own translations from this edition of the novel.

8. Rilke, *Sämtliche Werke* (Frankfurt am Main: Insel, 1955), I: 347. All references to volume I refer to this edition of Rilke's works.

9. *Rainer Maria Rilke—Lou Andreas Salomé, Briefwechsel*, ed. Ernst Pfeiffer (Zürich: Niehans, 1952), p. 55.

10. Ernst Fëdor Hoffmann, in his study "Zum dichterischen Verfahren in Rilkes 'Aufzeichnungen des Malte Laurids Brigge,'" *Deutsche Vierteljahrsschrift für Literaturwissenschaft und Geitesgeschichte* 42 (1968): 202–30, denies that the castaways are capable of achieving the transformation of misery into feeling. According to his view, they signify a danger for Malte. However, it seems to me impossible not to concede to the blind newspaper vendor, and by extension, therefore, to all the castaways, an exemplary function for Malte. Their "exhibitionism" does not serve vanity, but indicates the opposite—a complete relinquishing and abandonment of the last remnants of self-regard.

11. Cf. Allemann, p. 13, and Fülleborn, p. 269. The latter sees in the blind newspaper vendor the "high point" of the entire notebooks.

12. Cf. Käte Hamburger's essay on the phenomenological aspect of Rilke's work in general. "Die phänomenologische Struktur der Dichtung Rilkes," in *Philosophie der Dichter. Novalis Schiller Rilke* (Stuttgart: Kohlhammer, 1966), pp. 179–275. Cf. also Hoffmann, pp. 213–14.

13. Cf. Buddeberg, 166.

14. Cf. Buddeberg, 168–70.

15. Cf. Herman Meyer's essay, "Rilkes Cézanne-Erlebnis," in *Zarte Empirie* (Stuttgart: Metzler, 1963), pp. 264–72, concerning Rilke's ideal of a noninterpretable art.

16. Fritz Martini shows that the false czar feels the refutation of his claim to the throne as a liberation and rebirth of his true self, for precisely the same reason. Cf. "Rainer Maria Rilke: Die Aufzeichnungen des Malte Laurids Brigge," in *Das Wagnis der Sprache* (Stuttgart: Klett, 1954), p. 168.

17. *Briefe aus den Jahren, 1914–1921* (Leipzig: Insel, 1937), p. 241. Cf. also *Rainer Maria Rilke et Merline, Correspondence* (Zürich: Niehans, 1954), p. 25.

18. *Rilkes Duineser Elegien* (Bern and Munich: Francke, 1962), p. 88.

19. We remember Rilke's special closeness to the world of Nietzsche's thought through his relationship to Lou Andreas-Salomé.

20. Otto Friedrich Bollnow, *Rilke* (2nd rev. ed., Stuttgart: Kohlhammer, 1956), p. 42.
21. Martin Heidegger, *Sein und Zeit* (11th unrev. ed., Tübingen: Niemeyer, 1967), p. 175.
22. Rilke writes to Witold von Hulewicz, his Polish translator: "Malte is not in vain the grandson of the old Count Brahe who simply assumed everything, past like future, as existing." *Briefe aus Muzot* (Leipzig: Insel, 1935), p. 319.

11

Rilke and the Problem of Poetic Inwardness

RICHARD JAYNE

Rilke's reputation as the poet of "Weltinnenraum" seems in many respects a latter-day variant of German Romanticism. His doctrine of transformation appears to be an attempt to salvage a tradition in poetry that was no longer historically feasible when he set out to transform the visible world into what he called "das Unsichtbare." From a contemporary perspective the approach to Rilke is enormously complicated by the presence of what looks like a secularized metaphysics of poetry lacking any genuine intellectual coherence. Rilke's tendency to use abstract language with distinctly philosophical, theological overtones has caused endless confusion among his critics and has produced the end result of alienating the rational, skeptical reader from a positive evaluation of his poetry. It is now a commonplace of Rilke scholarship that his critics can be divided into those who accept the "message" of the poems as philosophical, theological, or metaphysical doctrine and those who reject Rilke's "Weltanschauung" as essentially false and then either relegate him to the position of a historical anachronism in modern poetry or accept him as a great poet who unfortunately held philosophically or theologically erroneous beliefs. Attempts to view him as a so-called absolute poet in the tradition of the French Symbolists, although they rescue Rilke from the whole problem of the interrelationship between language and belief, fail to demonstrate convincingly that his poems are simply the exposition of an *l'art pour l'art* standpoint. If this were the case the formidable obstacle to a full understanding of his work presented by his elaborate network of statements on the mission of the poet would not exist. The essence of his late poetry cannot be discovered by dismissing the "ideas" as if they were a superaddendum to the "lyrical" structure, because Rilke, like all other poets of rank, engaged in the act of thought, but in that peculiarly complex mode characterized by a dynamic fusion of thought and emotion, idea and image, which distinguishes poetry from other forms of discourse. His late poetry, with its abstract, "ontological" statements, is not to be viewed as a departure from a canonical norm which defines the nature of poetic discourse by reducing it to its "lyrical" essence—such as Staiger's lyrical prototype, the "Lied," derived from German Romantic poetry. It belongs to that order of poetry which seeks to burn away the dross of the empirical world by means of a continuous process of poetization.

The poet Yeats expressed this ultimate aim of poetry in the figure of the poet who, longing to escape from the "sensual music" of earthly existence, beseeches the "sages standing in God's holy fire" to gather him "into the artifice of eternity."[1] Yeats's "artifice of eternity" symbolizes that realm of aesthetic perfection which, in the poem "Byzantium," becomes a "starlit or a moonlit dome which disdains / All that man is, / All mere complexities, / The fury and the mire of human veins." Yeats's images of an aesthetically self-bounded universe may stand for the whole tradition of the Symbolist and post-Symbolist movements which grew out of the secularized theology of German Idealism and the visionary poetry of the Romantics. Poetry from Romanticism to Rilke took upon itself the task of redemption; the work of art was elevated to the status of an autotelic aesthetic entity invested with absolute ontological value. Rilke is the heir of this tradition; he carried to their ultimate consequences the aesthetic doctrines of Symbolism. However, his exploration of the limits of the poetry of "inwardness" links him to the specifically "Romantic" movement inaugurated by Novalis. His late poetry is no longer focused on the aesthetics of the "Kunst-Ding," but on a prophetic vision:

> Erde, ist es nicht dies, was du willst: *unsichtbar*
> in uns erstehn?—Ist es dein Traum nicht,
> einmal unsichtbar zu sein?—Erde! unsichtbar!
> Was, wenn Verwandlung nicht, ist dein drängender Auftrag? [*SW*, I: 720][2]

> Earth, isn't this what you want: to arise
> invisibly in us? Is it not your dream
> to be one day invisible? Earth! invisible!
> What is your urgent command, if not transformation?

The empirical world of the things is to be transformed, or "aufgehoben" (in its threefold sense in Hegel's philosophy: to annul, to preserve, and to transcend), into the inwardness of poetic subjectivity. The doctrine of poetic inwardness ("Nirgends, Geliebte, wird Welt sein, als innen") has its historical antecedent in German Romanticism, whose greatest philosopher, Hegel, anticipated the subsequent evolution of modern poetry toward an increasingly "inward," spiritual quest for the ultimate meaning of existence. For Hegel the quintessence of Romantic poetry, which embraces the entire tradition of European poetry since the end of the classical age of Greek poetry, is its absolute inwardness. The distinction Hegel makes between the "classical" art of ancient Greece and the "Romantic" art of Christian Europe is a remarkably prescient foreshadowing of Rilke's late poetry, as Erich Heller has shown in an essay on Hegel and modern poetry.[3] The basis for the affinity between Hegel and Rilke is Hegel's critical insight into the dialectical movement of the spirit ("Geist"), which is the Hegelian equivalent of poetic inwardness, from the synthesis it achieved with its empirical mode of appearance in classical art to the negation of this synthesis in Romantic art. For "Geist," in its Romantic, postclassical stage, withdraws from the realm of its self-objectification as "äußere Erscheinung" to its own proper sphere. In the section of his *Ästhetik* entitled "Die romantische Kunstform" Hegel defines the ideal of classical art and goes on to state the dialectical necessity for its "Aufhebung":

> . . . the perfection of art reached its peak here precisely because the spiritual was completely drawn through its external appearance; in this beautiful unification it idealized the natural and made it into an adequate embodiment of spirit's own substantial individuality. Therefore classical art became a conceptually adequate representation of the Ideal, the consummation of the realm of beauty. Nothing can be more beautiful. Yet there is something higher than the beautiful appearance of spirit in its immediate sensuous shape, even if this shape be created by spirit as adequate to itself. For this unification, which is achieved in the medium of externality and therefore makes sensuous reality into an appropriate existence (of spirit), nevertheless is once more opposed to the true essence of spirit, with the result that spirit is pushed back into itself out of its reconciliation in the corporeal into a reconciliation of itself within itself.[4]

The movement of "Geist" away from its sensual appearance toward its "Versöhnung seiner in sich selber" is what Hegel calls the fundamental principle of Romantic art, for the "Innigkeit" of "Geist" is a higher end of art than any manifestation of beauty in its classical form. The spirit "only becomes sure of its truth by withdrawing from the external into its own intimacy with itself and positing external reality as an existence inadequate to itself."[5] The spiritualization of beauty in Romantic art, which Hegel designates as a movement from the outer beauty of sensual form to the "spiritual beauty of the absolute inner life as inherently infinite spiritual subjectivity,"[6] although it raises art to a higher level, produces a division between inner and outer worlds which ultimately leads to the dissolution of art: "Thus in romantic art we have two worlds: a spiritual realm, complete in itself, . . . on the other side, the realm of the external as such which, released from its fixedly secure unification with the spirit, now becomes a purely empirical reality by the shape of which the soul is untroubled."[7]

The fundamental paradox in Romantic art is that while empirical reality is used as a means of expressing the "Innigkeit" of the spirit, it is simultaneously reduced to a mere cipher which points beyond itself to the "inner" realm of spirit. In Romantic-Christian art, as Hegel defines it, the empirical must be made transparent; it must always negate itself in order to bring to fulfillment the self-reconciliation of the spirit. This process of spiritualizing art leads to its self-negation at that point when the spirit no longer finds any need for the forms of empirical reality. For according to Hegel's dialectical logic the limitation of art lies in its dependence on the element of form, and, in the Romantic stage of art, the spirit has already passed beyond its *ideal* objectification, thereby anticipating the end of all art. Hegel says that art can no longer fulfill the needs of the modern age, because intellect and reflection, themselves products of the Romantic stage of art, have made art in its ideal, classical form impossible. This leads Hegel to conclude: "In all these respects art, under the aspect of its highest destination, is and remains for us a thing of the past."[8]

The substitution of abstract reason for the immediate perception of truth in the sensual forms of art leads to the alienation of the artist from reality. He finds himself caught up in the "reflexiveness" of the modern age which effectively destroys that primacy of unmediated vision without which great art cannot come into existence. The artist, who already belongs to the past from Hegel's standpoint, exists in a state of alienated consciousness. We find in the works of the German Romantic poets a latent awareness of the precariousness of the union of inner and outer reality in the inwardness of poetry which seems to verify Hegel's statement that art in its postclassical stage cannot overcome the split between spirit and its outward appearance. In a fragment from "Das allgemeine Brouillon," Novalis reflected this split between art and empirical reality by pointing out the curiously ambivalent nature of the "inner" world of poetry in its relation to empirical reality: "The inner world is as it were more than the outer. It is so intimate, so home-like—one would like to live completely in it—it is so familiar and native. It is a pity that it is so dreamlike, so uncertain. Must then of all things the best, the truest appear so apparent ["scheinbar"]—and the apparent so true? What is outside me is precisely in me and vice versa."[9] The Romantic postulate of the "higher" world of the dream, or "Märchen," is, on the one hand, superior to empirical reality, but on the other it is "so dreamlike, so uncertain" and its truth is, from the standpoint of the empirical world, only "apparent."

The passage ends with a reinstatement of the essential identity of inner and outer reality: "What is outside me is precisely in me and vice versa." Although Novalis was aware of the possibility that the "inner" world might be illusory when viewed from the standpoint of the outer world of empirical reality, his belief in the power of the poetic imagination to transfigure reality remained unaffected. In the paralipomena to *Heinrich von Ofterdingen* he states his doctrine of the "poetization of the world" as a prophecy of the triumph of poetry over the empirical, historical world: "At the end the poetization of the world—creation of the fairy-tale world . . . men, animals, plants, stones and stars, flames, tones, colors must at the end speak and act in unison, like a family or society, like a race."[10] According to the eschatological premises of Novalis's poetry, nature and history will be reconciled with man in this visionary state of the apotheosis of poetry or, as he states in the text above, in the "poetization of the world—creation of the fairy-tale world." The poet is empowered to anticipate this apotheosis of poetry by virtue of the uniqueness of his vision. As he is described in *Die Lehrlinge zu Sais*, he is contrasted with other men in terms of his ability to see and hear what does not exist for them. It is the nature of the poet that he sees and hears ". . . what others do not see and hear and [that he] can deal with the real world at will in a state of sweet delirium."[11] The poet is compared to a child who plays with the magic staff of his father and, in the same context, is identified with the figure of Orpheus in the statement "Is it not then true that stones and woods obey music and, tamed by music, submit to every will like domestic animals?"[12] Nature is in harmony with man when viewed from the perspective of the Orphic vision of the poet as magician. Thus Novalis can say that the empirical realm of nature expresses the inner reality of man in the same way as the face and his gestures. A magic correspondence or preestablished harmony exists between the human and the natural world: "Does not all nature as well as the face and gestures, the pulse and colors, express the state of each of those higher, wondrous beings whom we call men? Does not the rock become a peculiar you precisely when I address it? And what am I other than the stream when I wistfully look down into its waves?"[13]

In another section of *Die Lehrlinge zu Sais* the specific quality of Orphic vision is defined from the standpoint of feeling. Novalis introduces the word "feeling" ("Gefühl") as a synonym for poetic perception: ". . . through feeling ["Gefühl"] the old, longed-for time would return; the element of feeling is an inner light which is refracted in more beautiful, deeper colors. Then the stars would rise in him [man], he would learn to feel the whole world more clearly and more diversely—far beyond the horizons and surfaces his naked eye now shows him. . . . Thinking is only a dream of feeling, a feeling which has died away."[14] "Gefühl" is the "inner light" of poetic perception, which sees nature not with the naked eye of the senses, but with the "inner" eye of the soul. Novalis's metaphor of the inner light is taken from the mystical concept of spiritual vision. Moreover, the intellect as the primary means by which man knows reality is subordinated to feeling as a higher mode of cognition. Using an analogical argument, Novalis maintains that the intellect is to feeling as ordinary sense perception is to spiritual vision.

The primacy of spiritual vision culminates in Novalis's categorical distinction between the inner universe discovered by feeling and the merely empirical world. Nature viewed in Orphic terms is in total harmony with man, but in other contexts it becomes an alien realm to be transcended. The outer world is to be negated in order to discover the depths of the human spirit: "We dream of travelling through the cosmos: isn't the cosmos in us? We do not know the depths of our spirit.—The secret path leads inwards. In us or nowhere is eternity with its worlds, the past and the future. The outer world is the shadow world, it casts its shadow on the realm of light."[15] Empirical reality as a "shadow world" is negated by the "cosmos," which is the spiritual universe within man himself. The philosophical background for Novalis's negation of empirical reality and his thesis that eternity is *in us* is the revolutionary concept of the subjectivity of all forms of knowledge, which both Kant and Fichte had made the basis of their epistemology. Kant had argued that we can only know reality as it is presented to us in its phenomenal mode of appearance, that our knowledge of empirical reality is determined not by the things in themselves, but by the *a priori* categories of perception and cognition. The world as it is remains inaccessible to us because we can only know it as it is structured by the *a priori* categories of time, space, and causality. Fichte went even further than Kant in his philosophy of the world-positing ego and virtually denied the existence of any reality not posited by the subjectivity of the ego. These philosophical concepts, which negate the empirical world of nature as an objective reality outside the inner world of human subjectivity, fused with Novalis's Orphic doctrine of the primacy of poetic vision. For Novalis, as for Kant and Fichte, the inwardness of human subjectivity effectively replaces the objective realm of nature.[16] It is only by looking at the world within us that we can understand the real essence of nature: "Why need we wander through the dim world of visible things? The purer world lies in us, in this spring. Here the true meaning of the great, colorful, confused spectacle manifests itself; and when, saturated with these sights, we step into nature, everything is familiar to us and surely we recognize every form."[17]

Novalis's inner light of feeling, his Orphic doctrine of a magic correspondence between man and nature, and his negation of the "dim world of visible things" in favor of the "purer world" that exists in us are elements of a Romantic theory of poetry that seems to be reinstated in Rilke's poetry. The celebrated statement "The secret path leads inwards" ("Nach Innen geht der geheimnisvolle Weg") seems to prefigure Rilke's lines from the seventh Duino elegy:

> Nirgends, Geliebte, wird Welt sein, als innen. Unser
> Leben geht hin mit Verwandlung. Und immer geringer
> schwindet das Außen. . . . [*SW*, I: 711]

> Nowhere, beloved, can world exist but within.
> Life passes in transformation. And, ever diminishing,
> outwardness dwindles. . . .

On a very general level the parallel between Novalis's concept of the "cosmos" that lies in us and Rilke's "Welt" which also exists only "innen" is valid. In both statements the primacy of the inner world of human subjectivity over empirical reality is categorically maintained. However, whereas Novalis negates the empirical realm in order to discover the universe within man, Rilke attempts both to explore the inner universe and simultaneously to affirm empirical reality by transforming it in such a way that it becomes part of this "inner" universe. The theme of the "inner" universe or the inwardness of feeling is dominant in Rilke's late poetry. It is most cogently expressed in the poem "Es winkt zu Fühlung fast aus allen Dingen." This poem may stand as a documentation of Rilke's reinstatement of essentially Romantic ideas concerning the relation of poet and nature or, more precisely, the Romantic notion that inner and outer reality are indistinguishable within the higher order of perception established by the poet. The relation between poet and nature is that of mutual recognition in an undifferentiated state where the self discovers its own image in nature:

Es winkt zu Fühlung fast aus allen Dingen,
aus jeder Wendung weht es her: Gedenk!
Ein Tag, an dem wir fremd vorübergingen,
Entschließt im künftigen sich zum Geschenk.

Wer rechnet unseren Ertrag? Wer trennt
uns von den alten, den vergangnen Jahren?
Was haben wir seit Anbeginn erfahren,
als daß sich eins im anderen erkennt?

Als daß an uns Gleichgültiges erwarmt?
O Haus, o Wiesenhang, o Abendlicht,
auf einmal bringst du's beinah zum Gesicht
und stehst an uns, umarmend und umarmt.

Durch alle Wesen reicht der *eine* Raum:
Weltinnenraum. Die Vögel fliegen still
durch uns hindurch. O, der ich wachsen will
ich seh hinaus, und *in* mir wächst der Baum.

Ich sorge mich, und in mir steht das Haus.
Ich hüte mich, und in mir ist die Hut.
Geliebter, der ich wurde: an mir ruht
der schönen Schöpfung Bild und weint sich aus. [*SW*, II: 92–93]

Everything beckons to us to perceive it,
murmurs at every turn "Remember me!"
A day we passed, too busy to receive it,
will yet unlock us all its treasury.

Who shall compute our harvest? Who shall bar
us from the former years, the long-departed?
What have we learnt from living since we started,
except to find in others what we are?

Except to re-enkindle commonplace?

O house, O sloping field, O setting sun!
Your features form into a face, you run,
you cling to us, returning our embrace!
One space spreads through all creatures equally—
inner-world-space. Birds quietly flying go
flying through us. Oh, I that want to grow,
the tree I look outside at grows in me!
It stands in me, that house I look for still,
in me that shelter I have not possessed.
I, the now well-beloved: on my breast
this fair world's image clings and weeps her fill.

The opening line of the poem introduces the key term "Fühlung"
as a metaphor for the process of mutual recognition between the things
and the poet. Rilke assumes the same magic correspondence between the
inner world of the poet and the outer world of empirical reality that we
have discussed above with reference to Novalis's theory of poetic perception. The lines "Was haben wir seit Anbeginn erfahren, / als daß sich
eins im anderen erkennt?" are remarkably similar to Novalis: "Does not
the rock become a peculiar you precisely when I address it?" However,
Rilke's exposition of the correspondence between inner and outer worlds
is not only predicated on an Orphic vision of nature magically transformed by the poet. It expresses the identity of inner and outer worlds
in terms of a physiognomic perception of reality. The third stanza states
that the self is mirrored in nature as a physiognomically perceived reality.
The things that are indifferent to man become an extension of his world
at that moment when they are perceived in physiognomic terms. Rilke's
"Gesicht" metaphor expresses the essential identity of self and nature
in terms of a perceptual experience that can be defined as mythical. The
"physiognomic" perception of nature, which is thematic throughout
Rilke's poetry, has been explained by Ernst Cassirer as the product of a
mythical mode of consciousness. In the world of mythical consciousness
man did not perceive an object in space subject to the laws of causality
and temporal succession. There was no "object" at the mythical stage of
human consciousness, but only what Cassirer calls the character of things
as pure expression: "The further we pursue perception back to its origin,
all the more does the form of the 'you' in it take precedence over the
form of the 'it'; all the more clearly does its character as pure expression
outweigh its character as object and thing."[18]
The critical distinction between the appearance of phenomena and

their essence, which has become the distinctive feature of modern consciousness, did not exist for man at this stage of consciousness: "Mythical consciousness does not infer essence from appearance, rather it possesses it, it resides in it. The latter does not recede behind appearance, it manifests itself in it."[19] Empirical reality is ". . . not the quintessence of things which are provided with certain 'characteristics' and 'distinguishing features' . . . but rather a multiplicity and abundance of primarily 'physiognomic' characteristics. . . . The world still has a 'face' peculiar to it which is comprehensible at every moment as a totality. . . ."[20]

Cassirer's definition of physiognomic perception provides a useful model in terms of which Rilke's physiognomic metaphor may be understood. One significant aspect of his late poetry is his distinctly physiognomic perception of nature. But the poem cannot be interpreted exclusively as a documentation of Cassirer's mythical consciousness. The physiognomic metaphor introduced in the third stanza is only one phase in the elucidation of the inner realm of consciousness. Stanza four introduces the concept "Weltinnenraum." The poem moves toward an abstract delineation of the relation between the self and nature within the framework of human consciousness. Rilke begins with the statement that all "Wesen" exist within an undifferentiated space: "Durch alle Wesen reicht der *eine* Raum: Weltinnenraum." This appears to be a reformulation in abstract language of the statements made in the opening three stanzas. The abstract term "Weltinnenraum" replaces the concrete metaphor "Gesicht" as a definition of the relation between inner and outer reality. Human consciousness seems to be identical to the unconscious world of the things. In order to make the abstraction "Weltinnenraum" comprehensible, Rilke introduces the image "Die Vögel fliegen still / durch uns hindurch." In such an undifferentiated state subject and object may be said to interpenetrate each other. There are additional texts that further document this suspension of the distance separating the realms of subject and object, inner and outer reality. In a letter of January 14, 1919, Rilke recorded a synthesis of two events, each of which expresses precisely the same convergence of the inner world of consciousness and the outer world of nature which is stated in the poem "Es winkt zu Fühlung fast aus allen Dingen":

> In the poem "Der Tod," however, the moment is finally evoked when . . .
> a star falling in a slow taut arc through cosmic space simultaneously . . .
> fell through inner-space: the dividing contour of the body was no longer
> there. And just as in this case this unity was announced to me through

the eye it had previously been announced to me through the ear: once on the isle of Capri, as I was standing in the garden at night under the olive trees and the cry of a bird, which made me shut my eyes, was at the same time in me and outside as in a single indistinguishable space perfect in its vastness and clarity![21]

One problem in determining the meaning of Rilke's concept "Weltinnenraum" is the extent to which he intended it as a purely "spatial" conception of the structure of consciousness. The poem contains specifically temporal determinations of the relation between the inner world of consciousness and empirical reality. In stanza one the verb "Gedenk" and the lines following suggest that the temporal modes of past and future are embraced by the magic present of "Weltinnenraum." Some scholars have attempted to define "Weltinnenraum" in terms of a specific conception of temporality. Jacob Steiner interprets the temporal references in the opening stanzas of the poem as meaning that the things are transposed into the dimension of

> "Weltinnenraum" in the sense that they are "interiorized" and "remembered" ["erinnert"]: "Weltinnenraum" is not simply a place of refuge from time; rather the latter is preserved in the former in a precise sense. Thus the world can only become transparent after the real encounter in time has preceded it. Like *die Straße von gestern* we are thus left with the past day; reference is made to the past years, to experience from the beginning—in short, the world is only "Weltinnenraum" as interiorized and remembered ["erinnert"].[22]

Steiner's explanation equates the process of "remembering" and "interiorizing." From the standpoint of his interpretation, the process of transposing reality into the terms of "Weltinnenraum" can be understood both spatially and temporally. The things are transposed into the "inner" space which is at the same time a kind of mythical present.

Beginning with the section "O, der ich wachsen will. . . ," a new stage in Rilke's exposition of the inner world of consciousness is introduced. The undifferentiated state of "Weltinnenraum" is examined with respect to the intentional structure of consciousness. The three statements, all of which express the relation between the I and the empirical world, represent a transition toward a purely abstract model of consciousness which clearly goes beyond the statements preceding them. Rilke shows how the abstract concept "Weltinnenraum" can be restated in terms of the intentional acts of consciousness. As Käte Hamburger points out in her essay "Die phänomenologische Struktur der Dichtung

Rilkes,"[23] Rilke poses the question concerning the relation of the ego to what *is* in essentially the same manner as Husserl. For Husserl consciousness is intentional; it creates an object, which is what he calls the "noematic correlate" of the intentional acts of consciousness. Within his system the object is constituted as an entity which is both immanent *and* transcendent with respect to consciousness. Rilke's line "ich seh hinaus, und *in* mir wächst der Baum" exactly parallels Husserl's definition of the manner in which a perceived object is given to consciousness. The ego and the empirical object are placed in a state of mutual recognition by the *intentional act* of consciousness. Rilke sees the image of the tree as being constituted by the act "ich seh hinaus." He insists that the external phenomenon "Baum" can be transformed by an "inner" intentional process, which in this instance is the intentional act: "O, der ich wachsen will." This act reconstitutes the ordinary object "Baum" in such a way that it corresponds to the inner process of "wachsen" as an inner image. The phenomenon "Baum" has been transformed into an inner, dynamic movement or process. Thus the image is no longer identical to the interiorized image of an empirical object presented to consciousness as a mental representation. As the equivalent of an inner process, it ceases to be an image in any conventional sense. This transformation of objects into a dynamic process of motion can be further demonstrated by the text of a letter Rilke wrote to Paula Becker. Here Rilke describes his memory image of a sketch shown to him by the artist. The objects represented in the sketch are figures of girls dancing around a tree. Whereas most observers of the sketch would distinguish between the subject of the dance, the figures of the girls, and the dance itself, Rilke sees these figures as having been transformed into a dynamic process: "Fortunately, I remember the girls dancing around the large tree very precisely. Even before color was added. But already completely finished in terms of movement. I remember almost every single figure (as movement) in this dance which, lightly woven, passed from the hands of joy into those of the wind and now draws shimmering circles around the large quiet trunk."[24]

The next statement "Ich sorge mich, und in mir steht das Haus" does not refer directly to the empirical object "Haus," but makes the existence of this object dependent on a process originating within consciousness. The *act* "Ich sorge mich" takes priority over the object "Haus" so that the latter only *is* insofar as it has been constituted by this act. The third statement: "Ich hüte mich, und in mir ist die Hut" moves one step further from a correlation between the "inner" realm of consciousness and empirical reality by positing the existence of an intentional object of consciousness which has no empirical equivalent. The entity "die Hut" comes into existence as the "noematic correlate" of an intentional act. That is, the act "Ich hüte mich" creates its own object without any reference to the empirical realm. If the analogy between Rilke's statements and Husserl's phenomenological theory of the intentional structure of consciousness is valid, we are justified in saying that the "inner" world of the self, in its intentional acts, knows itself in the act of constituting what Husserl calls the "noematic correlate" of consciousness. Viewed from the perspective of Husserl's theory, the problem of determining how subject and object are related appears to be resolved.

The poem ends with a recapitulation of the state of mutual recognition of poet and world which we attempted to define in terms of a mythical-physiognomic mode of consciousness and perception. In this instance the poet recognizes himself in the image of creation. Rilke uses the device of personification in order to restate the dominant theme of the poem. The "Bild" of creation is conceived of as a person. Moreover, Rilke's use of the word "Bild" suggests that the relation of the inner world of the I and empirical reality is not merely an undifferentiated state, which is the tenor of the first three stanzas, but rather a state in which nature becomes the poet's lover. Here the emphasis seems to have shifted away from the concept of the priority of the I over empirical reality. It is now the image of creation which becomes the active partner in the constitution of the state of "Weltinnenraum."

Rilke's introduction of the term "Bild" may be intended to point beyond the immediate context of the poem. It might be construed to mean that only insofar as the things are transformed into "Bild" do they become part of "Weltinnenraum." Read in this way, the poem is more than an attempt to define the relation between the inner world of consciousness and the outer world of things. It is also a definition of "poesis" as the transposition of the elements of empirical reality (the things in their purely contingent, sensual mode of appearance) into the inwardness of poetry. There are other poems which use the term "Bild" as a synonym for "poesis." For example, the poem "Für Max Picard" states this meaning of "Bild" in the framework of an imaginary situation in which the poet is seen as holding up a mirror to reality:

Da stehen wir mit Spiegeln:
einer dort. . . ., und fangen auf,

und einer da, am Ende nicht verständigt;
auffangend aber und das Bild weither
uns zuerkennend, dieses reine Bild
dem andern reichend aus dem Glanz des Spiegels.
Ballspiel für Götter. Spiegelspiel, in dem
vielleicht drei Bälle, vielleicht neun sich kreuzen . . . [*SW*, II: 255]

And so we stand with mirrors: someone here,
and someone there, with no agreement reached;
but catching, though, and passing the reflection
we've singled out from far, that pure reflection,
on to another from the gleaming mirror.
Ball-game for gods! A mirror-game, in which
three balls, perhaps, perhaps even nine, will cross . . .

The poetic image as presented here is identical to a mirror which captures the true image of reality in a free play with the unknown forces which come to the poet and are transformed by him:

Unsichtbar kommt es durch die Luft, und dennoch
wie ganz der Spiegel ihm begegnet, diesem
(in ihm nur völlig Ankunft) diesem Bild . . . [*SW*, II: 255]

It comes invisibly through the air, and yet
how absolutely the mirror meets it!—this
(only there fully advent), this reflection . . .

The positive resolution of the relation between subject and object or inner and outer reality in "Es winkt zu Fühlung fast aus allen Dingen" represents Rilke's affinity with the tradition of German Romantic poetry. The similarity between this poem and the passages from Novalis quoted above is unmistakable. However, this is only one aspect of Rilke's conception of the nature of inwardness. In other poems he negates the thesis that the self is recognized by nature. The idea that the transposition of the things into the dimension of the poetic image as expressed by the metaphor "der Schöpfung Bild" is the highest form of mutual recognition between poetic inwardness and empirical reality is shown to be an illusion, a misconception of the true nature of reality. Poetic subjectivity, which is seen as in harmony with nature in the context of "Weltinnenraum," is confronted by the problem of transcendence. Hegel's notion that the spirit in its Romantic stage ". . . wird sich seiner Wahrheit nur dadurch gewiß, daß er sich aus dem Äußeren in seine Innigkeit mit sich zurückführt und die äußere Realität als ein ihm nicht adäquates Dasein setzt" is ironically negated by Rilke's discovery that the inadequacy of empirical reality to express the truth of "Geist" or inwardness can be dialectically reversed. In such poems as "Waldteich," "Vor Weihnachten 1914," and in the first, second, and eighth Duino elegies the inwardness of poetic subjectivity, its attempt to project itself into the empirical realm, becomes acutely problematical. A crisis arises out of the failure of consciousness to transcend itself toward the empirical world, which is experienced as a wholly other, transcendent sphere. The poet asks the ultimate question as to whether poetry is a form of transcendence or merely an empty, self-reflexive game the poet plays with himself. The poet as Narcissus confronts the absolute transcendence of the angel.

In the eighth Duino elegy Rilke introduces the theme of consciousness in its relation to nature and uses the term "Schöpfung" in precise analogy to the metaphor "der schönen Schöpfung Bild":

> Der Schöpfung immer zugewendet, sehn
> wir nur auf ihr die Spiegelung des Frein,
> von uns verdunkelt. Oder daß ein Tier,
> ein stummes, aufschaut, ruhig durch uns durch.
> Dieses heißt Schicksal: gegenüber sein
> und nichts als das und immer gegenüber. [*SW*, I: 715]

> Always facing Creation, we perceive there
> only a mirroring of the free and open,
> dimmed by our breath. Or that a dumb brute's calmly
> raising its head to look us through and through.
> For this is destiny: being opposite,
> and nothing else, and always opposite.

Whereas in the "Weltinnenraum" poem Rilke maintains that the poet is embraced by the "Bild" of creation, in this context he reverses his position and makes the reflection of empirical reality in consciousness a negation of the possibility of genuine knowledge of reality in its essence. In contrast to the mutual recognition of poet and nature in the poetic image, Rilke argues that the very structure of our consciousness prevents us from seeing and knowing nature as that dimension beyond the categories of subject and object he calls "das Offene." Consciousness is negatively defined as the state of "Gegenüber sein / und nichts als das und immer gegenüber." Because of our imprisonment within the categories of subject and object we can never see the true image of nature. The symbol of this state of consciousness alienated from reality is the figure of Narcissus, who, instead of reconciling empirical reality to poetic subjectivity, imprisons it within the magic circle of self-reflexive consciousness:

Narziss

Narziss verging. Von seiner Schönheit hob
sich unaufhörlich seines Wesens Nähe,
verdichtet wie der Duft vom Heliotrop.
Ihm aber war gesetzt, daß er sich sähe.

Er liebte, was ihm ausging, wieder ein
und war nicht mehr im offnen Wind enthalten
und schloß entzückt den Umkreis der Gestalten
und hob sich auf und konnte nicht mehr sein. [SW, II: 56]

Narcissus

Narcissus pined. The nearness of his being
kept on evaporating from his beauty
like scent of essenced heliotrope. But, seeing
that just to see himself was all his duty,

he loved back what had been in him before,
reconquered what the open wind had captured,
short-circuited perception, and, enraptured,
cancelled himself, and could exist no more.

The tragic situation of the poet as Narcissus is that he sees only his own image in nature. Rilke uses this traditional motif as a means for stating the limits of poetic subjectivity. The image created by Narcissus is something inert and unrelated to that reality which lies beyond self-reflection:

Was sich dort bildet und mir sicher gleicht
und aufwärts zittert in verweinten Zeichen,
das mochte so in einer Frau vielleicht
innen entstehn; es war nicht zu erreichen,

wie ich danach auch drängend in sie rang.
Jetzt liegt es offen in dem teilnahmslosen
zerstreuten Wasser, und ich darf es lang
anstaunen unter meinem Kranz von Rosen.

Dort ist es nicht geliebt. Dort unten drin
ist nichts, als Gleichmut überstürzter Steine,
und ich kann sehen, wie ich traurig bin.
War dies mein Bild in ihrem Augenscheine? [SW, II: 57]

What forms itself there, and resembles me,
and trembles upwards in a tear-stained sketch,
may at some time, perhaps, have come to be
within a woman, but beyond my stretch,

hard though I struggled for it into her.
Now, in unfeeling water, it exposes
itself completely, and I may confer
with it for hours under my crown of roses.
It is not loved down there. There's nothing there
but pebbles rolling round indifferently.
And I can see my melancholy stare.
Was this the image in her eyes of me?

The projection of the self into empirical reality as expressed in the metaphor of the self-reflected image of Narcissus is negated by the "Gleichmut überstürzter Steine." In the poem "Waldteich" the same problematical relationship between the subjectivity of the poet and the empirical realm is explored. In this poem mediation between the two realms becomes impossible, because the chaos of conflicting impulses within the poet prevents any form of self-objectification:

Soll ich mich des Sturmmeers jetzt entsinnen
oder Bild des Teichs in mir behüten
oder, weil mir beide gleich entrinnen,
Blüten denken—, jenes Gartens Blüten—?
Ach wer kennt, was in ihm überwiegt.
Mildheit? Schrecken? Blicke, Stimmen, Bücher? [*SW*, II: 80]

Oh, which image shall I now retain,
sea at rage or pool at rest within?
Or, since neither will remain,
think of gardens I have wandered in?
Who knows his more prevailing tendency?
Composure? Terror? Faces? Voices? Reading?

The poet admits the total fortuitousness of those images that express the inner world of subjectivity. The poet as Narcissus is in the predicament of art in its Romantic stage, which finds no empirical content that could adequately express subjective inwardness. In this context Hegel provides a pertinent analysis of precisely this predicament: "The true content of romantic art is absolute inwardness, and its corresponding form is spiritual subjectivity with its grasp of its independence and freedom. This inherently infinite and absolutely universal content is the absolute negation of everything particular, the simple unity with itself which has dissipated all external relations. . . ."[25] The essential distinction between the classical and Romantic stages of art lies in the absence of any genuine mediation between the inwardness of the spirit and its objectification in empirical reality in the latter. Rilke compares the situation of the modern, Romantic artist with that of the artist in classical Greece, concluding that the ideal objectification of the inwardness of subjectivity achieved in classical art is no longer possible:

> . . . Denn das eigene Herz übersteigt uns
> noch immer wie jene. Und wir können ihm nicht mehr
> nachschaun in Bilder, die es besänftigen, noch in
> göttliche Körper, in denen es größer sich mäßigt. [*SW*, I: 692]

> . . . For our own heart still transcends us
> even as theirs did. And we can no longer
> gaze after now into pacifying image, or godlike
> body, wherein it achieves a grander restraint.

Because the modern poet can no longer find that ideal content of art that, as Rilke states, was manifested in "Bilder" and in "göttliche Körper," he must renounce his claim to objectify poetic inwardness in images taken from the empirical realm of nature. In the poem "Wendung" (1914) Rilke distinguishes between the kind of poetry which attempts to realize a classical synthesis between subject and object (with reference to the *Neue Gedichte*) and a poetry which comes to terms with the problem of the subject's inability to achieve such a synthesis:

> Denn des Anschauns, siehe, ist eine Grenze.
> Und die geschautere Welt
> will in der Liebe gedeihn.
>
> Werk des Gesichts ist getan,
> tue nun Herz-Werk
> an den Bildern in dir, jenen gefangenen; denn du
> überwältigtest sie: aber nun kennst du sie nicht. [*SW*, II: 83–84]

> For gazing, look, has a limit.
> And the on-gazeder world
> wants to mature in love.
>
> Work of sight is achieved,
> now for some heart-work
> on all those images, prisoned within you; for you
> overcame them, but do not know them as yet.

The images which are "Werk des Gesichts" are imprisoned within the poet's subjectivity. This refers to the problem of aesthetic self-reflexiveness as this is stated in the Narcissus poems. Rilke further explored the limits of aesthetic Narcissism in the poem "Vor Weihnachten 1914." Using his childhood experience of the doll as a point of departure, he reflects on the nature of poetic subjectivity as a process of projecting feeling into the realm of the empirical object. The doll serves as a symbol of an object which has been made into an extension of the inner world of imagination and feeling. Against this background Rilke explores the relation between the aesthetic world of the poem and the empirical world of the object. Art is interpreted as the construction of an artificial world of "Kunst-Dinge" which becomes the model for an assimilation of empirical reality into the aesthetic sphere. In the essay *Puppen* the doll as a symbol for the "Kunst-Ding" is characterized as inferior to the real things, but superior to them as the embodiment of subjective inwardness: "The doll has no imagination and is precisely so much less than a thing as the marionette is more than a thing. But this being-less-than-a-thing, in all its incurability, contains the secret of its superiority" (*SW*, VI: 1069).

Rilke describes the doll as that object by means of which the relationship between the self and empirical reality was first explored with the result of a splitting of the self into two halves: "Confronted with the doll we were compelled to assert ourselves. . . . It did not reply and thus we were put in the position of taking over its work, of splitting our gradually broader being into part and counter-part, of as it were warding off the world . . . through it. . . . it was exceedingly lacking in imagination that our imagination became inexhaustible through it" (*SW*, VI: 1067).

The self which has projected itself into an artificial substitute for a genuine object, which has substituted the doll for the things, creates a world which can be infinitely extended because it encounters no resistance. By splitting the self into "part and counter-part" it produces an artificial universe composed of the aesthetic entities, of the "Kunst-Dinge," which has no counterpart in the empirical realm. The distinction Rilke makes between this artificial world and the actual world rests upon his consciousness of the necessary alienation of the self from the empirical object in order for the aesthetic object to come into existence. It is only because the self enters into an imaginary dialogue with itself, which is in reality pure self-projection, that the construction of the artificial universe of art becomes possible. The implication is that poetry is essentially a monologue which takes the form of dialogue. The doll can stand for the image reflected back to the self; it is virtually identical to the image of the self stated in the Narcissus poems. In "Vor Weihnachten 1914" the doll as a symbol for the aesthetic realm is described as an object whose illusory existence is projected into the things themselves:

. . . Um jeden Gegenstand
nach dem ich griff, war Schein von deinem Scheine,
doch plötzlich ward aus ihm und meiner Hand
ein neues Ding, das bange, fast gemeine
Ding, das besitzen heißt. [SW, II: 96]

There played round every new
object I grasped at something of your light;
yet suddenly from it and my hand grew
another thing, that timid, almost trite,
thing called possessing.

The "Schein" world of the doll is used as a model for the construction of a world enclosed within the circle of aesthetic illusion. Those things which are assimilated into the "Schein" world of art lose their authentic existence and become objects in the negative sense of something possessed:

O wie doch alles, eh ich es berührte,
so rein und leicht in meinem Anschaun lag.
Und wenn es auch zum Eigentum verführte,
noch war es keins. Noch haftete ihm nicht
mein Handeln an; mein Mißverstehn; mein Wollen
es solle etwas sein, was es nicht *war*. [SW, II: 96]

How all, though, till it felt my hand's oppression,
would purely, lightly, in my gaze abide;
and, even if it tempted to possession,
stay unpossessed. Unhampered in those days
by my doing, my mistaking, my unsouling
wish it were something that it could not be.

The paradox expressed in these lines is that only prior to the assimilation of the empirical object into the inner realm of subjective inwardness can a pure relation exist between poet and world. In contrast to the definition of human subjectivity in terms of consciousness given in the poem "Es winkt zu Fühlung . . . ," which makes the existence of the object dependent on an intentional act of consciousness, Rilke says here that it is the very fact of the intentional structure of consciousness that prevents the self from knowing reality. The lines "Noch haftete ihm nicht mein Handeln an; mein Mißverstehn; mein Wollen / es solle etwas sein, was es nicht *war*" reverse the positive definition of consciousness as an intentional process.

In section two of "Vor Weihnachten 1914," Rilke attempts to reinstate the Romantic aesthetics of "Weltinnenraum." Having negated the aesthetic realm as a "Schein" which alienates the self from reality, he now imagines himself in a state of undifferentiated harmony with reality:

> Doch laß durch mich wie durch die Luft den Flug
> der Vögel gehen. Laß mich, wie aus Schatten
> und Wind gemischt, dem schwebenden Bezug
> kühl fühlbar sein . . . . [*SW*, II: 96]

> Through me as through the air let none the less
> birds take their flight. Make me, as though combined
> of wind and shade, to swaying relatedness
> coolly perceptible . . . .

Section three rejects this Romantic state of being in harmony with "dem schwebenden Bezug." The possibility of transcending the closed circle of self-reflexive consciousness by a return of consciousness to an undifferentiated state is revealed as a form of self-deception. The mutual reflection of self and object in "Weltinnenraum" presupposes a harmony which does not exist. The self in its inwardness fails to transcend itself in order to achieve a genuine relation to the real world, which would necessitate the dissolution of its self-created aesthetic universe:

> Auch dieses Fest laß los, mein Herz. Wo sind
> Beweise, daß es dir gehört? Wie Wind
> aufsteht und etwas biegt und etwas drängt,
> so fängt in dir ein Fühlen an und geht
> wohin? drängt was? biegt was? Und drüber übersteht,
> unfühlbar, Welt. Was willst du feiern, wenn
> die Festlichkeit der Engel dir entweicht?
> Was willst du fühlen? Ach, dein Fühlen reicht
> vom Weinenden zum Nicht-mehr-Weinenden.
> Doch drüber sind, unfühlbar, Himmel leicht
> von zahllos Engeln. Dir unfühlbar. [*SW*, II: 97]

> This festival, my heart, relinquish too.
> Where are the proofs that it belongs to you?
> Just as a rising wind will bend and chase,
> some feeling rises up in you to race
> whither? Chase what? Bend what? And beyond feeling
> loom worlds on worlds. What feast would you be keeping,
> so witless of angelic festiveness?
> What would you feel? Your feelings but progress
> from one that weeps to one no longer weeping.
> Above, though, light with angels numberless,
> hangs heaven. For you unfeelable.

The attempt of the self to assimilate empirical reality into the inner sphere of consciousness (Rilke uses the word "Fühlen" as a synonym for the intentional acts of consciousness) is negated by the fact that the empirical world is fundamentally alien to consciousness: "Und drüber übersteht, / unfühlbar, Welt." Moreover, "Welt" is equated with the transcendence of "Himmel leicht / von zahllos Engeln," because both realms remain "unfühlbar," inaccessible to the sphere of consciousness. The juxtaposition of consciousness and the empirical world, as this is presented in section one of the poem, with its contrast between the artificial world of the aesthetic object, the doll, and the genuine empirical object, now appears to take the form of a dialectical relationship between the self and a nonempirical, transcendent order of being. With the introduction of the angels ("Was willst du feiern, wenn die Festlichkeit der Engel dir entweicht?") Rilke redefines the problematical situation with which the poem began. The focus is no longer on the distinction between art and empirical reality, but on the total alienation of the self from an absolute transcendence symbolized by "Himmel leicht von zahllos Engeln."

In order to grasp the intention of Rilke's reference to "Welt" and "Himmel" some consideration of the nature of the transcendence these words stand for is necessary. It is clear that Rilke intends to posit a sphere of being which is not merely a projection of consciousness. However, how can this transcendent sphere be defined? According to the traditional philosophical definition of consciousness, there can be no transcendent ontological sphere outside consciousness since we cannot conceive of such a sphere except in the most hypothetical terms. The only way in which transcendence can be a meaningful ontological concept is if it is defined in terms of the self's knowledge of itself in the ceaseless movement of consciousness toward the limits of reality. In this context the definition of transcendence given by Karl Jaspers provides a useful clarification. Jaspers defines transcendence as a negation of the "tenet of consciousness" ("Satz des Bewußtweins") which says that "Everything which is, insofar as it is present *for me*, must be present for my consciousness, to which it becomes present."[26] Transcendence is a movement of existence toward being which can be defined neither as pure immanence ("In-der-Welt-sein"), nor as pure transcendence in its theological sense of "Außer-der-Welt-sein." It arises out of a consciousness of a possible world of transcendence experienced in what Jaspers calls the "boundaries" ("Grenzen") of existence: ". . . we attempt *to push to the frontiers* which we expect because the world, which does not repose in itself as appearance, is not self-originated."[27] The model

212

for Jaspers's concept of "Grenzen" is not that scientific exploration of reality which expands human knowledge ever further toward an ultimate grasp of the structure of the universe, but an existential process he calls "objectless self-certainty in freedom and unconditionality."[28] Transcendence is the discovery by existence that consciousness is not the whole of reality; that there is a realm lying beyond our conscious knowledge of the world which cannot be comprehended as a datum of consciousness. It can only be defined negatively as the antithesis of consciousness; as the transcendence of the subject-object structure of human knowledge in what Jaspers calls the "disappearing of the object." In one of the critical passages of his *Philosophische Weltorientierung* he defines transcendence as follows:

> Transcendence . . . is not something which is immanent in the object; it arises in the disappearing of the object. For existence comprehends itself not only as incomplete, but also in every form of transcendence it comprehends its *lack of consciousness*. It may be said: presumably all thought arising from possible existence wills its greatest possible expansion as knowledge and imagination, but only so as to be able to destroy itself in the end; consciousness, comprehending itself in its deepest ground, wills its own destruction when the absolute is the transcendent.[29]

Transcendence as a negation of consciousness arises out of that process of the self's total knowledge of itself which is identical to self-annihilation. It is the result of a dialectical movement within consciousness itself: "This process of negating is *dialectical*. . . . Every statement, moreover, erroneously presupposes that the absolute is something existent concerning which something could be said, whether positive or negative; thus it must also annul itself altogether as a statement. . . . This dialectic leads to permanent contradictions. Their resolution would annul transcendence for us."[30]

Jaspers's dialectics of transcendence applies to Rilke's juxtaposition of the inwardness of subjectivity and the realm of transcendence he defines as "Welt" and as "Himmel von zahllos Engeln." The terms Rilke uses for all forms of reality lying beyond the inner reality of consciousness comprise a realm of transcendence. As we have seen, he transposes the problematical relationship of consciousness and empirical reality onto a higher, transcendent plane in the section of the poem which introduces the theme of "Fühlen." Mediation between the inner world of consciousness and the outer world of things is negated by their absolute otherness, by their "Für-sich-sein." Rilke suggests in a late poem dedicated to

Hedwig Zapf that the only escape from the imprisonment of the self in the sphere of consciousness would be to accept the radical otherness of empirical reality:

> Wir wenden uns an das, was uns nicht weiß:
> an Bäume, die uns traumvoll übersteigen,
> an jedes Für-sich-sein, an jedes Schweigen—
> doch grade dadurch schließen wir den Kreis,
> der über alles, was uns nicht gehört,
> zu uns zurück, ein immer Heiles, mündet. [*SW*, II: 235–36]

> We turn to what is ignorant of us:
> to all the dreamfully transcendent trees,
> the self-sufficingnesses, silences—
> completing, though, the mighty circle thus,
> which, over all we can't appropriate,
> runs back into us uncontaminated.

The world as "Für-sich-sein" is described in the poem "Waldteich" as "Erscheinung":

> Oh, ich habe zu der Welt kein Wesen,
> wenn sich nicht da draußen die Erscheinung,
> wie in leichter vorgefaßter Meinung,
> weither heiter in mich freut. [*SW*, II: 81–82]

> Oh, the world's remote from my existence,
> unless all that appearance outside me,
> as though it always meant to be inside me,
> gleams from afar into me gladsomely.

We can contrast this definition of "Welt" with its definition as "Schein von deinem Scheine" in the first section of "Vor Weihnachten 1914." The world which has been reduced to the category of an object or assimilated into the artificial universe of the "Kunst-Ding" is the antithesis of "Erscheinung." For this word expresses a transcendent dimension manifested by the things as they are *for themselves*. Viewed from this perspective, the ordinary objects of empirical reality, those "Bäume, die uns traumvoll übersteigen," are transparent ciphers for the inaccessible realm of transcendence.

The dichotomy between self and "Welt" has as its larger context the relationship between man and the angel in the first and second Duino elegies. Rilke's lament over the inadequacy of "Fühlen" in "Vor Weihnachten 1914" has its origins in the dramatic confrontation between the finite consciousness of man and the infinite consciousness of the angel.

The angel is characterized as infinite consciousness in Rilke's letter to Hulewicz: "The angel of the Elegies is that being which guarantees that the invisible will be recognized as a higher plane of reality. . . .—All the worlds of the universe plunge into the invisible as their next deeper level of reality; a few stars rise immediately and disappear within the *infinite consciousness* [emphasis mine] of the angels."[31] In the first Duino elegy the angel is described as a being who exists beyond the realm of empirical form. What the angel *is* remains inaccessible to man; and if man were to be united with the angel, he would be utterly destroyed:

> Wer, wenn ich schriee, hörte mich denn aus der Engel
> Ordnungen? und gesetzt selbst, es nähme
> einer mich plötzlich ans Herz; ich verginge von seinem
> stärkeren Dasein . . . . [*SW*, I: 685]
> Who, if I cried, would hear me among the angelic
> orders? And even if one of them suddenly
> pressed me against his heart, I should fade in the strength of his
> stronger existence . . . .

What Rilke expresses in the metaphor "und gesetzt selbst, es nähme / einer mich plötzlich ans Herz" is, in abstract philosophical language, what Jaspers means when he speaks of the self-annihilation of consciousness at that ultimate stage when it grasps itself in its essence: ". . . consciousness, comprehending itself in its deepest ground, wills it own destruction when the absolute is the transcendent." If the angel is "infinite consciousness," its union with the finite consciousness of man can only be conceived in negative terms as a destruction of man's existence. The angels exist in a state of absolute self-reflexiveness. They are: "Spiegel: die die entströmte eigene Schönheit / wiederschöpfen zurück in das eigene Antlitz"—"Mirrors, drawing up their own / outstreamed beauty into their faces again" (*SW*, I: 689). Because their consciousness is coextensive with the whole of being, the angels see nothing but the reflected image of their own perfection. At the level of angelic consciousness there can be no dichotomy between subject and object since the two realms are identical. Paradoxically, what constitutes an absolute realm of self-reflexive existence in the case of the angels is a projection of that negative self-reflexiveness which characterizes the poet as Narcissus. Whereas Narcissus "schloß entzückt den Umkreis der Gestalten / und hob sich auf und konnte nicht mehr sein" (*SW*, II: 56), the angel regenerates its image in a continuous process of self-reflection. The imprisonment of the self in the closed circle of aesthetic perfection is transformed into transcendence. The angel as pure self-reflexive existence is essentially identical to the self-contained universe of the "Kunst-Ding": "No matter how great the movement of a work of art may be it must . . . return to it, the great circle must be completed . . ." (*SW*, V: 158).

In the *Duino Elegies* the problem of man's radical transience as compared with the absolute transcendence of the angel is resolved by the doctrine of the transformation of the things into the inwardness of human subjectivity, as stated in the ninth elegy. However, the first and the second elegies, which were written in 1912, do not resolve the dialectical tension between the realms of human and angelic existence. They express the crisis in Rilke's conception of the poet's role during the period 1912–14, and "Vor Weihnachten 1914" is in many respects a restatement of the theme of transience in these opening elegies.

Rilke attempts to solve the problem of the self's alienation from "Welt" and "Himmel" in the passage from section three which begins:

Oh wie dich, Herz, vom ersten Augenblicke
das Übermaß des Daseins übertraf.
Du fühltest auf. Da türmte sich vor dir
zu Fühlendes: ein Ding, zwei Dinge, vier
bereite Dinge. Schönes Lächeln stand
in einem Antlitz. Wie erkannt
sah eine Blume zu dir auf. Da flog
ein Vogel durch dich hin wie durch die Luft. [*SW*, II: 97]

From your first beat, my heart, from your first beat
the excessiveness of being surpassed you so.
You started feeling, there would tower before you
a thing, two things, four things, all ready for you
to feel them. Now a smile materialized
within a face. As it were recognized,
a flower looked up at you. A bird
would take its flight through you as through the air.

We may rightfully question the poetic logic involved in Rilke's shift from the dialectical tension between "Fühlen" and "Welt" to the totally undialectical statement that the "Übermaß des Daseins" is "zu Fühlendes." There is no logical transition between these antithetical definitions of the relation between poetic inwardness and the transcendence of "Welt." A further shift occurs in the closing section of the poem. Rilke constructs an imaginary self-transcendence in the form of a projection of the self into an *unio mystica* with the cosmos. This section reflects the

influence of the cycle of poems *Gedichte an die Nacht* written during
the same period:

> Schwächliches Herz. Was soll ein Herz aus Schwäche?
> Heißt Herz-sein nicht Bewältigung?
> Daß aus dem Tier-Kreis mir mit einem Sprung
> der Steinbock auf mein Herzgebirge spränge.
> Geht nicht durch mich der Sterne Schwung?
> Umfaß ich nicht das weltische Gedränge?
> Was bin ich hier? Was war ich jung? [*SW*, II: 98]

> Weak heart! Can hearts consist with hesitation?
> Is not heart's essence so to domineer
> that from the Zodiac in one career
> the He-Goat onto my heart's crest comes leaping?
> Unless in me the rising stars appear,
> unless through me the crowded world is sweeping,
> why was I young? Why am I here?

This union of self and cosmos, stated in the metaphor of the imaginary
leap of the constellation Capricorn onto the mountains of the heart, is
the dominant theme of *Gedichte an die Nacht*. Rilke explored the possibility of self-transcendence in these poems without achieving any final
resolution.

The problem of assessing Rilke's conception of the relation of inwardness to empirical reality within the framework of transcendence is
perhaps insoluble. Ultimately we are confronted with the fundamental
ambivalence of his poems, which can be defined in aesthetic, existential,
theological, or ontological terms, depending on the bias of the critic.
There is, however, considerable evidence in his poetry that the surface
complexities which allow all of these contexts of interpretation are
grounded in Rilke's supreme belief in art as a mode of transcendence.
Beneath the dialectical tension between the self and the otherness of
reality lies Rilke's aesthetic doctrine of art as self-redemption. The existential dilemma of the "disinherited mind" which is cut off from transcendence is resolved by Rilke's equation—poetry and existence: "Gesang
ist Dasein" (*Sonnets to Orpheus*). This is the most concise formula for
virtually all of Rilke's poetry. It is his aesthetic imperative and represents
the apotheosis of art as religion. The premises of Rilke's aestheticism are
grounded in a radical affirmation of the immanence of reality as a form
of transcendence. This aesthetic doctrine is stated in the ninth elegy in
answer to the question "warum dann / Menschliches müssen—und,

Schicksal vermeidend, / sich sehnen nach Schicksal? . . ." ("oh, why / have to be human and, shunning Destiny, / long for Destiny? . . .").

> Aber weil Hiersein viel ist, und weil uns scheinbar
> alles das Hiesige braucht, dieses Schwindende, das
> seltsam uns angeht. Uns, die Schwindendsten. *Ein* Mal
> jedes, nur *ein* Mal. *Ein* Mal und nichtmehr. Und wir auch
> *ein* Mal. Nie wieder. Aber dieses
> *ein* Mal gewesen zu sein, wenn auch nur *ein* Mal:
> *irdisch* gewesen zu sein, scheint nicht widerrufbar. [*SW*, I: 717]

> But because being here amounts to so much, because all
> this Here and Now, so fleeting, seems to require us and strangely
> concerns us. Us the most fleeting of all. Just once,
> everything, only for once. Once and no more. And we, too,
> once. And never again. But this
> having been once, though only once,
> having been once on earth—can it ever be cancelled?

The transience of existence has become the condition for its transcendence. The paradox of the *Duino Elegies* and of the late poetry as a whole is that Rilke categorically affirms the possibility of transcendence after having shown its virtual impossibility in the face of the total otherness of that absolute realm of transcendence symbolized by the angel. The paradox is formulated in a letter to Ilse Jahr of February 22, 1923, in which Rilke characterizes the transformation of earthly existence into a form of transcendence: "Only to that person for whom the abyss has also become a home will the *heavens sent in advance* [emphasis mine] return and everything deeply and inwardly earthly which the Church has taken away and given to the beyond will return; all the angels will resolve to return singing praises to the earth."[32] The "heavens sent in advance" is Rilke's metaphor for transcendence which, in a dialectical reversal caused by the poetic transfiguration of existence, is assimilated to the realm of pure immanence.

The historical background for Rilke's radical attempt to redeem the earth, to transform empirical reality into the inwardness of poetry, is the loss of transcendence occasioned by the death of God. Rilke shared with Nietzsche the "disinherited" situation of the writer who no longer believes in the validity of a traditional body of ideas concerning the nature of human existence. Like Nietzsche, he sought to re-ground man's existence by proclaiming the right of poetry to become a legitimate substitute for religious belief. The aesthetic mode of existence had to be made an equivalent to those Christian ideas which no longer appeared tenable to the skeptical minds of Rilke and Nietzsche. Erich Heller has characterized the spiritual crisis of Rilke and Nietzsche as an attempt to reinstate transcendence after having accepted the terrible consequences of the death of God:

> The enormous complexity of their works must not deceive us; the structure behind it is consistently simple; it has the simplicity of that immense single-mindedness with which they . . . dedicated their lives to the one task: to re-assess and re-define all experience in thought and feeling; to show that the traditional modes of thought and feeling, in so far as they were determined, or decisively modified, by Christian transcendental beliefs . . . had been rendered invalid by the end of religion; to replace them; to overcome the great spiritual depression, caused by the death of God, through new and ever greater powers of glory and praise; to adjust, indeed to revolutionize, thought and feeling in accordance with the reality of the world of absolute immanence; and to achieve this without any loss of spiritual grandeur.[33]

Rilke's aestheticism is, then, the instrument by means of which the spiritual value of existence, which had been posited in the realm of an otherworldly transcendence by Christian theology, thereby resulting in a despiritualization of existence, is to be re-created. Rilke set out to disprove Hegel's assertion that art no longer speaks to us as an ideal, transcendent medium of the truth of spirit. He attempted to realize the "poetization" of existence which had been proclaimed as the ultimate historical-eschatological goal of poetry by Novalis. However, despite the resemblances between Rilke and his Romantic predecessor Novalis, there is a major difference between their respective historical positions. Novalis wrote in an age when the secularized theology of German Idealism provided a philosophical framework within which poetry could rise to previously inconceivable heights. Rilke's position is that of the disinherited mind confronted by a substantial loss of reality caused by the total disintegration of "that reservoir of fundamental intellectual certainties . . . from which the poetic impulse must be sustained if it is not to be in danger of breaking under a burden too heavy for its delicate constitution," as Erich Heller states.[34]

We have seen in the analysis of the problem of poetic inwardness that Rilke was far from consistent in his attempt to define how the self, abandoned by the certainties of those transcendental ideas provided by Christian dogma, is to accomplish the superhuman task of restoring to

219

the empirical world the ontological value it has lost in the modern age. His poems represent experiments in the resolution of the problem of inwardness in its potentially alienated relation to reality. Some of these, such as the "Weltinnenraum" poem, appear highly questionable when set in relation to those poems in which Rilke reflects on the limits of inwardness. In such poems as "Vor Weihnachten 1914," in the first and second Duino elegies, as well as in the *Gedichte an die Nacht*, the harmonious unity of poetic subjectivity and the empirical-transcendent world (the realms of "Welt" and "Himmel leicht / von zahllos Engeln") is not taken for granted. Here a countermovement sets in which dialectically negates the claim of the self to extend itself into the domain of the things. In these poems there are signs of a profound spiritual crisis in Rilke which cannot be ignored by pointing to the doctrines of "Weltinnenraum" and "Verwandlung." Art is not interpreted as a transfiguration of existence. The poet views himself not as the rival of the angel, which is the position taken in the seventh and ninth elegies, but as the fabricator of aesthetic illusion. Art as "Schein" does not fit into the doctrine of "Weltinnenraum," because Rilke became painfully conscious of the possibility that his art might be nothing more than the emptiness of a self-infatuated aestheticism. Measured against the aesthetic doctrines of the *Duino Elegies* and his self-interpretations in the letters, the poems themselves remain experiments doomed to failure. What Rilke actually wrote was poetry *in extremis* in that he was compelled to create the spiritual conditions for the existence of poetry in a sustained effort to redeem its subject matter, the elements of empirical reality, in an age which denies to poetic inwardness its claim to speak the language of truth.

NOTES

This essay appeared previously in German as "Rilke und das Problem der Innerlichkeit," in *Rezeption der deutschen Gegenwartsliteratur im Ausland*, ed. Dietrich Papenfuss and Jürgen Söring (Stuttgart: Kohlhammer, 1976), pp. 309–27. Reprinted by permission of the publisher.

1. W. B. Yeats, *The Collected Poems* (London: Macmillan and Co., 1952), pp. 217–18.

2. Rainer Maria Rilke, *Sämtliche Werke*, ed. Ernst Zinn (Wiesbaden: Insel, 1955–66). (All references to Rilke, *Sämtliche Werke*, are cited as *SW*.) The

translation of Rilke's *Duino Elegies* used is taken from R. M. Rilke, *Duino Elegies*, trans. J. B. Leishman and Stephen Spender (New York: Norton, 1963). All other translations of Rilke's poems are taken from R. M. Rilke, *Poems, 1906 to 1926*, trans. J. B. Leishman (London: Hogarth, 1957). The translations of his prose texts are my own. Unless otherwise indicated all other translations of German texts are mine.

3. See Erich Heller, *Die Reise der Kunst ins Innere* (Frankfurt am Main: Suhrkamp, 1966), pp. 123–98.

4. Hegel, *Ästhetik*, ed. Friedrich Bassenge (Frankfurt am Main: Europäische Verlagsanstalt, 1966), I: 498–99. The English text of Hegel's *Aesthetics* is from the translation of T. M. Knox (Oxford: Clarendon Press, 1975), pp. 517–18.

5. Ibid., p. 518.

6. Ibid., p. 518.

7. Ibid., p. 527.

8. *Aesthetics*, p. 22.

9. Novalis, *Schriften*, ed. Richard Samuel, Hans-Joachim Mähl, and Gerhard Schulz (Darmstadt: Wissenschaftliche Buchgesellschaft, 1960–1968), III: 376–77.

10. *Schriften*, I: 347.

11. Ibid., p. 100.

12. Ibid., p. 100.

13. Ibid., p. 100.

14. Ibid., p. 96.

15. *Schriften*, II: 417.

16. See Hugo Kuhn, "Poetische Synthesis oder ein kritischer Versuch über romantische Philosophie und Poesie aus Novalis' Fragmenten," in *Wege der Forschung*, vol. 248 (*Novalis*), ed. Gerhard Schulz (Darmstadt: Wissenschaftliche Buchgesellschaft, 1970), pp. 203–59.

17. *Schriften*, I: 89–90.

18. Ernst Cassirer, *Philosophie der symbolischen Formen* (Berlin: B. Cassirer, 1923–29), III: 74.

19. Ibid., p. 79.

20. Ibid., p. 80.

21. Rilke, *Briefe*, ed. Karl Altheim (Wiesbaden: Insel, 1950), II: 120.

22. *Rilkes Duineser Elegien*, 2nd ed. (Bern and Munich: Francke, 1969), pp. 24–25. See also Beda Allemann, *Zeit und Figur beim späten Rilke* (Pfullingen: Günther Neske, 1961), pp. 18–19.

23. See *Rilke in neuer Sicht*, ed. Käte Hamburger (Stuttgart: Kohlhammer, 1971), p. 123.

24. Rilke, *Gesammelte Briefe*, ed. Ruth Sieber-Rilke and C. Sieber (Leipzig: Insel, 1930–37), I: 151–52.

25. *Aesthetics*, p. 519.

26. *Philosophie* (Berlin: Julius Springer, 1932), I: 45.

27. Ibid., p. 50.

28. Ibid., p. 51.
29. Ibid., p. 51.
30. Ibid., pp. 51–52.
31. Rilke, *Briefe*, II: 484–85.
32. Rilke, *Briefe aus Muzot*, ed. Ruth Sieber-Rilke and C. Sieber (Leipzig: Insel, 1937), p. 186.
33. Erich Heller, *The Disinherited Mind*, 4th ed. (London: Bowes & Bowes, 1975), pp. 159–60.
34. Ibid., p. 153.

12

Rilke's and Walter Benjamin's Conceptions of Rescue and Liberation

ANDRAS SANDOR

I

Walter Benjamin's conception of rescue, or rescuing ("Rettung"), was central to his thinking. It might even be said that it formed the very center of his preoccupation with questions literary, social, philosophical, and historical alike.[1] The word does not appear in his theses "Über den Begriff der Geschichte," but it well expresses its messianistic message. The historical materialist, he says in Thesis XVII, is involved in a struggle for the liberation of the oppressed past. The Jews were forbidden to inquire into the future but were instructed in remembering: "This broke for them the magic spell of the future to which all those fall victim who turn to soothsayers for information" (Thesis VII). "Remembrance," then, is the act by which the oppressed past is rescued and liberated. In English one may say that to remember means to make something torn into the past a member again of present time, to re-member it with present-time. He who remembers is the Messiah of people and things of the past; "present-time" is fulfilled time: it is time fulfilled by the act of rescue. This conception of rescue and liberation is based on Benjamin's contention, expressed in Thesis VIII, that the historical world is a continuous disaster: "The tradition of the oppressed teaches us that the 'state of emergency' in which we live is regular."[2] The temporal world, the world of measurable time and space, is oppressive, negative; it is to be broken open, in order to free all those people, experiences, and things which have been trapped in it.[3]

223

Rilke held a basically similar view of the historically and socially given world. In a letter of August 8, 1903, to Lou Andreas-Salomé, he said: "Things are definite, things of art must be even more definite. Being removed from all contingencies, being placed beyond all ambiguity, having been lifted out of time and having been given to space, they have come to be lasting, capable of eternity. Models *seem*, things of art *are*."[4] This was written between the two volumes of *Das Buch der Bilder* (1902 and 1906) and about six months before he began to write *Die Aufzeichnungen des Malte Laurids Brigge* (1904–1910), which deals mainly with the idea and the problem of rescue. Malte's vision of the world closely resembles the one just presented; it is a world of measurable time and space, of constant manipulation and abuse, of oppression. It is a world in which both things and humans are abused to the point of losing their being. Only animals appear to be immune. "The things have been watching it [the abuse] for centuries. Small wonder that they are corrupt and have lost their taste for their natural and quiet ends; that they would like to exploit existence ["Dasein"] the way they see it exploited around themselves. They make attempts to avoid being used."[5] At another place, Malte speaks of the terrible time which "absent-minded sleepy things were having." They broke easily, "because these things, spoilt as they were, could not bear any kind of fall" (116–17). Malte himself is one of these absent-minded, sleepy, and spoilt things; his notebook records his intended self-awakening and his attempt to rescue, indeed to recapture, his own very being which he feels he has largely lost. Malte tries to do this by writing; and even if he does not think of writing a literary work, Rilke did and was trying to solve with it his own problems.[6] Rilke's novel deals with the rescuing of things, of a human being, and of a literary work.

The rescuing is done by the "saint" who carries out his task by throwing his "glance" at things (279). "Seeing" them, he brings their "image" into himself, but this self is not a particular social being's self. The saint frees the things from the uses to which they have been put, that is, he liberates them as pure things, things in themselves; and he does this by producing an "image." He transforms, in fact re-forms, "things" into "images." "To see" means, therefore, "to restore being." Individuals, too, are things and can be rescued the same way. Malte writes of Bettina Brentano: "You *were* just now, Betinne; I see you into myself" (297). This is an odd way of using the verb "to see, to comprehend, to realize ["einsehen"]" but Rilke's Malte uses the verb, which means both "to imagine" and "to be conceited ["sich einbilden"]," in a similarly odd fashion: "Abelone, I conceive, you are there" (229). And Malte tries to undertake a similar rescue operation when he conceives that he is the Prodigal Son, and, as Ziolkowski has pointed out,[7] tries to rescue himself, his very being, by turning himself into a third person, into an image.

"Image" for Rilke in *Die Aufzeichnungen* is "timeless" (254); it connotes "being" (297), and a totality ("Vollzähligkeit") from which nothing is missing (123). It is a clearly Platonic concept: "image" means "idea." Besides Bergson and Mallarmé, another probable source for Rilke was Pater, whose book *The Renaissance* he highly praised in a review in 1902. Platonistic is the dualism of measurable time-and-space and timeless space, although we must note that Plato was at least equivocal about the world of generation, the world of measurable time and space. Rilke's unequivocal stance was bound to lead to an uncompromising rejection of the world of measurable time and space, that is, the historically determined world. Malte notes that the world of antiquity was a perfect sphere, but that this "complete realization" was merely a "simile" ("Gleichnis"): a "massive planet which, having lost its weight, ascended into space; and the sorrow over that which has not yet been mastered was reticently reflected in its golden curve" (329). This "sorrow," or "mourning," is the same idea and the same word ("Trauer") which dominates Benjamin's book on Baroque drama: it is a sorrowful mourning of that which has not been rescued and is still trapped in the historical world of generation.

In the *Duineser Elegien*, too, Rilke introduces the word "rescue" in an analogous context. "Praise the world to the angel," he says in the ninth elegy. "Show him that which is simple . . . And these things, which live by departing, understand that you are praising them. Perishable (as they are), they trust that we, who are most perishable, have the power to rescue" ("traun sie ein Rettendes uns zu"). We are reminded here of the saint from *The Notebooks* who has cast his glance (279). But this time the act of "saying," not of "seeing," is the highest human act of rescuing things.

"Glance" and "image" appear as insufficient in the *Elegien*; "speaking" supersedes "seeing," and, by the same token, "sorrow" is superseded by "lament" ("Klage"). "Lament," too, is a term used by Benjamin, and it is used by him in his later works.[8] Sorrow arises from seeing the image of the dead; lamenting breaks that image and transcends it. Benjamin's "remembrance" was conceived as "lament," not as "sorrow," which he associated both in the book on Baroque drama and in the essay "Über den Begriff der Geschichte" with indolence, *acedia*.

II

There are very few references to Rilke in Benjamin's writings. His letter to Rilke (July 3, 1925) contains little information.[9] Rilke was supposed to translate Saint-John Perse's *Anabasis*, but he withdrew and, on the suggestion of Hofmannsthal, recommended Benjamin to the publisher. Benjamin enclosed seven translated chapters with his letter and asked Rilke for a critical comment. He also promised Rilke a copy of his essay on Goethe's *Elective Affinities*.

More important than this letter is a short note, written in Moscow in 1927, in which Benjamin attacked Franz Blei for his speech at Rilke's burial. Blei was critical and condescending; Benjamin considered such an attitude both in bad taste and of ill judgment. For although Rilke, in his view, "could never quite master his own corrosive inwardness" ("verwesende Innerlichkeit"), and "the harvest among the pages diminished with each subsequent raid through his work," still, he produced some exquisite poems, which affected a whole generation, and thus he did not deserve ungratefulness. He was a true sufferer; his weaknesses were those of his generation.[10] We learn from this note that Benjamin knew Rilke's work, and that he cherished poems like "L'Ange du Méridien" and "Archaïscher Torso Apollos"; but we do not learn whether he even read *Die Aufzeichnungen* and the *Elegien*. It seems that he preferred the *Neue Gedichte* to Rilke's later work. At the same time, Benjamin's praise for "L'Ange du Méridien" is noteworthy, especially if one is to consider this poem as the prefiguration of the angel in the *Elegien*.[11]

A third document to consider is a letter to Carla Seligson on August 4, 1913. Benjamin speaks in it about "loneliness" ("Einsamkeit") and contends that "a person can only be really lonely in a community, indeed in the closest community of believers; in a loneliness in which one opposes one's self [Ich] against the Idea, in order to reach oneself. Do you know Rilke's 'Jeremia': it is beautifully said there." Benjamin adds: "The deepest loneliness is that of the ideal human being in his relationship to the Idea which annihilates his humanness. And we can only expect such a deeper loneliness from a perfect community." He concludes: "By wishing to rid ourselves, individuals, of the loneliness among human beings, we bequeath / transmit ["vererben"] our solitude to the many who had not known it. And we learn about a new loneliness, that of a very small community before its Idea."[12]

Benjamin speaks here in fact of three different conceptions of loneliness, of the loneliness one feels in a society which does not make a community, that is to say, which is not formed by an Idea; of the loneliness which one feels in a perfect community; and of the loneliness which one feels in anticipation of such a community. There can be no question that Benjamin himself suffered from the first kind—Paris offered him a nearly identical experience as to Rilke—and that he hoped to experience the third kind. It is equally beyond doubt that the conception of loneliness and the word "loneliness" are central to *Die Aufzeichnungen,* and it is more than probable that he encountered both there. For in *Die Aufzeichnungen* the saint is called again and again the lonely one; he is lonely on account of his "labor" ("Arbeit"), which is his road to God (279). Malte tries to be such a saint. Only "the real" matters to him; and he notes: "My God, if only it could be shared. But would it *be* in that case, would it *be?* No, it only *is* at the price of solitude" (176).

All in all, the evidence of Rilke's influence on Benjamin is not conclusive in itself, especially since they shared the same ancestors, first of all Baudelaire and Nietzsche. It is at the same time undeniable that there are significant correspondences between key terms and conceptions, just as it is undeniable that Benjamin read Rilke and not conversely. "Rescue" and "loneliness" can be supplemented by "angel," "puppet," "image," "story telling" ("Erzählen"), and "experience" ("Erfahrung"); and although there were, of course, others who made use of these terms, there hardly was another who used them all and, what is more, used them in an obvious relationship to the conception of rescue. This is the term that in fact forces one to think of an influence, and, what matters much more, to compare their thoughts and attitudes to one another. The pointing out of an influence of one person on another only makes sense if it sheds more light on either or both; and a mere comparison, no doubt, can serve the same purpose.

Benjamin's interpretation of "loneliness" corresponds to Malte's, and to the later Rilke's; but it also suggests a certain difference. Loneliness for Rilke was a personal affair in which only two parties were involved, an individual and God or an angel. Benjamin, however, reckoned with a plurality of lonelinesses both as the cause of the bad kind and the source of the good one. "The lover is always superior to the beloved one, because life is greater than destiny," said Malte (299). Rilke retained the second half of the sentence in the *Elegien*, but replaced the first half: "the loving ones hold each other" (tenth elegy). Benjamin, it seems, never thought that the beloved was inferior to the lover; but, to vary Rilke's phrase, he held that the loving ones held each other by emphasizing the distance between themselves: love could only be consummated by being consumed. The meaning of this discrepancy will be clearer after the discrepancies between Rilke's and Benjamin's conceptions of "puppet," "angel," and "image" have been discussed.

III

The puppet or doll ("Puppe") is introduced in the fourth elegy. It is necessary, however, first to have a look at Rilke's article "Some Reflections on Dolls," published in *Die weißen Blätter* in 1913/14, a year and a half before the fourth elegy was written (November, 1915). The article was occasioned by an exhibition of wax dolls, and Rilke's associations center mostly around children's dolls.

Rilke places the doll between the marionette and the "thing": "A poet might succumb to the domination of a marionette, for the marionette has only imagination. The doll has none, and is precisely so much less than a thing as the marionette is more. But this being-less-than-a-thing, in its utter irremediability, is the secret of its superiority."[13] Dolls are completely passive, "allowing themselves to *be dreamed*" and "to be lived unwearyingly with energies not their own" (44). They share this silence and passivity with destiny and even God who both "have become famous above all because they answer us with silence." The dolls had already performed the dubious service of preparing the child for adult experience "at a time when everyone was still intent on giving us a quick and reassuring answer." Malte said in *The Notebooks* that life was larger than destiny; but here we read that silence is larger than life: "The doll was the first to inflict on us that tremendous silence (larger than life) which was later to come to us repeatedly out of space, whenever we approached the frontiers of our existence" (46). Kleist entitled his famous essay "Über das Marionettentheater," but the popular name of this institution, the name commonly used by children, is "puppet stage" or "puppet show." Rilke reassesses in the fourth elegy the childhood experience by considering not its possible failure, but its possible, if approximate, success. In the article, the encounter with dolls taught the child the first lessons of the failure of adult life in a world emptied of God and order; the

228

fourth elegy, by contrast, shows that the encounter with puppets teaches the child the first lessons of a possible, if incomplete, redemption of adult life. Rilke did not consider it a real rescue.

Benjamin, too, had an article on puppets, "In Praise of Puppets." It was a review of Max V. Boehn's book *Puppen und Puppenspiele* and was published in 1930. Benjamin criticizes Boehn who, in his view, does have some knowledge of "the globe of puppets, love and play," but who does not really know the spirit of either playing or love, the latter of which he treats under the name "puppet-fetishism."[14] He says in the article that Kleist's essay on the marionette theater presents "an unforgettable image" of how "the marionette confronts God, with man helplessly hanging between the two in his reflective confines" (215). If "things" needed a glance and a vision to rescue them from the usages to which they have been put on the one hand, and from the destruction by time on the other, man equally needed a glance and a vision to rescue him from his reflective confines. He had to be made a puppet, but a God was needed for this task, and, as already young Benjamin noted, a community of believers was needed to have a god.

It has puzzled some why Benjamin associated in Thesis I of "Über den Begriff der Geschichte" historical materialism with a puppet.[15] The mystery, it is hoped, can be cleared up now. The puppet this time is an automaton; and if Benjamin had been reminded at the time of the article "In Praise of Puppets" of Hoffmann's Olympia, he seems to have been reminded at the time of his theses on history of Hoffmann's Talking Turk (from the short story "The Automaton"). Benjamin, in other words, must have had the very same automaton in mind, which had already served Hoffmann's purposes, Kempelen's chess-player, which was dressed as a Turk and was reputed to be animated by a hidden dwarf. This dwarf, Benjamin says, was an excellent chess-player and controlled the puppet with cords. Benjamin's message is: "The puppet called 'historical materialism' should always win. It can challenge anybody without any difficulty, provided it employs theology which these days, as is known, is small and ugly, and which anyway must not show itself." The paradox of Benjamin's allegory is disguised. We are made to think of the puppet and the dwarf hidden in it, although we should, of course, think of the puppet and those who play with it. The paradox consists in the circumstance that the player wins if he is defeated. (This paradox, by the way, strongly suggests that Benjamin must have been thinking of Hoffmann's Talking Turk.) He wins if he can activate the puppet properly; if he can play with it truly, with love; if he can rescue historical materialism by imparting to it his own hidden power which is the power of present-time, of a love (universal *eros*) which alone can disrupt the inevitability of the historical process.[16] The successful player who can force the dwarf called theology to move the puppet is analogous to the successful spectator of the puppet-show in Rilke's fourth elegy who can force the angel to appear and to bring about an approximately pure process. Rescuing, however, is not carried out by either that angel or the dwarf; it has another agent with both Rilke and Benjamin.

IV

The agent of rescue is paradoxical with Rilke and ambiguous with Benjamin; what they offer us is problematic. Understandably, since to name the agent means, at least in one of its aspects, not merely to say how synthetic judgments *a priori* are possible (Kant), but also how synthetic judgments *a priori* can coincide with liberation, that is, a rescue which is not a new entrapment. Nobody has been able to give an answer to this combination of questions to general satisfaction, and Rilke's and Benjamin's attempts must be judged with this situation in mind.

Rilke's angel in the *Elegien* is connected with rescuing in the ninth elegy where the rescue is carried out while the angel listens. The actual agent is the speaker, a human being, but he would not speak to himself. (Only the angels are content with self-mirroring.) We have, in other words, one agent and yet two.

This paradoxical situation is prefigured in the fourth elegy where no real rescue is achieved. The visionary spectator forces the angel to appear and to participate, but the moment the angel appears the spectator ceases to be active and the angel comes to be the agent: "Angel and puppet: it finally comes to a performance." Spectator and angel meet and part on a demarcation line; they stay on either side of it. In the ninth elegy, where rescue finally commences, the paradox is fully developed. The speaker addresses an angel that merely listens, but this listening apparently is a constitutive part of the speech. We have no reason to question the identity of the angel in the *Elegien*, it must be the same angel in different situations. The inactive angel of the ninth elegy, therefore, must be the terrible angel of the first two elegies who provokes Rilke to speak. He calls and lures ("Lockruf," first elegy) "the nearly lethal birds of the soul" (second elegy), because, we must assume, he knows about them. The angels provoke him by their existence to break out of himself, to speak; and this provoking, in a way, is action, although it is none. Rilke's inactive angel from the *Elegien* resembles his earlier angel from the poem "Der Engel" who "breaks you out of your form," but the breaking is done in the *Elegien* by the speaker; the angel merely provokes and listens. There is no way to reduce this dualism of speaker and angel, of activity and inactivity, and one is left with the paradox that the two are one, the passive angel is aggressive. This paradox is present in the human agent himself: he is human by fulfilling his humanity, which is self-transcendence.

Benjamin's rescuing, too, is connected with an inactive-yet-active angel, the helpless angel of history, described in Thesis IX of "Über den Begriff der Geschichte" on the basis of Klee's picture "Angelus Novus." The angel faces the world and sees "a single catastrophe piling incessantly ruins upon ruins, and hurling them to his feet. He would like to stay, to awaken the dead, and to fit together what has been broken to pieces. But a strong wind blows from paradise and is so powerfully caught in his wings that he cannot close them. The storm irresistibly forces him into the future, on which his back is turned, while the pile of ruins grows to heaven. What we call progress is this storm." In Benjamin's view, the revolutionary act consists in breaking out of this storm. For the angel of history is helpless; more helpless than the angel summoned to control the puppets in Rilke's fourth elegy. The angel there obeys the bidding of the spectator, whereas Benjamin's angel of history obeys some stronger, nonhuman power, and the rescuer's task is to defy this stronger power. The inactivity of the helpless angel resembles the inactivity of the angel that listens in the ninth elegy, in spite of the obvious differences; for it is equally provocative.

Benjamin's revolutionary rescuer is human, as is Rilke's, but in his essay on Karl Kraus he likens him to the very same angel of Klee's picture: "One must have seen . . . Klee's 'New Angel,' who would liberate people by taking from them rather than make them happy by giving them, in order to grasp a humanity which proves itself against destruction." This new angel is not the angel of history, but an angel that makes the escape from history possible:

> Not purity and sacrifice have mastered the daemon; but its rule is over whenever origin and destruction meet. The one who conquers it faces it as a creature comprised of a child and a man-eater: not a new man, but a monster [human and inhuman: "Unmensch"], a new angel. One of

those, perhaps, who, according to the Talmud, are created new in innumerable hosts at every instant, so as to grow silent and pass into nothingness after they have raised their voice before God. In lament, to accuse, or in jubilation? It is all the same.[17]

Benjamin was not inconsistent in using Klee's angel twice. The helpless angel of history, who merely would like to rescue, and the perishing angel of humanity, who does the rescue, belong together. It is an ambiguous situation. For the power driving the angel of history comes from paradise, and the power in the rescuer, too, must come from the same source: his act of rescue is messianistic. By forcing the angel of history to fly into the future, the wind from paradise enables the rescuer, who stares into his own image in the angel of history, to interrupt also his own flight by breaking out of it for quiet moments, short spans of quietude.[18]

Benjamin's agent of rescue is ambiguous rather than paradoxical. The circumstance that Klee's angel is both the helpless angel of history and the perishing angel of humanity merely helps us notice that paradise makes the rescue both necessary and possible. This ambiguity is inherent both in the rescuer and in the rescue. He rescues by perishing, and the thing rescued perishes itself. Present-time is a discontinuous quantum. The paradox that the player wins if he is defeated must be reinterpreted in the ambiguity that the player wins while he is being defeated. Benjamin combines in a single instance that which Rilke divided and left on the two sides of the demarcation line of rescue, aggressiveness and peace. Benjamin's message was in part: "messianistic quietening," "quietude," and in part: "The determined and seemingly brutal grip belongs to the image of rescue."[19] Benjamin, by the way, has as little room for a creative God as Rilke, but he at least suggests his reasons for such an omission: "The average European is unable to unite his life with technology [or technique] because he has held on to the fetish of creative existence ["schöpferisches Dasein"]."[20]

Benjamin's perishing agent, who represents a humanity that asserts itself by effacing itself, very closely resembles Rilke's speaker from the ninth elegy, who stands for self-transcending humanity. Both of them rescue by speaking out before a listener who is of a higher stature. There are two differences, however. Benjamin's listener is God, for whom he fails to account. If this was his reason for omitting the perishing angel from "Über den Begriff der Geschichte," he achieved little. For he equally failed to give an account of paradise, its wind, and the angel of history.

This is a fundamental defect of his scheme. Rilke's listener is the angel, although Rilke knows of gods. Rilke's rescuer, in other words, does not speak out before the highest powers whose role remains completely undefined in the *Elegien*. This is their major defect. Secondly, Benjamin combines rescuing and perishing, whereas Rilke merely notes that the rescuer is "most perishable." It may even be said that Rilke contrasts with one another the permanence of rescue and the transience of the rescuer. (At the time of his book on Baroque drama, Benjamin still shared a view similar to Rilke's but later he moved away from it.) Whereas pure, timeless space is a continuous realm of being for Rilke, and a thing can be transposed there for good, Benjamin's spaceless present-time is a discontinuous realm of being. Both of them inadvertently suggest that there could be a more powerful agent of rescue, but they fail either to consider him or to stop suggesting such a possibility.

V

It has been mentioned at the outset that "image" was Rilke's means and product of rescue in *Die Aufzeichnungen*. Rescuing was done by "seeing" and by "recounting" the full-countable image. Rilke's aim at that time was to make the invisible visible.[21] The book ended in an impasse because Malte could not complete his own full-countable image all by himself. In the *Elegien* seeing is retained, in connection with the more dynamic conception of "play," but it is assigned to the angel, not to man; for seeing is a thing not of the earth ("kein hier Ereignetes," ninth elegy). Rescuing now is attributed to man and is carried out by "saying," which in this way replaces both "seeing" and "recounting." Rilke's aim has changed to making the visible invisible.[22]

Rilke bids himself in the ninth elegy to address the angel—"Say the things to him"—because the things want to be transformed "within the invisible heart," and "into us," humans. What should be said is "action without image" ("Tun ohne Bild"), something supra-countable: "supra-countable existence springs up in my heart" ("überzähliges Dasein"). But this transcendence of visible things into an invisible existence is also a self-transcendence of the human heart: "our heart transcends us. . . . And we can no longer follow it with images" (second elegy). The supra-countable existence is also that of man. Man rescues himself by rescuing the things—that is, by making them his. Human self-transcendence, this particular human quality not shared by the more perfect angels, is being established in and by the act of rescue.

In the invisible context, past and future, dead predecessors and unborn descendants, childhood and old age to come, all coalesce, and Rilke's message this time is that this coalescence begins here on earth. "Here" is a key term in the *Elegien*; it corresponds to Benjamin's "now." Rilke wrote in his letter on the *Elegien*: "We from here and of today, are not satisfied in the world of time for a moment, nor are we tied to it; we continuously transcend to the earlier ones, to our origins, and to those who seemingly follow us. In that largest *'open'* world, all of them *are*, one cannot say 'simultaneously,' since exactly the disappearance of time entails it that they all *are*. Transience everywhere plunges into a profound being."[23] Rilke introduces the idea that the dead must be really dead, in order to be rescuable, to *be*. They must be "infinitely dead," in the words of the tenth elegy. This reminds one of Benjamin's later assertions that the rescue can only be accomplished by perceiving that which is being lost irretrievably (cf. p. 226). In the ninth elegy, Rilke says that the earth wants to be invisible, and he pledges to help its transfiguration. This pledge is paradoxical. Loyalty to a thing consists in changing it; changing it means completing it; and completing it means to make it more than it is.

Obviously, Rilke associated no conception of image with rescue by "saying." Supra-countable existence is not an image. Still, he conceived the transcendence from the visible into the invisible as a process simple rather than complex. The paradox that his two agents of rescue were one can also be defined—now that the demarcation line between spectator and angel is known to be Rilke's "here"—as the paradox that a thing rescued is the same thing on either side of the demarcation line as well as on it. It retains its own identity, although in an enriched form. Supra-countable existence may be said, therefore, to be the form in which the full-countable image appears when leaving the terrestrial context. A thing only appears full-countable in the angelic context of pure space, in "the other context" ("der andere Bezug," ninth elegy).

Benjamin's rescue in his book on Baroque drama was carried out by the establishment of the origin and the idea of a particular thing. "Origin" meant for Benjamin the prehistory and the posthistory of a thing, its natural-historical quality, its being part of the world of generation. "Origin" ("Ursprung") means not a single fixed source, but the process by which a thing has come about; it might be called "originality."[24] (This is how the title of the book must be understood: *The Origin of German Tragedy* purports to discover, not the sources from which German Baroque tragedy sprang, but what it was like. The book is a rescue attempt.) "Idea" meant for Benjamin that the originality of a thing was shown as a totality, and thus as rescued. He called ideas "monads," representative parts of the world of ideas.[25] Later, Benjamin introduced the conception of "dialectic image" as the means and the product of rescue. This change resulted from his conversion to historical materialism, which forced him to abandon his formerly idealistic position of the existence of a world of ideas. His "dialectic image" more or less corresponds to his former conception of "origin"; it combines prehistory and posthistory, or an earlier and a future period, in a discontinuous flash of present-time that replaces the former continuum of ideas.

For the later Benjamin, as for the earlier Rilke, the "image" constitutes the act of rescue; he is not ready to accept that the visible world must change into an invisible one. But his conception of image had to include the transcendence of the later Rilke's "supra-countable existence" or "saying"; it had to include action and two images. Accordingly, his dialectic image was complex. We can read in the essay "Paris—Die Hauptstadt des XIX. Jahrhunderts" that the images produced in a given period contain in part the vision of the subsequent period and in part certain elements of the vision of primordial times, of the times of classless society. These are images in which the old and the new mingle; they are "wishful images" ("Wunschbilder").[26] "Ambiguity is the imaginal appearance of dialectic; the law of dialectic is quietude. This quietude is utopia, and the dialectic image, therefore, is a dream image."[27] One should add to this the fragment from the collection of fragments published under the title *Zentralpark*: "The dialectic image is a flash. In this way, as an image flashing up in the Now of cognizability, it is to be captured as an image of something past ["des Gewesenen"], in this case as that of Baudelaire. The rescue accomplished this way, and this way alone, can only be carried out by perceiving that which is being lost irretrievably."[28] Thesis V of "Über den Begriff der Geschichte" says the same, but says it of historical events in general: "The true image of the past rushes by. The past can only be arrested ["festhalten"] as an image which flashes up in the second of its cognizability, so as not to be seen again."

"Wishful image" is the same name that Benjamin applied to the puppet that was being loved (cf. p. 229). That love did not rescue the beloved one; and it did not really rescue, therefore, the lover either. Benjamin thought to solve the problem when he conceived that the wishful image of the dialectic image, which united rescuer and thing to be rescued, was an instantaneous act, flaring up in a unique flash of present-time. It was the instantaneousness of the act that rescued the thing in question from the entrapment in some continuous state of alleged liberation. Benjamin would have found heaven just as oppressive as Shaw's Don Giovanni found it at about the same time.

Benjamin distinguished in his book on Baroque drama allegoric image from symbolic image, the latter of which in his view suggested a "false appearance of totality."[29] This distinction was based on that between symbolic dialectic, which is that of essence and appearance,[30] and allegoric dialectic, which is that of being and meaning.[31] The symbolic image presenting a symbolic totality is deceitful in his view in suggesting a self-contained whole. It is the form of myth which, too, is deceitful in suggesting timelessness in time, the suspension of historical time within the historically given world. The allegoric image presents the dualism of an insufficient, limited being and a reflection upon it, pointing to a beyond. Such an allegoric image, the totality of the emblem, only exists in the flash of the vision, or rather of the experience in which thing and reflection, image and notion meet to point to a beyond. It is easy to see that the allegoric image so conceived holds out the hope of rescue rather than carries it out. It has sufficient power to show that a thing is in need of rescue, but it lacks the power to rescue it. The symbolic image, by contrast, rescues the thing but rescues it in the form in which it appears; this means that it entraps the thing in this form for good. Rilke and Benjamin may be said to have been at one in trying to produce images that were neither allegoric nor symbolic, that is to say, which did rescue things but rescued them without accepting the contemporary world in its social-historical manifestation.

Rilke's full-countable image, to be conceived in the angelic context of pure space, and its terrestrial form, supra-countable existence, are a conception that is neither allegoric nor symbolic. Since the angel is at home in "that largest 'open' world," the saying that introduces things to him opens them up; it is a productive process in which a thing is enlarged, opened into its own full notional quality, which includes its death. ("Notional" is to be conceived in the realist rather than in the nominalist tradition.) This activity does not connect an image with a meaning, which would mean to produce an allegory, or establish the essence within an appearance, which would mean to produce a symbol; it develops a notion out of a thing.[32] The command from the ninth elegy—"Say the things to him"—should be complemented with the command from *Die Sonette an Orpheus*—"Know the image." It must be *known*, because the voice can only be eternal in the double context:

Mag auch die Spieglung im Teich
oft uns verschwimmen:
Wisse das Bild.

Erst in dem Doppelbereich
werden die Stimmen
ewig und mild.[33]

Though the reflection in the pool
often swims before our eyes:
Know the image.

Only in the dual realm
do voices become
eternal and mild.

If the dilemma posed for us in Plato's *Timaeus* is how the world of generation can be an imitation of the world of being, the dilemma to which Rilke has treated us seems to be the opposite, how the world of being can be an imitation of the world of generation. But in fact the dilemma is different. For "to say the things," this act of rescue, is not imitation, it is not re-presentation, but presentation: "to say in such a way as the things inwardly never meant to be" (ninth elegy). Completing a thing, to repeat, means to make it more than it is by adding to it its non-being, death.

Whether or not such a notional image is a trick is the same question whether or not Rilke's angel is trick, and it cannot be discussed here.[34] At any rate, it has been the intended formula of much of twentieth-century poetry. According to Rilke's intentions, lovers holding each other, thing and man, were one, although they could only be one by leaving the terrestrial context in self-transcendence.

Benjamin's dialectic image is an equally well-known twentieth-century attempt to veer clear between symbolic image and allegoric image; it is metaphoric blending, montage, in which two distinct components are forced to be one. Benjamin's lovers hold each other by distance. His dialectic image, too, has been called a trick, but this question cannot be discussed here either.[35] Many a twentieth-century poet has tried to rescue poetry by a similar method, but the existence of certain concatenations of words is by itself no proof. The meaningless generosities of language are as much a fact as are its limitations.

VI

Rilke's notional image ("to say the things" and "to know the image") and Benjamin's "dialectic image" are attempts to get at grips with the same problem, but Benjamin tried to unite by distance that which Rilke identified on the one hand and kept apart on the other. Rilke did not want to conceive of the pure action of the speech, the "saying," as a complexity produced in part by the historically determined mind of the spectator and speaker, because he believed he was able to liberate himself from historical determinations. He did not feel obliged to get involved with the problems that troubled Benjamin. He does not seem to have realized that Malte could only choose his *oppressive* disguises from the garments and masks available to him, and that he, Rilke, too, could only choose his own *liberating* disguises, such as "angel" and "space," from an equally determined storage room. But even if he realized it, the most he could do was to refrain from speaking about rescue when he distributed in the fourth elegy the production of the pure process of the puppet-show between the human spectator and the angel, itself a notional image. But, in the ninth elegy—where the speech produced the speaker no less than the speaker produced the speech—the speaker, although seemingly alone responsible for the speech, was fully dependent on a listener, the angel, who himself had to be conceived. The exchange of seeing for saying did not alter the fact that the speaker, too, confronted an angel, an image and notion which he was *not* constituting by the very same act of saying. If Benjamin landed himself in, perhaps, empty ambiguities and in incoherence, Rilke seems to have been entrapped in paradoxes and in solipsism.[36]

Rilke's rescue by continuous space is as problematic as Benjamin's rescue by discontinuous quanta of present-time. Rilke could only conceive of his own plan by discarding the notion of time altogether; Benjamin, by discarding the notion of space altogether. Since Rilke's "space" is a notion corresponding to Bergson's *durée*, a conception of absolute time, the polarization between Rilke and Benjamin, "space" and "time," "here" and "now," is indicative of their different conceptions of the sphere of being to which it was their common intention to rescue things. Whether continuous or discontinuous, this sphere of being was equally essential to both of them. Benjamin's conception of "recounting" ("Erzählen"), which in his view has become impossible, does not differ at all from Malte's conception by the same name; and his conception of "experience," which "recounting" should impart to others, too, repeats Malte's conception by the same name. Both Rilke and Benjamin abandoned "recounting" and replaced it each with his own conception of rescue. The problem with the thought of both Rilke and Benjamin lies in this replacement. If earlier people still could tell a story—that is, recount an experience and impart it to others—the historical world cannot be the same homogeneous continuum of entrapment, and the possible liberation from it, too, must be different at different times.

This criticism can also be formulated this way. The conception of liberation as "rescue" is fundamentally defensive; it is a conception in which matters are counteracted and rectified, whereas the liberation that both Rilke and Benjamin had in mind can only be brought about by an offensive, a power that can constitute a world. They, too, did not quite have such a power, the power to associate with others. Rilke did not want to be a social revolutionary, but he might have been a religious one, a man with a community. This he could do, however, as little as Benjamin. The later Benjamin, with all his unquestionably activist, social, and revolutionary tendencies, did not really transcend Rilke's basically defensive attitude. Indeed, the later Rilke, in a fantastic-imaginary and paradoxical way, succeeded in ridding himself of it to a larger extent than the later Benjamin whose attachment to historical materialism and the revolutionary proletariat was and remained ambiguous.

Rilke, after all, was an odd kind of prophet, and Benjamin was an odd kind of revolutionary Marxist.[37] A religious person can believe in a hidden god, and in a hidden community. But a prophet, the man with a real power of rescue, must know both; he must be able to confront them. He cannot have his God and his community replaced by angels. And a historical materialist, and a Marxist revolutionary, can hardly find himself musing, however refreshing it may affect us to hear: "Marx says that revolutions are the engines of world history. But it is, perhaps, quite otherwise. Revolutions, perhaps, are grasps at the emergency brake by mankind travelling on the train."[38] Benjamin's preoccupation with theology, on the other hand, did not take him further either. He could be a prophet no more than Rilke; the prophet-rescuer he approximated was of Rilke's kind rather than Jewish.[39] Our image of Benjamin is bound to remain an image of his own making, a dialectic image, in which, however, the faith of the man will never come for us to a rest, to quietude; only his effort will. The same is true of Rilke.

NOTES

1. Cf. Rolf Tiedemann, *Studien zur Philosophie Walter Benjamins, Mit einer Vorrede von Theodor W. Adorno* (Frankfurt am Main: Suhrkamp, 1975), p. 112. Cf. also Jürgen Habermas, "Bewußtmachende oder rettende Kritik: die Aktualität Walter Benjamins," in *Zur Aktualität Walter Benjamins*, ed. Siegfried Unseld (Frankfurt am Main: Suhrkamp, 1972), pp. 175–223.

2. Walter Benjamin, *Gesammelte Schriften* (Frankfurt am Main: Suhrkamp, 1974), I/2: 693–704. The title of this work earlier was "Theses on the Philosophy of History," which, however, is not genuine. Cf. the editor's note in *Gesammelte Schriften*, I/3: 1254—further referred to in text by the number of the theses.

3. Walter Benjamin, *Ursprung des deutschen Trauerspiels* (Frankfurt am Main: Suhrkamp, 1963), pp. 55–56 and 60–66.

4. Rainer Maria Rilke, *Briefe* (Wiesbaden: Insel, 1950), I: 55.

5. Rainer Maria Rilke, *Werke in drei Bänden* (Frankfurt am Main: Insel, 1966), p. 277. Further references are by page number in the text. The last sentence is a reference to "the malice of objects," a phrase set in currency by Vischer's novel.

6. Rilke, *Briefe*, I: 324–29.

7. Theodore Ziolkowski, *Dimensions of the Modern Novel: German Texts and European Contexts* (Princeton: Princeton University Press, 1969), pp. 3–36.

8. *Gesammelte Schriften*, I/3: 1231.

9. Walter Benjamin, *Briefe*, ed. Gershom Scholem and Theodor W. Adorno (Frankfurt am Main: Suhrkamp, 1966), I: 390f.

10. *Gesammelte Schriften* (Frankfurt am Main: Suhrkamp, 1972), IV/1: 453.

11. For this view, cf. Käte Hamburger, "Die phänomenologische Struktur von Rilkes Dichtung," in *Rilke in neuer Sicht*, ed. Käte Hamburger (Stuttgart: Kohlhammer, 1971), p. 120.

12. *Briefe*, I: 85f.

13. Rainer Maria Rilke, *Selected Works*, trans. G. Craig Houston, with an introduction by J. B. Leishman (New York: Hogarth, 1967), I: 47. Further references are by page number in the text. Cf. Anthony Stephens, "Rilkes Essay 'Puppen' und das Problem des geteilten Ich," in *Rilke in neuer Sicht*, p. 168. Stephens considers the article only and says that its negative assessment of the experience with dolls counterbalances Rilke's conception of "world-space," which he conceived at about the same time. Stephens repeats this point by analyzing the doll's soul in his " 'Puppenseele' and 'Weltinnenraum,' " *Seminar*, vol. 6, no. 1 (March, 1970).

14. *Gesammelte. Schriften* (Frankfurt am Main: Suhrkamp, 1972), III: 214, further referred to by page number in the text.

15. Cf. Tiedemann, p. 119; Gerhard Kaiser, "Walter Benjamins 'Geschichtsphilosophische Thesen,' Zur Kontroverse der Benjamin-Interpreten," *Deutsche Vierteljahrsschrift* 46(1972): 586. Further references are given by Kaiser.

16. Kaiser (p. 586) does not know of Benjamin's article "In Praise of Puppets" and misses the point about the paradoxical quality of the puppet. While at the beginning of his article Kaiser says that the puppet with the dwarf is "the real and true" historical materialism (p. 586), at the end he says it is "the true theology" (p. 624).

17. *Illuminationen*, p. 407f. Cf. the lines from *Die Aufzeichnungen* (p. 313) in which Pope John XXII "had prescribed for himself and those around him the *angelus* against the daemons of twilight."

18. Kaiser, p. 603, mentions both angels, but he does not relate them to one another. His interpretation that the historian sees only the angel of history, whereas the angel saw god (p. 598), is a good point and emphasizes the analogy to Rilke's speaker in the ninth elegy; but Kaiser does not realize that the speech of the historians, if it rescues anything, means a breaking away from the angel of history and the activating of the angels that perish after they have raised their voice.

19. *Illuminationen*, p. 257.

20. Ibid., p. 407.

21. Rilke, *Briefe*, I: 498.

22. Ibid., II: 482. Curiously enough, Rilke still spoke of making things visible, however impossible the task had come to be, shortly before completing the *Elegien*; cf. *Briefe*, II: 298.

23. Ibid., II: 481–2.

24. *Ursprung*, p. 29f.

25. Ibid., p. 32. On p. 31 we are told that a thing in its idea is a totality, and that "That is its Platonic 'rescue.' "

26. Ibid., p. 187.

27. Ibid., p. 196.

28. Ibid., p. 261.

29. *Ursprung*, p. 195.

30. Ibid., p. 175.

31. Ibid., p. 182.

32. Hamburger, *Rilke in neuer Sicht*, p. 102, says that Rilke dealt with "things," not "symbols," but she may have been more unequivocal in this question. For this is but the other side of her basic contention that Rilke was a phenomenologist, not a metaphysician. Cf. ibid., p. 147f: "For this poet is a phenomenologist, not a metaphysician."

33. R. M. Rilke, *Sonnets to Orpheus* (New York: Norton, 1942), pp. 32–33.

34. Hamburger, *Rilke in neuer Sicht*, p. 121f, criticizes Rilke's conception of "angel" as mere invention. Her more or less rhetorical question whether the combination of the angel with the puppet in the fourth elegy shows their common origin, however, should be answered in the negative. There is no sign that Rilke realized that his "angel" was an "image." His explanations to Hulewicz, it seems to me, in disagreement to Käte Hamburger, do fit the angel of the ninth elegy, so far as Rilke's intentions were concerned. Stephens, too, speaks of the insufficiency of the solutions found by Rilke, op. cit., p. 170.

35. Tiedemann, *Studien,* p. 129.
36. Stephen speaks of a "quasi-solipsism" in a different context, cf. his essay in *Rilke in neuer Sicht,* p. 168.
37. Cf. Habermas, in *Zur Aktualität,* p. 207. Habermas argues that Benjamin's attempt to unite historical materialism and the "messianistic conception of history" did not succeed; the idea that it did "was Benjamin's mistake, and the wish of his Marxist friends." Ibid., p. 206. Gerhard Kaiser, who obviously could not have read Habermas's article, which appeared the same year, comes to a basically similar conclusion, although he tries to be less critical towards Benjamin and covers a different and smaller ground (see p. 624 of his article on Benjamin). His conclusion is that theology and class struggle are equally indispensable constituents of Benjamin's thinking and intention.
38. *Gesammelte Schriften,* I/3: p. 1232.
39. The religious and Jewish aspect has been emphasized by many; Kaiser is one of the last in the line.

13

R. M. Rilke's Dreams and
His Conception of Dream

ERICH SIMENAUER

I

The symbolism of dreams is an essential characteristic of the *condito humana*. The dream is almost as important for human existence as speech. The features of the dream and of speech are determined by the different organizational forms of the unconscious and conscious thought processes. Symbolization and speech can be understood to stand in a dialectical relationship to one another according to their origins. It is of utmost significance that the language of dream speaks out so distinctly in Rilke's writing.

The intimate permeation of his works and thoughts with dream creations may well be explained by the fact that he was a prodigious dreamer, one who, at times, even felt himself to be afflicted by his dreams. Dream events simultaneously preoccupied and disturbed him. One should recall the larger historical and literary framework in which these phenomena are imbedded, as well as the place which the dream occupies in human history. In particular, one should consider the dreams and the dream productions of other writers and the influence that they exerted on Rilke. He always tended to incorporate his own feelings and thoughts in the depicted dreams and dream-like events of others. These, above all, claim our interest in this investigation of Rilke's dreams and of dream production in his works.

His conception of the dream is like an echo of diverse ideas about dreams from different epochs up until modern notions and the psychoanalytical theory of dreams. In this discussion paraphrases of Rilke's dream thoughts will be given in common psychoanalytical terminology. However, an attempt will also be made to trace these dream thoughts to their subconscious sources and motives. Insofar as basic psychoanalytical interpretations are profiled in this manner, the question as to the legitimacy of the applied method naturally arises, since, conceived as it is as a part of the analytical process in the dual physician-analysand relationship, it is based on the free associations (and their processing) of the latter. However, sometimes even under optimal conditions—that is, in the clinical doctor-patient situation—the work of interpretation must go on without the help of the dreamer's associations, because they cannot be made by him. Stekel, a pioneer in symbolic interpretation, was convinced that he would never have learned of certain connections "just from what had occurred to the dreamer."[1] Freud, who had recognized the significance of dream symbolism from the beginning, came to a full appreciation of its extent only through Stekel and, at that, gradually.[2]

For our purposes Freud's views are particularly meaningful:

> . . . since the relationship between a symbol and the idea symbolized is an invariable one, the latter being, as it were, a translation of the former, symbolism in some measure realizes the ideal of both ancient and popular dream-interpretation, one from which we had moved very far in our technique. Symbols make it possible for us in certain circumstances to interpret a dream without questioning the dreamer, who, after all, can tell us nothing about the symbols. If we know the symbols commonly appearing in dreams as well as the personality of the dreamer, the conditions under which he lives, and the impressions in his mind after which his dream occurred, we are often in a position to interpret it at once, to translate it at sight.[3]

This applies above all to the study of historical personalities, from whom the information of random thoughts and associations is not available. It lends the validity we seek for symbolic interpretation of the arts. In Freud's *Traumdeutung* there are many such interpretations.[4] He did not hesitate to present a psychological explanation for the well-known dream of writer Peter Rosegger in this manner.[5] For other authors, too, he approved such a procedure. We may refer in particular to his endorsement of an analysis by O. Rank, entitled "A Dream that Interprets Itself,"[6] although the interpretation, carried out in detail, ensued "to a considerable extent without the aid of the dreamer."[7]

There is much that allows us to interpret Rilke's dreams. There are the testimonies of Rilke's contemporaries, who deserve our respect through their own cultural achievements. Above all, however, there are his own statements concerning himself and his intellectual world. These are minutely detailed descriptions of his experiences, aspirations, and fantasies concerning the way in which the world was reflected in a thousand facets in his views and emotional states, all set down in his diaries and in an almost overwhelming abundance of letters. All of these allow us to make statements concerning the dreams and dream visions intimately linked with them through motif. In addition, he wrote a little-known *Traumbuch*.[8]

Does, however, the license to symbolically interpret actual dreams also extend to literary dreams? If one is mindful of the conditions of the "Traumarbeit," of the transformation of the psychic material in the dreamed dreams, as well as of the psychological peculiarities of dream, and of activity of the fantasy in its development and of the relationship to other psychic accomplishments, including those which are culturally valuable, one will not be surprised to learn that fictional dreams follow the same rules as do naturally occurring ones. They, too, may be subjected to an interpretation in the same manner.[9] Whether we like it or not, writers make use of dream psychology in their work, usually without knowing it. Literary dreams also disclose their hidden meanings, albeit outside the strict frame of reference of the classical analytical situation. The ubiquity and universal validity of dream symbolism make this possible. With its help an investigation of the surface of the psychic mechanisms can penetrate deep into the structure, functions, and contents of the personality.

II

Anyone writing about Lessing would have to do without this interpretation. According to his own admission, Lessing never dreamed.[10] On the other hand, Robert Louis Stevenson maintained that most of his themes were presented to him in his dreams. He saw himself as a remarkable dreamer and speaks of the "dream factory" that his "little people" ran. He describes a process in which he, the writer, dozed away in his "box seat" while his "little people" did his work.[11]

And Rilke? He was such a strong dreamer that at times he suffered most deeply under the frequency and influences of his dream visions and felt himself to be helplessly at their mercy. His existential real dreams, not those directly shared in his writings, he entrusted to his closest friends.

In her book on Rilke, Lou Andreas-Salomé mentions one of his boyhood dreams and subjects it to interpretation. The boy René dreamed amid shudders of terror that he was lying next to an open tomb, into which a tall gravestone standing right before him threatened to push him at the slightest movement. This dream rightfully reminds Lou Andreas-Salomé of certain dream fears of boys at the time of puberty, or "das Miteinander von Erleiden und Vergewaltigen" in a "Gefühl von beirrender Doppelgeschlechtlichkeit."[12] This nightmare returned to Rilke from time to time, pointing to the fact that the emotional conflict leading to the release from fear was by no means ended when he reached physical maturity. I have tried to show elsewhere what a strong role bisexuality played in Rilke's psyche; it was not unlike that of the mythological Narcissus in Pausanias's version.[13] The elements of this bisexuality, which occurs in certain parts of his work, are in agreement with the interpretation that Salomé had given Rilke's dream. She reports three further dreams of Rilke's from the year 1913. They seem to be incompletely reported, and the interpretative discussion is fragmentary. From her words, however, it follows that we have lost no new viewpoint, since she writes: "This is especially reminiscent . . . of the nightmare of childhood about the gravestone next to the grave opening at which Rilke saw himself lying."[14]

Except for this dream, and one recorded by the Princess of Thurn und Taxis, which we shall examine later, we find hardly another mention of specific dreams over a period of three decades. Since Rilke was otherwise hardly reticent concerning his experiences and sufferings, it is possible that he wished to avoid having a dream symbol "key" applied to himself, since his reluctance to be subjected to biographical—much less psychological—examination is well known. He even wants to set up a taboo, in order to protect himself against that.[15] This attitude indicates that dreams are not a matter of indifference to him, not merely froth and tricks of the imagination, but meaningful and of deep significance. Quite early (1899), he was conscious that the content of dream speech is not directly accessible to the waking reason:

Vielleicht, daß Etwas bald geschieht,
das du im Traum begreifst.[16]

Something perhaps will happen soon
that you will understand in a dream.

In his sense of mission as a poet he must have perceived this expectation as a challenge, as if here a possible handhold were opening up for his

246

endeavor to express the inexpressible. About the same time, Ewald Tragy hears from the befriended writer Herr von Kranz: "Splendid . . . really splendid! You should express this in verse, it's worth while. This altogether your personal idiom—."[17] Although one may expect no systematic discussion of this problem by Rilke, nor find one in his scattered meditations, a progressive development in his views of dreams can be established. Hieatt's remarks concerning a just evaluation of dream psychology among nineteenth-century English poets are also valid in regard to the young Rilke's approach: "I do not mean to imply a full-blown post-Freudian system of dream interpretation, but, simply, those facts about the way dreams work which are readily observable by any human being who takes interest in the matter. The main reason why modern analyses of dream psychology are convincing is the plain fact that they are in accordance with what we all know from our own experience, if we have given that experience any thought. . . ."[18]

The young Rilke's deliberations about dreams, and the knowledge he derives from them, must be understood. The following thoughts are stimulated through his reading of Maeterlinck's "Tod des Tintagiles":

> We have learned from dreams that feelings are great and spacious. Under the protection of sleep actions occur that one would expect to find in separate areas of feeling and that could be reflected in reality only after the locality of action had been changed. But in a dream everything occurs in one scene, a single feeling seems to expand as a sky and remain, at times cloudy, at times clear, stretched curved above all occurrences, even if these may be strange and lost in this atmosphere. Thus, for example, out of fear one becomes acquainted with worldly joys and moments of happiness that seem very touching in their naïve vulnerability, in the manner of children and girls who visit lions with smiles and affection . . . This great fear [i.e., of Maeterlinck's play] . . . appears to be eternal in contrast to the occurrences. . . .[19]

Here we find (still purely descriptively) important elements of the dream event. The apparently irrational and illogical elements are reproduced through the confrontation with that which would have to occur naturally and in reality—that is, according to the understanding of waking reason, strengthened through the reference to that incomprehensible behavior "of children and girls." Like an underground rumble of fate's great powers, the world of fear ("aus Angst") may already be sensed in the dreams, the "große, graue Angst," which plays such an important and frequent role. Rilke wrote these sentences in November, 1900, at about the same time that Freud's *Die Traumdeutung* and *Über den Traum* appeared, and they almost read like an intuitive introduction to their causal-genetic linking of dream and subconscious psychic activity—although the assumption that he knew *Die Traumdeutung* that early is highly unlikely. It would hardly have made any difference, for it would be an unfortunate misjudgment to assume that the poet treated results of scientific observation in his works. Freud came, by the evaluation of the poetic process of creation, to the conclusion ". . . that the poet need not know anything about such rules and motivations so that he could renounce them with good conscience [as Wilhelm Jensen had done to Freud]; nevertheless, everything in his works is consistent with these rules and motivations." Freud finds the difference of the methods of the psychoanalyst and the poet in the fact that the former applies the conscious observation of abnormal mental processes of others in order to be able to guess and pronounce their laws.

> The poet, to be sure, uses a different approach; he focuses on the unconscious of his own soul, perceiving its potentialities and granting them artistic expression rather than suppressing them with criticism. Thus, he learns from himself what we learn from others, which laws the activity of the unconscious must obey, but he need not articulate these laws nor be entirely aware of them; they are contained in his creative works because his mind tolerates them.[20]

Around the same time that Rilke portrays dream feelings on the basis of "Tod des Tintagiles," he describes the peculiar state in which his own dreams held him prisoner for a long time. "Perhaps it is not a good thing that you pay so much attention to your dreams. You often awake with difficulty and live the entire forenoon looking backwards. . . . Only now that I know how much I love this state of being I realize its great danger."[21]

Some years later, in anticipation of the ominous "Fluten der Herkunft" in the *Duino Elegies*, the unconscious processes of dreams are given expression in *Buch der Bilder*:

> drin träumt das Weinen der Weiber,
> drin rührt sich im Schlafe der Groll
> ganzer Geschlechter . . .[22]

> therein dreams the weeping of women,
> therein stirs in its sleep the anger
> of entire races . . .

In the play *Weiße Fürstin*, Rilke describes other peculiarities of the dream:

> bedenke, das ist alles unser Traum;
> da kann das Kurze lang sein, und das Lange
> ist ohne Ende. Und die Zeit ist Raum.[23]

> Consider: all that is our dream;
> there what is short can be long, and what is long
> is without end. And time is space.

More than twenty years later he alludes to this characteristic "da kann das Kurze lang sein" in a letter: ". . . I admit that I myself was quite near to this danger (of considering your visit a dream), lead astray by the truly phantastic brevity of your stay as well as by its strange inner expanse."[24]

In *Ewald Tragy*, which may be seen as an autobiography of the young Rilke, we read:

> "When are dreams?" he asked himself out loud. And this is what he tells Herr von Kranz who comes to visit him at dusk: "Life is so wide, and yet there are only so very few things placed here and there, just one for each eternity. They are tiring and frightening, these transitions. I was in Italy once as a child. I don't know much about it. But when you ask a peasant there when walking in the country: "How far is it to the village?" he'll say: "un mezz' ora." And the same with the next one, and the third one too, as though by agreement. And you walk all day long, and still there's no village. That's how it is with life. But in the dream everything is quite close. There one isn't afraid at all.[25]

The statement "Und die Zeit ist Raum," from the *Weiße Fürstin*, in connection with this representation of a childhood memory opens up a striking parallel to that aspect of the workings of the "Primärvorgang," under whose rule stand dream events—timelessness.[26] Out of the three major categories of waking human thought there remains space—in the poem: "Und die Zeit ist Raum."

Before he could have become acquainted with Freud's doctrine of the wish-fulfillment function of dream he states:

> Unsere Träume sind Marmorhermen,
> die wir in unsere Tempel stellen,
> und mit unseren Kränzen erhellen
> und mit unseren Wünschen erwärmen.[27]

> Our dreams are marble hermae,
> which we place in our temples,

and which we decorate with our wreaths
and which we warm with our wishes.

These verses awaken our interest through the appearance of the words "marble hermae." Hermae represented fertility symbols in antiquity and were always phallic.[28]

Seen from the perspective of psychoanalysis, it is certainly neither coincidental nor surprising to find the association with the sphere of sexuality in a statement about dreams. In the original general reception of psychoanalysis this essential part of the theory found the most ambivalent and generally adverse judgment. But Freud attenuated his formulation in 1920 after the most varied reactions to his theory: "Thus, the libido of our sexual instincts would correspond with the Eros of poets and philosophers, which holds everything living together."[29] And even more explicitly: ". . . we recognize the sexual instinct as Eros, the all-sustaining. . . ."[30] This is also one reason why one can observe everywhere among various thinkers (especially Schopenhauer and Nietzsche) and writers, an anticipation of psychoanalytical conclusions, and it is in agreement with the conception of psychoanalysis concerning the nature of the true poet.[31] This condition makes it difficult to determine at which point Rilke became acquainted with Freud's dream interpretation. In subsequent creative periods of the poet the correlations to this doctrine become increasingly manifest, and in his late work the direct influence is quite evident. To leave out the poet's contemporary world, the indications and accomplishments of society in the areas of scientific and cultural activity in general would be a serious omission. Or should one consider such influences as those of Jacobsen, Maeterlinck, Rodin, von Hofmannsthal, d'Annunzio, George, Tolstoy, Valéry, Jammes as indispensable, while dismissing Freud and his inestimable role in the cultural accomplishments of his time? He was a formative influence on Rilke, and his dynamic inspirations changed his life views.[32]

In characterizing the pain, the torment, and the horror which are unavoidably part of human existence, Rilke says in *Malte Laurids Brigge*: "People would like to be allowed to forget much of this; sleep gently flies over such grooves in their brains, but dreams drive sleep away and trace the designs again. And they wake up gasping and let the gleam of a candle melt into the darkness, and drink, like sugared water, the half-light solace. But, alas, on what a ledge this security rests!"[33] Again the subject is the "Welt aus Angst," but in addition to this irrational element found in many dreams there is expressed here for the first time, even if only in passing, that in the dream a "Tagesrest" is always included which normally elicits it—part of a particular real daily experience, which, for the type of dream Rilke is speaking of here, lies in the sphere of the dreadful, the horrible, and the torturous. Malte Laurids Brigge admonishes us furthermore that rationalization of fears is illusory, a precarious mollification, a security balanced on the extreme edge, which can tumble down at any moment.

The same thoughts can be pursued more clearly (albeit only after they have been translated from the idiom of poetic imagery into ordinary language) in the poem "Weißes Pferd-wie? . . . ." which emerged more than ten years later.[34] This poem, a creation of great complexity, requires clarification through paraphrase. We cannot understand it at all without the psychology of the unconscious and must reduce the "lyrical sums" to their individual components.[35]

Rilke, so it seems, begins with the everyday experience of the extraordinary transitoriness of the dream event with the often sudden loss of memory of the images, both of which are so perfect in the experience of the poet that he wonders in amazement whether the image that remained to him in waking had been a white horse or such a heterogenous phenomenon as a torrent. He compares this highly vague memory-image with the unclear reflection cast by the dull surface of a leftover drink in a cup. In order to better approach the dream happening, the poet pursues his external experiences of the preceding day: "der Tag, der mich nach außen trieb." This suggests that an important part in the structure of dream exists in the residue of the experienced impressions of the day. That is the return ("Wiederkehr") in the poem, which takes place at night, when the sleeper "schwerhaft in sich einfällt." This is an excellent description of the process of the beginning of the dream, of falling into dream's own forgotten depths, into the chambers of the unconscious, out of which the "Schlaf-Koch," as sovereign artificer of dreams, concocts the fantastic play from experienced reality and submerged memories.

We touch upon the frequent sexual roots of dreams in the analysis of the same poem. In the end "fadet der Moder," that which is lowly, abhorred, and therefore repressed, through the "ausgeschmeckten Saft" of the dream potion. The passion which wells up again from these "versunkenen Hügeln," from the great power-center of the psyche, the id, wins out over the ego in dream. The sexual-instinctiveness of primitive times breaks abruptly to the surface of his poetry in the third Duino elegy:

Ach, da *war* keine Vorsicht im Schlafenden; schlafend,
aber träumend, aber in Fiebern: wie er sich einließ
     . . . Wie er sich hingab—. Liebte.[36]

Alas! there *was* no caution within that sleeper; sleeping,
yes, but dreaming, yes, but feverish: what he embarked on!
     . . . How he gave himself up to it! Loved.

The image of the herbalist who prepares the strong draught does not occur here for the first time in Rilke's writings. It belongs to his ever-present store of thoughts, out of which he derives his poetic fantasies, as he always had. Twelve years earlier he had written: "I am like one who gathers mushrooms and medicinals among the herbs; one looks bent and busied with very small things then. . . . But the time will come when I shall prepare a potion. And that other time, when for its strength's sake I shall take it up, this potion which all is condensed and combined, the most poisonous and most deadly. . . ."[37] Rilke himself was a "Schlaf-Koch," who prepares the potion of his poetic dreams out of the ingredients from such healing and cooking herbs, "in dem alles verdichtet ist." We all do in dream, what poets do in their poetry.

III

The confrontation with the phenomena of life (with the manifestations of the human intellect, as well as with all of the experiences of the times) always occurs in Rilke via poetic treatment and specifically in instances where it conventionally has nothing to do with poetic "themes." The inclusion of such new territory, especially of modern intellectual and technical acquisitions in the area of poetry, is not the least of Rilke's originality, but one might have expected from the outset that such an *inventum novum* would force the possibilities of language to the outer limits of the expressible: hence the unusual effect of many lyrical Rilkean formulations which, in their deviation from traditional aesthetic norms, have a deeply disquieting influence. One will gain a relevant instrument, independent of the degree of responsiveness of our emotion, for rationally comprehending at least one aspect of Rilke's mastery, only when one conceives of the artistic task as a remolding of Freud's strictly rationalistically oriented doctrine of the essence of dreams into a form of presentation so essentially foreign to it as lyrical writing (as Rilke did it in the first poem "Aus dem Nachlaß des Grafen C.W."). The decision to concern oneself with such an "unpoetic" object is, in Rilke's case, conditioned through many circumstances and pressures. He was quite familiar with psychoanalysis through Freud's writings, through his reading of the journal "Imago," as well as through psychoanalysts, above all, Lou Andreas-Salomé, von Gebsattel, and the circle around publisher H. Heller. Moreover, it was through several personal analyses that psychoanalysis influenced him deeply. But that is not sufficient grounds for its permeation of a significant part of his writing. E. C. Mason has called the third Duino elegy Rilke's confrontation with psychoanalysis.[38] Other authors have found parallels of a more general nature. In reality, Rilke's lyrical reworkings of sober Freudian doctrine are even more numerous.[39] In order to understand the transsubstantiation from scientific theory into a work of art one must remain aware of the fact that the revolutionary discoveries of psychoanalysis could not remain caught in the peripheral layers of the mind of such an impressionable intellectual medium as Rilke. They motivate his avid striving toward appropriation of the world with all its phenomena; they strike at the very center of his being; they demand imperiously to be assimilated by it.[40]

Naturally, Rilke had not "intended" to represent psychoanalytical concepts in his work, nor even to produce the cycle of poems from the Castle of Berg am Irchel. This cycle was so alien to him that he claimed these poems were given to him by the unexpected apparition of Count C.W.,[41] whose dictation he had only copied down.[42] This occurred as though in an hallucinatory semiconscious state,[43] and for that reason also the remaining poems of the cycle closely resemble dream happenings. Rilke himself felt this; he says what was granted him in Berg—that is, these poems—was condensed within the "Traumrahmen einer Nacht."[44] The process is completely different from the "dictation" of the *Duino Elegies*, the *Sonnets to Orpheus*, or the *Vergers*.[45] In these, aside from a remark about the opening verses of the first elegy, there is no mention of optical or acoustical hallucinations. At least in the *Elegies* we are dealing with a project of long duration, a conscious effort spanning ten years. They ruled his life during this long period of time, they represented his thinking and writing almost exclusively, and he waited agonizingly for the "intuition," which was to inspire him with the final form.

Rilke was inclined towards a detailed and lengthy pursuit of dream events not only because he was a strong dreamer, but also because he was often plunged into a state of complete confusion by his dreams, and because the enigma of the dream experience troubled him. He reports: "Only the nights are bad, filled with dreams, dream after dream, so that in the morning I am sometimes quite confused . . . perhaps it is a kind of transition, all old and superfluous dreams streaming forth. Of course, that would be a good thing."[46]

Rilke ascribes to dream events the ability to project the future. On the seventh of October, 1912, he describes the dream of Pascha, the son of Princess Marie of Thurn und Taxis.[47] One remarkable thing here is that Pascha dreams a dream which Rilke should actually have dreamed. Another is that Rilke, when he went to Toledo a month later, really traveled "au Sud," from there, that is, to Ronda, a city on a bare hill, "eingeschlossen in Mauern und an den Mauern sehr viele Thürme." He writes from there to the Princess Marie: "I immediately sent a few pictures of it to Pascha, for it seems more than probable to me that the incomparable apparition of this town, surmounting two steep massifs of rock divided by the deep, narrow chasm of the river, corresponds to that he saw in his dream. . . ."[48]

Even years later he extols to Merline the divinatory character of the dream,[49] and what Rilke writes to Countess Sizzo is similar. She had had a dream image of an aunt, who lived far away, during the night the aunt died which resembled in every detail the appearance of the deceased in her last hours. Rilke, deeply impressed by this occurrence, accepted its verity in the words: "L'initiation sublime de ce rêve."[50] Through Ewald Tragy he expressed his conviction as early as 1896 that the "first" dreams in a new dwelling place have special significance, and he regrets having "forgotten" to dream when he spent the first night in Munich. Rilke's estimation of dreams is occasionally so intense that he ascribes to them the same intensity as to real existence. He has the Weiße Fürstin say: "Consider: is any life *more* experienced / and more your own than the images of your dreams?"[51] He remains true to this conviction and still expresses it in 1924: "Simply dream it or do it—: / both mean to exist."[52] This statement is interesting through its similarity to ideas which we meet in ancient cultures and in today's primitive tribes.

Another time he speaks of "Mächentraum der Wahrheit."[53] Dreams have the essence of real events, they draw their powers from the sap of life.[54] In the following verses, too, the substratum of ancient beliefs breaks through:

Du bist der Vogel, dessen Flügel kamen,
wenn ich erwachte in der Nacht und rief.
Nur mit den Armen rief ich, denn dein Namen
ist wie ein Abgrund, tausend Nächte tief.
Du bist der Schatten, drin ich still entschlief,

und jeden Traum ersinnt in mir dein Samen,—
du bist das Bild, ich aber bin der Rahmen,
der dich ergänzt in glänzendem Relief.[55]

You are the bird whose wings come
whenever I awoke in the night and called.
I simply called with my arms, for your name
is like an abyss, thousand nights deep.
You are the shadow in which I fell asleep quietly,
and your seed conceives each dream in me,—
you are the picture, but I am the frame
complementing you in splendid relief.

Here the guardian angel is addressed. The poet calls him a bird, a metaphor which he will use much later for the angel of the *Elegies*: "fast tödliche Vögel der Seele."[56] The guardian angel is for him the source of all his dreams; these emanate from him, a superhuman spiritual force. The metaphor which Rilke uses, "und jeden Traum ersinnt in mir dein Samen," points on the other hand to the libidinous source of dreams. Rilke calls to the guardian angel, just as he "cries" after the angel in the *Elegies*, and here we see, still only suggestively and tentatively, the identification which the poet takes up in his major lyrical work with the figure of the angel: "der dich ergänzt in glänzendem Relief."

Rilke goes further than to equate dream with reality, he awards it an even stronger reality: "When—as sometimes happens—you are in a dream of mine, then that dream and its afterring on the following day are more real than all daily reality, are world and happening."[57] Indeed, Rilke believes that through dreams we are transmitted to the other side of nature, as he experienced it in "Erlebnis."[58]

J. von Uexkuell reports Rilke's statement:

"Rilke: Is the little girl sleeping?
Gudrun Uexkuell: She is dreaming.
Rilke: She is shaping the stuff of which her life will consist."[59]

That only repeats what Shakespeare expressed in the lines

. . . We are such stuff,
As dreams are made on, and our little life
Is rounded with a sleep.[60]

and confirms once again, how in Rilke the most varied ideas of humanity are transmuted into form.

IV

May we expect a deeper meaning every time Rilke uses the word "dream" in his works, in which the meaningful human ideas about dreams seem to be fully represented? The word occurs so extraordinarily frequently, particularly in the writing of the young Rilke, that it often has only an everyday and inexact metaphorical meaning, no different from the generally accepted view of the poet as dreamer. The non-committal use of the word "dream" in Rilke must not, however, obscure the fact that dream events concealed meaningful existential secrets for him and held him in their sway. We have seen how he was victimized by his dreams. He attributed to them serious disturbances of his health, nervous disorders, and painfully felt restraints in his work and in life. Such neurasthenic complaints occur often. His special relationship to the dream world characterizes, too, the impression which he made on others and even on those who knew him most intimately.

Lou Andreas-Salomé describes him as glowing with "dream-certainty" and as a person in whom dreams represent a "second, actual soul."[61] Kassner claims that for Rilke there is no difference between dreaming and seeing.[62] Benvenuta chooses as the title for the book edition of her letters from Rilke his words: "so laß ich mich zu träumen gehen."[63] Karin Michaelis reports that Rilke showed remarkable behavior at social gatherings during the time of his military service at Vienna: during the first half hour he did not speak or else he mumbled incomprehensibly. Only then did he seem to awaken from his dreamlike state;[64] and to Antonina Vallentin he appeared "comme si sa présence supprimait la frontière entre le rêve et le réel."[65] His poetry moves along this borderline. Even the prose of his early years is laced with images, gestures, and actions such as occur in dreams, and it treats these elements no differently from the real occurrences and reflections of waking thought, so that both dream and reality often come to stand directly next to one another. By means of this technical aid he succeeds in turning back that which is normally rationally conceptualized into its prior stages and in dissolving it into visual images, through which an enormous amplification of the artistic effect is reached.

V

In the memoirs of Princess Marie of Thurn und Taxis-Hohenlohe we find another of the dreams mentioned at the beginning of this essay, one which Rilke communicated to her in Vienna during the war.[66] He dreamed that he held in his hand a clump of damp, dirty earth, out of which he was ordered to create something, a form or an image. While he was struggling with it disgustedly and scratching around on the clump with a small knife, suddenly a beautiful, iridescent butterfly separated itself from a bare area and flew away. An unusual dream, but may one agree with the interpretation of Rilke and the princess that he has been mandated to redeem and transform the horrible? This interpretation deals only with surface action. The symbolic level is a much deeper one. It is the well-known symbolism of many fairy tales and reminds one vividly of other disgusting objects or life-forms that suddenly are transformed into precious figures. For example, a damp, dirty, repulsive creature turns into a "splendid, glittering prince." Not only are the symbols often the same, even the language is often interchangeable, as in the case of Rilke's dream with that of the fairy tale "Der Froschkönig oder der eiserne Heinrich." The same symbolism is found in the fairy tale "Der verwunschene Prinz," in which an ugly, fearsome, and loathsome boar appears as a suitor and turns into a young, handsome prince the moment Gretchen overcomes her disgust and loathing for the wild pig.

With these enchantments of the fairy tales it is always the ambivalence of desire and disgust, a matter of marriage and procreation. The sexual desires, repressed because they are perceived as ugly and mean, are projected into the external world and take on real form there. In that moment when the suppression is overcome, the pleasantness of the instinctual satisfaction makes itself felt. Even more heavily accompanied by moral demands and taboos, and correspondingly more strongly suppressed, are the infantile, anal-erotic impulses that are concealed in Rilke's dream of clumps of damp, dirty earth. The equation of excrement with gold and gifts in folklore traditions, which have their exact correspondence in unconscious mental life, gives us the key for the interpretation of this dream.[67] The beautiful, iridescent butterfly, which flies away from the lump, is itself an informative symbol belonging to this group. It represents the transformation of the original drive into a morally and culturally valued activity. In this respect the dream really presents itself to Rilke as an inner assignment, but not that of salvaging and transforming something horrid projected in the external world; rather that of sublimating his own repressed instinctual impulses, which were the content of the projection, into valuable energies and integrating them with his higher ego.

Presented with Rilke's ceaseless and inescapable addiction to dreaming one might easily be tempted to speak of a flight from reality into dream. But such stereotyped thinking overlooks the complexity of the situation. If one changes this sentence into its exact opposite, as A. Vallentin does, such a statement seems to express the truth just as well.

Although Rilke's work is extremely rich in symbolism, it would not do to place it in the same classification as the art critic's concept of symbolism, as explained above. The choice of metaphorical and imaginative language occurred unintentionally with him, as pure transcription of his thoughts. One would not be doing justice to the extent of the symbolism in his work if one wanted to simply reduce it to a universal trait of poets in general. Certainly the genuine poetic word is not direct. It is token, reference, and image, pregnant with meaning and full of associations. Only Lou Andreas-Salomé's superlative label for that which was the most important to Rilke brings out his unique relation to symbolism. She writes to him in January of 1921: "For it is certainly true that from the time of your youth you experienced life only as such a symbol. . . . Ah, you did not need to fret about anything; what you need will be given to you and with greatest certainty on those occasions when you appear helpless, since, after all, it happens without your intention, with the help of signs and miracles."[68]

This attempt at an elucidation of Rilke's being is of direct importance for the dream theme, for this symbolic language of poetry is born of the same matrix as is that of dream. Indeed, poetic language is identical with it when it occurs spontaneously and unintentionally. Its elements belong to the same universal and archetypal patterns of human thought with their eternally constant worries and fears, wishes and desires. For that reason it speaks to men with an irresistible force; it touches upon older and anthropologically more elementary interests than those which rational speech of logical intellect can ever reach. Andreas-Salomé's observation that Rilke was one of the most symbolic of men discloses in a word an essential reason for the response that his poetry and personality have found.[69]

In one respect many elusive and obscure passages in Rilke's poetry often prove to be blessings in disguise. That is, they could lead to the initiation of a decidedly fruitful interdisciplinary effort between literary criticism and psychoanalysis. Despite many attempts at interpretation on the part of literary criticism and philosophy, many difficulties in Rilkean texts have led to an unsatisfactory situation. Often it seems that only one missing link is needed to complete understanding. No aesthetic investigation seems to be able to help, no philological precision to find the reason. Simile and metaphor are not enough, comparison of style remains inadequate, and contexts of meaning come from preconceived viewpoints that do not extend to the depths of the creative processes. Such investigations can only get as close to their object as their models allow. The true dimensions of the inner eye will not be accessible before the perspective of the unconscious thought processes is introduced—a revolution much like that which the method of Leonardo affected. In understanding the symbols within the poet and their treatment in the secondary process, dream symbolism proves helpful by airing one corner of the secret of his *ars poetica*. With its help, that which was otherwise obscured can step out into the light, revealing, to name only one example, the amalgamation of the beautiful and the terrible into a quasi concept in the Rilkean angel.

NOTES

Ann Bollinger translated Dr. Simenauer's German manuscript. In an expanded form the essay has appeared previously in German in Erich Simenauer, *Der Traum bei Rainer Maria Rilke* (Bern: Haupt, 1976). Reprinted by permission of the publisher.

1. W. Stekel, *Die Sprache des Traums: Eine Darstellung der Symbolik und Deutung des Traumes in ihren Beziehungen zur kranken und gesunden Seele* (Wiesbaden: Bergmann, 1911). Unless otherwise indicated, the English translations of German quotations were supplied by Frank Baron.
2. S. Freud, *Zur Geschichte der psychoanalytischen Bewegung*, in *Gesammelte Werke* (London: Imago, 1949), X: 58 (henceforth *GW*).
3. S. Freud, *Vorlesungen zur Einführing in die Psychoanalyse: Die Symbolik im Traum*, in *GW*, XI: 152.
4. Ibid., pp. 259–62.
5. Ibid., pp. 476–80.
6. O. Rank, "Ein Traum, der sich selbst deutet," *Jahrbuch für psychoanalytische und psychopathologische Forschungen* 2 (1910).
7. S. Freud, *Die Traumdeutung*, p. 340. Cf. Freud's *Vorlesungen zur Einführung in die Psychoanalyse*, in *GW*, XI: 189ff.
8. R. M. Rilke, *Gesammelte Werke* (Leipzig: Insel, 1927), IV (henceforth *GW*). Also in *Prager Presse*, Beilage "Dichtung und Welt," 49 (1925), and *Sämtliche Werke* (Leipzig: Insel, 1966), VI: 989–98 (henceforth *SW*).

9. S. Freud, *Die Traumdeutung, GW*, II: 101n. Cf. Anna Freud, in *International Journal of Psychoanalysis* 46 (1965).

10. It would be more accurate to say that he never remembered his dreams.

11. Cf. E. Aserinksy and N. Kleitman, "Regularly Occurring Periods of Eye Motility and Concomitant Phenomena during Sleep," *Science* 118 (1953): 273–74. See also N. Kleitmann, *Sleep and Wakefulness* (Chicago: University of Chicago Press, 1963).

12. Lou Andreas-Salomé, *Rainer Maria Rilke* (Leipzig: Insel, 1929), p. 14.

13. E. Simenauer, *Rainer Maria Rilke: Legende und Mythos* (Bern: Haupt, 1953), p. 631ff.

14. Lou Andreas-Salomé, *Tagebuch eines Jahres 1912/1913: Aus der Schule bei Freud*, ed. E. Pfeiffer (Zürich: Niehans, 1958), p. 213.

15. Simenauer, p. 97ff.

16. *SW*, I: 410.

17. R. M. Rilke, *Ewald Tragy* (London: Vision Press, 1958), p. 49.

18. C. B. Hieatt, *The Realism of Dream Vision* (The Hague: Mouton, 1967), p. 12.

19. R. M. Rilke, *Briefe und Tagebücher aus der Frühzeit* (Leipzig: Insel, 1933), p. 383. Entry of November 10, 1900.

20. S. Freud, "Der Wahn und die Träume in W. Jensens 'Gradiva,'" in *GW*, VII: 120.

21. *Briefe und Tagebücher*, p. 259f. Entry of April, 1900.

22. *SW*, I: 401.

23. *SW*, I: 211.

24. Rilke's letter of March 10, 1922. Unless otherwise indicated, letters of Rilke are quoted from *Gesammelte Briefe*, ed. Ruth Sieber-Rilke (Leipzig: Insel, 1936–39).

25. *Ewald Tragy*, p. 49.

26. S. Freud, *Die Traumdeutung, GW*, II–III: 571–73 and 593–616; *Das Unbewußte, GW*, X: 286; *Jenseits des Lustprinzips, GW*, XIII: 35f.

27. *SW*, I: 191.

28. O. Hiltbrunn, *Kleines Lexikon der Antike* (Bern: Francke, 1946), pp. 198 and 359.

29. S. Freud, *Jenseits des Lustprinzips*, p. 55.

30. Ibid., p. 56.

31. Kierkegaard recognized the wish-fulfilling nature of dream long before Freud. "Ich bin in diesen Tagen in dem Grad unglücklich, daß ich in Träument unbeschreiblich glücklich bin." *Tagebücher* (Innsbruck: Brenner, 1923), I: 130.

32. E. Simenauer, "Rilke und die Psychoanalyse," in *Legende und Mythos*, pp. 115–38.

33. *SW*, IV: 776.

34. The first poem of the cycle "Aus dem Nachlaß des Grafen C. W.":

> Weißes Pferd-wie? oder Sturzbach . . ? welches
> war das Bild, das übern Schlaf mir blieb?

Spiegel-Schein im Neige-Rest des Kelches—
und der Tag, der mich nach außen trieb!

Wiederkehr—, was find ich mir im Innern,
fall ich abends schwerhaft in mich ein?

Traum, trag auf jetzt: wird der Teller zinnern—,
wird die fremde Frucht eröffnet sein?

Werd ich wissen, was ich trinke—, oder
ists versunkner Hugel Leidenschaft?

Und wem klag ichs, wenn am Schluß der Moder
fadet durch den ausgeschmeckten Saft?

Gnügts mir, daß ich noch nach auswärts schaue,
braucht der Schlaf-Koch noch ein Suppenkraut?

Oder wirft er schon in ungenaue
Speisen Würzen, denen er nicht traut? [*SW*, II: 112]

35. Rilke's letter of December 22, 1923, in *Briefe aus Muzot* (Leipzig: Insel, 1935).

36. R. M. Rilke, *Duino Elegies*, trans. J. B. Leishman and Stephen Spender (New York: Norton, 1963), p. 36.

37. Rilke's letter of September 4, 1908, in *Briefe* (Leipzig: Insel, 1933), IV.

38. E. C. Mason, *Lebenshaltung und Symbolik bei R. M. Rilke* (Weimar: Böhlau, 1939), p. 153.

39. E. Simenauer, *Legende und Mythos*, pp. 115–38.

40. Rilke was certainly not the first to use new scientific ideas in his poetry. They were to be found in the work of Arno Holz and other writers of German Naturalism. Similar tendencies may be noted some three hundred and fifty years earlier in the poetry of John Donne.

41. *Aus dem Nachlaß des Grafen C. W.*, p. 38.

42. Rilke's letter of December 15, 1920.

43. E. Simenauer, "Rilkes Beziehung zum Fallen und zur Fallsucht," *Der Psychologe* 7 (1955): 309–14 and 373–78.

44. Rilke's letter of May 31, 1921, in *Briefe* (Leipzig: Insel, 1937), V.

45. The three works, respectively, were mentioned in Rilke's undated letter from Muzot; his letter of April 20, 1923; and his letter of December 18, 1925.

46. Rilke's letter of April 10, 1903.

47. In the "Protokollen der vier Séancen," in *Rainer Maria Rilke und Maria von Thurn und Taxis, Briefwechsel* (Zürich: Niehans, 1951), II: 914: "In der Nacht auf den 7. Oktober hat P. [Pascha, the son of the Princess Marie of Thurn and Taxis] folgenden Traum: Wir befinden uns auf einem Schiff, die Fürstin, die Grfn. Regina, er und ich. Das Schiff erscheint im Verlauf sehr ausgedehnt, 'wie eine Allee.' Ich wende mich zu ihm und sage:

'Vous savez que vous rêvez?'
'Non.'
'Eh bien,' trage ich ihm auf, 'dites-moi demain que je ne resterai pas à Tolède, que j'irai au Sud—' und zeigend: 'là.' Und es war eine Stadt

zu sehen, kahle Hügel und auf dem einen eine Stadt, 'wie ausgegossen,'
eingeschlossen in Mauern und an den Mauern sehr viel Thürme.

"(Diesen Traum erzählte Pascha mir heute morgen.)"

48. Rilke's letter of December 17, 1912. *Letters*, II: 79.
49. Rilke's letter of February 20, 1921. *Lettres françaises à Merline* (Paris: De Seuil, 1950), p. 62. "Chérie, j'ai lu 'le rêve' tel que vous me l'avez confié et je vous remercie de l'avoir fait, c'est si curieux—dans la domaine de vos rêves tout est permis, parce que tout y est divinatoire, grand et fatidique."
50. *Die Briefe an Gräfin Sizzo* (Leipzig: Insel, 1950), p. 62.
51. *SW*, IV: 536, and I: 208.
52. *Briefwechsel mit Erika Mitterer* (Wiesbaden: Insel, 1950), p. 37.
53. *Briefe an Baronesse von Oe* (New York: Johannispresse, 1945), p. 53.
54. *SW*, I: 36.

    Träume scheinen mir wie Orchideen.—
    So wie jene sind sie bunt und reich.
    Aus dem Riesenstamm der Lebenssäfte
    ziehn sie just wie jene ihre Kräfte,
    brüsten sich mit dem ersaugten Blute,
    freuen in der flüchtigen Minute,
    in der nächsten sind sie tot und bleich.

55. *SW*, I: 381.
56. *SW*, I: 689.
57. Rilke's letter of April 15, 1904. *Letters*, I: 146.
58. "Erlebnis," *SW*, VI: 1036–42.
59. J. von Uexkuell, *Niegeschaute Welten* (Berlin, 1936), p. 258.
60. *The Tempest*, IV, Scene 1, lines 155–57.
61. Lou Andreas-Salomé, *Lebensrückblick: Grundriß einiger Lebenserinnerungen* (Zürich: Niehans, 1951), p. 142, and *Briefwechsel mit Rilke*, p. 243.
62. R. Kassner, *Buch der Erinnerung* (Leipzig: Insel, 1938), p. 318.
63. Magda von Hattingberg (Benvenuta), *R. M. Rilke: so laß ich mich zu träumen gehen* (Gmunden: J. Mader, 1949).
64. K. Michaelis, *Der kleine Kobold* (Vienna, 1948), p. 204.
65. A. Vallentin, *Les Temps Modernes* (Paris, 1952), p. 402.
66. Marie von Thurn und Taxis-Hohenlohe, *Erinnerungen an R. M. Rilke* (Munich: Oldenburg, 1932). Cf. Christiane Osann, *Rainer Marie Rilke: Der Weg eines Dichters* (Zürich: O. Fussli, 1941), p. 265.
67. S. Freud, "Über Triebumsetzungen, insbesondere der Analerotik," in *GW*, V: 268ff.
68. *Rainer Maria Rilke—Lou Andreas-Salomé, Briefwechsel*, p. 445.
69. Cf. E. Simenauer, "Betrachtungen über den Ruhm Rilkes," *Deutsche Universitätszeitung* 4 (1952): 21.

List of Contributors

BERNHARD BLUME (d. 1978), who taught at Harvard and the University of California (San Diego), edited a book of Rilke's correspondence: *Briefe an Sidonie Nádherný von Borutin* (1973). His interpretation of Rilke's poetry has appeared in a number of articles.

ULRICH FÜLLEBORN, University of Erlangen, Germany, has written extensively on Rilke. He is the author of *Das Strukturproblem der späten Lyrik Rilkes* (1973).

HANS EGON HOLTHUSEN, Northwestern University, has written a number of books about Rilke. He is the author of *Rilkes Sonette an Orpheus* (1937), *R. M. Rilke: A Study of His Later Poetry* (1952), and *Rainer Maria Rilke in Selbstzeugnissen und Bilddokumenten* (1958).

RICHARD JAYNE, University of Göttingen, Germany, has traced the evolution of Rilke's poetry in *The Symbolism of Space and Motion in the Works of Rainer Maria Rilke* (1972).

WALTER KAUFMANN, Princeton University, has interpreted Rilke's place in modern intellectual history in *Existentialism from Dostoevsky to Sartre* (1956). His translations of Rilke's poetry appear in his *Twenty German Poets* (1962).

LEV KOPELEV, Germanist and author living in Moscow, has published articles and books on modern German literature. His books include *Zwei Epochen deutsch-russischer Literaturbeziehungen* (1973).

HERBERT LEHNERT, University of California (Irvine), has written about Rilke in a number of articles and books.

DARIA ROTHE, University of Michigan, has completed the dissertation *Rilke and Russia: A Re-examination.*

List of Contributors

ANDRAS SANDOR, Howard University, has published many articles and books on modern poetry and literary theory.

ERICH SIMENAUER, psychoanalyst in Berlin, is the author of *Rainer Maria Rilke: Legende und Mythos* (1953) and *Der Traum bei Rainer Maria Rilke* (1976).

WALTER SOKEL, University of Virginia, has treated the problems of artistic creativity in Rilke's time in many articles and books.

STEPHEN SPENDER, University of London, was instrumental in introducing Rilke to the English-speaking world through the translation (with J. B. Leishmann) of Rilke's *Duino Elegies* (1939).

WALTER STRAUSS, Case Western Reserve University, has interpreted Rilke's poetry in his book *Descent and Return: The Orphic Theme in Modern Literature* (1971).

ANDRZEJ WARMINSKI, Yale University, has published articles on modern German poetry.

Index

Admoni, Vladimir, 129
Aksakov, Sergej, 119
Alleman, Beda, 172
Andersch, Alfred, 95
Anderson, Marian, 19
Andreas-Salomé, Lou, 4, 5, 10, 12, 13, 14, 114, 117, 120, 121, 125, 127, 129, 130, 137, 146, 172, 175, 224, 246, 253, 256, 258
Arnim, Bettina von, 8, 11
Arnold, Matthew, 57
Aquinas, Saint Thomas, 50
Asadovskij, Konstantin, 132 n, 133 n
Auden, W. H., 31, 32, 36, 42, 44
Auerbach, Erich, 86

Babbit, Irving, 54
Bach, Johann Sebastian, 87
Bachelard, Gaston, 85
Balzac, Honoré de, 85
Barth, Karl, 186
Batterby, K. A. J., 125
Baudelaire, Charles, 65–67, 78, 81, 86, 96, 98, 102–5, 107, 227, 235
Baxtin, M., 131
Becker-Modersohn, Paula, 202
Beethoven, Ludwig van, 52
Bellman, Carl Mikael, 38
Benjamin, Walter, xi, xiii, xv
Benn, Gottfried, 5–6, 13, 22, 33, 42
Benois, Aleksandr N., 115, 120
Benvenuta. See Hattingberg, Magda von
Berdjaev, Nikolaj A., 131
Bergson, Henri, 225, 238
Blake, William, 86, 90
Blei, Franz, 226

Blok, Aleksandr A., 130
Blume, Bernard, xiv
Bodman, Emanuel von, 14 n
Boehn, Max V., 229
Bogatyrev, Konstantin, 136 n
Braque, Georges, 72, 73, 77, 81, 85, 87
Brecht, Bertolt, 29, 33, 42, 109–10
Brehm, Alfred Edmund, 32
Brentano, Bettina, 224
Brooks, Cleanth, 34
Brutzer, Sophie, 116, 125, 128
Buddha, 18, 20, 26
Bülow, Frieda von, 137
Bunin, Ivan, 118

Čaklais, Maris, 136 n
Cassirer, Ernst, 200
Černosvitova, Ženja, 118
Cetlin (Amari), M., 118
Čertkov, L., 132 n, 134 n
Čertkov, V. G., 135 n
Cézanne, Paul, ix, 4, 8, 64, 67–68, 72–73, 86, 104, 105, 106
Champigny, Robert, 85
Chardin, Jean-Baptiste Simeon, 68, 72, 87
Charles XII, 138
Chekhov, Anton, 120, 121, 122, 138
Chernyshevsky, Nikolaj, 121
Claudel, Paul, 78, 88
Coleridge, Samuel Taylor, 53
Čvetaeva, Marina, 118, 119, 134 n, 136 n

D'Annunzio, Gabriele, 250
Dante, Alighieri, 50, 51
David-Rhonfeld, Valerie von, 114

Index

Dehmel, Richard, 114
Dehn, Fritz, 31
Donne, John, 76, 261
Dostoevsky, Fjodor, 113, 120, 128, 130, 131
Drožžin, Spiridon, 116, 117, 119, 120, 121

Ehrenburg, Ilya, 118
Eisner, Kurt, 30
El Greco, 38
Eliot, T. S., xi–xii, 32–35
Éttinger, P., 115, 120

Fet, Afanasi, 114
Fichte, Johann Gottlieb, 197
Fitzgerald, Edward, 48
Flaubert, Gustave, 85
Florenne, Yves, 111
Fofanov, Konstantin, 120
Francis of Assisi, Saint, 80
Franco, Francisco, 31
Frank, Simon, 132 n
Freud, Sigmund, 15, 244, 248, 250, 252
Fülleborn, Ulrich, 172, 189 n

Gallerati-Scotti, Aurelia, 30
Garshin, Vsevolod, 121, 129
Gautier, Théophile, 87
Gebsattel, E. von, 253
George, Stefan, x, 42, 114, 250
Gide, André, 41
Glade, Henry, 133–34 n
Goethe, Johann Wolfgang, 9, 11, 15, 17, 21,
    34–35, 37, 40–43, 96, 226
Gogol, Nikolaj, 121, 122
Gončarov, Ivan A., 121, 128, 129
Gorky, Maxim, 121
Grimm, Hermann, 40–41
Guardini, Romano, 31

Hamburger, Käte, 241 n
Hattingberg, Magda von (Benvenuta), 12, 256
Hauptmann, Gerhart, 11, 114
Hegel, Georg Wilhelm Friedrich, xii, 39–40,
    90, 193–94, 204, 207, 219
Heidegger, Martin, 89, 181, 187
Heine, Heinrich, 15
Heller, Erich, xii, 17, 34–35, 39–40, 57–58, 61,
    80, 86, 90, 193, 219
Heller, H., 253
Heydt, K., 121
Heym, Georg, 178
Hieatt, Constance B., 247
Hippius, Zinaida, 120
Hitler, Adolf, 108

Hoffmann, Ernst F., 189
Hoffmann, E. T. A., 96, 229
Hofmannsthal, Hugo von, 11, 13, 14, 42, 114,
    226, 250
Hölderlin, Friedrich, ix, 86, 90
Holthusen, Hans Egon, ix, xii, xiv, xv
Holz, Arno, 261 n
Horace, 29, 42, 103
Huf, Fritz, viii
Hulewicz, Witold von, 54, 128, 190
Husserl, Edmund, 89, 202

Ibsen, Henrik, 11, 113, 115
Ilya of Murom, 139, 149
Isherwood, Christopher, 31
Ivan IV (the Terrible), 139, 140, 141, 142, 144
Ivanov, Aleksandr, 122, 123, 128
Ivanovich, Fëdor (Czar), 138–48

Jacobsen, Jens Peter, 113, 114, 172, 173, 250
Jahr, Ilse, 218
Jammes, Francis, 180, 250
Jančevetskij, V., 120
Jaspers, Karl, 212–13, 215
Jayne, Richard, xii, xiv
Jensen, William, 248
John, Saint, 145
Jonas, Klaus W., viii
Joyce, James, 33

Kafka, Franz, 33
Kaiser, Gerhard, 240–42 n
Kant, Immanuel, 79, 196
Kappus, Franz Xaver, 10
Karl August of Sachsen-Weimar, 7
Kassner, Rudolf, 3, 34, 256
Kaufmann, Walter, xiv
Keats, John, 50
Key, Ellen, 116
Khayyám, Omar, 48
Kierkegaard, Sören, 42, 172, 173, 182, 260 n
Kippenberg, Anton, 7–8
Klee, Paul, 73, 231, 232
Kleist, Heinrich von, 228, 229
Klopstock, Friedrich Gottlieb, ix
Klossowska, Baladine (Merline), 12, 254
Kočur, Grigorij, 136 n
Kopelev, Lev, xi, xii, xiv
Korovin, Konstantin A., 122
Kostomarov, Nikolaj I., 121
Kotetišvili, Vaxtang, 136 n
Kotošixin, G. K., 121
Kramskoj, Ivan, 122, 123
Krauss, Karl, 231

Index

Kropotkin, Petr A. (Prince), 121
Kuhlmann, Quirinus, 43

La Fontaine, Jean de, 87
Larousse, Pierre, 82
Lehnert, Herbert, xii, xiii
Leishman, J. B., 31, 151
Lermontov, M., 114, 115, 120
Lessing, Gotthold E., 245
Levik, V., 134 n
Levitan, I., 122
Liliencron, Detlev von, 114
Littré, Maximilien-Paul-Émile, 79, 81
Lohner, Edgar, 103
Lorca, Garcia, 33
Lowell, Robert, 19
Ludwig II, 7
Lukaš, Mikola, 136 n

Maeterlinck, Maurice, 121, 247, 250
Malherbe, Daniel François, 87
Maliutin, Sergej, 122
Maljavin, Philipp A., 122
Mallarmé, Stéphane, 48, 52, 66, 81, 85–86, 88, 107, 112
Man, Paul de, 163
Mann, Heinrich, 11, 109
Mann, Thomas, 11, 33, 35, 96, 98, 109
Martini, Fritz, 189 n
Marx, Karl, 35, 96, 239
Masaryk, Tomáš Garrigue, 30
Mason, Eudo C., x, 253
Matisse, Henri, 78, 81
Merline. See Klossowska, Baladine
Meyer, Herman, 67
Michaelis, Karin, 256
Mikuševič, Vladimir, 133 n, 136 n
Mitterer, Erika, 38
Montaigne, Michel de, 173
Mörike, Eduard, 37
Moses, 16, 24
Musil, Robert, 36, 40, 42
Mussolini, Benito, 30, 108

Napoleon III, 103
Nekrasov, Nikolaj, 114, 128
Neruda, Pablo, 33
Newton, Sir Isaac, 42
Nietzsche, Friedrich, xiv, 15, 17, 21, 57, 61, 115, 127, 172, 185, 218–19, 227, 250
Novalis (Friedrich von Hardenberg), 192, 195–97, 204, 219

Pasternak, Boris, 118, 136 n

Pasternak, Leonid O., 113, 115–20, 125, 131, 133 n, 150 n
Pater, Walter, 225
Pausanias, 246
Perse, Saint-John, 88, 226
Petrov, Sergej, 136 n
Philotheus, 145, 148
Picasso, Pablo, 72–73, 87
Pitoev, Georgij, 118
Plato, 225, 237
Ponge, Francis, xi
Proust, Marcel, 33, 57, 65, 86–87
Pushkin, Alexandr, 114, 128
Pypin, Aleksandr N., 121

Rameau, Jean Philippe, 87
Rammelmeyer, Alfred, 127
Rank, Otto, 244
Rathenau, Walther, 30
Reinhart, Werner, 9
Repin, Ilja, 122
Richard, Jean-Pierre, 89
Rilke, Clara, 67, 102, 104, 105, 130, 138
Rimbaud, Jean Nicolas Arthur, 17, 64, 78
Rodin, Auguste, ix, 8, 10, 32, 64–67, 86, 98, 102, 125, 250
Rogalskij A., 125
Romanelli, Mimi, 11–12
Rosegger, Peter, 244
Rothe, Daria, xiii, xiv
Rožanskij, Ivan, 131, 133 n
Rudnicki, Adolf, 132 n
Runge, Philipp Otto, 134 n
Russell, Bertrand, 15

Sakharov, Aleksandr, 118
Sakharov, Andrej D., 131
Sakharov, Chlothilde, 118
Sandor, Andras, xi, xiii, xv
Sartre, Jean Paul, 89, 181
Sazonova-Slonimski, Julia L., 118
Schalk, Lili, 3
Schill, Sofia, 115, 117, 120, 146
Schiller, Friedrich, 5, 9, 37, 52
Schopenhauer, Arthur, 250
Schuler, Alfred, 108
Schwarz, Egon, 30–31, 108
Sedlakowitz (General), 149
Seligson, Carla, 226
Serov, Valentin, 122
Shakespeare, William, 255
Shaw, George Bernard, 236
Shelley, Percy Bysshe, 61
Simenauer, Erich, xii, 11
Sizzo, Countess L. M. von, 254

Index

Šklovskij, Victor, 36
Sokel, Walter H., xii, xiv–xv
Sollers, Philippe, 89
Solovjëv, Vladimir, 130, 131
Solzhenitsyn, Aleksandr, 131
Somov, Konstantin A., 122
Sontag, Susan, 89
Spender, Stephen, xi, xii, 31
Staiger, Emil, 192
Steiner, Jacob, 184, 201
Stekel, W., 244
Stephens, Anthony, 240
Stevens, Wallace, 85
Stevenson, Robert Louis, 245
Storck, Joachim, 112 n
Strauss, Walter A., xi, xii
Suvorin, A., 120, 121

Thurn und Taxis, Marie von, 7, 9, 11, 34, 38, 246, 254
Thurn und Taxis, Pascha von, 254, 261–62 n
Tieck, Ludwig, 96
Toller, Ernst, 30
Tolstoy, Leo, 115–16, 119–22, 124, 126, 127–29
Tolstoy, Nikolaj, 116, 250
Trubetzkoy, Paolo, 115
Turgenev, Ivan, 113–15, 122, 128–29

Uexkuell, Gudrun von, 255

Uexkuell, J. von, 255

Valéry, Paul, 33, 67, 86–87, 250
Vallentin, Antonina, 256, 258
Vasiljev, Feodor, 122, 128
Vasnetsov, Apollinarij, 121
Vasnetsov, Viktor, 122
Velásquez, Diego, 81
Velikij, Ivan, 115
Verlaine, Paul, 65–66
Vermeer, Jan, 81
Vitkovskij, Eugenij, 136 n
Vladimir (Prince of Kiev), 139
Vogeler, Heinrich, 117, 134 n
Voronina, Elena, 115, 118

Wackenroder, Wilhelm Heinrich, 96
Wagner, Richard, 96
Warminski, Andrzej, xii, xiv
Wassermann, Jakob, 114
Westhoff, Clara, 3–4, 10
Wittgenstein, Ludwig, 8
Wolzogen, Caroline von, 5
Wunderly-Volkart, Nanny, 22, 24

Yeats, William Butler, 20, 42, 53, 192

Zapf, Hedwig, 214
Zernov, Nicolas, 144, 146
Zeyer, Julius, 114
Zinn, Ernst, 102
Ziolkowski, Theodore, 225